ESPECIALLY FOR

....

FROM

....

DATE

....

DAILY WISDOM FOR WOMEN

2023

Devotional Collection

BARBOUR
PUBLISHING

WELCOME TO *DAILY WISDOM FOR WOMEN*

On any given day, our thought patterns (both negative and positive) have a major impact on us as individuals. It's a cycle that's always in flux: our thoughts influence our heartfelt emotions, which, in turn, influence our attitudes and actions, which then influence our circumstances. At other times it is our circumstances that work to influence our thoughts, influencing our heartfelt emotions and our attitude and actions.

In either scenario, problems arise when our thoughts are stuck in a negative pattern. We find ourselves trapped in worry, discontentment, anxiety, fear, and a slew of other bleak and unhealthy emotions and attitudes. The evil one thrives on keeping us in the negative and self-fulfilling prophecy thought cycles. But God's Word provides us a way out, not only highlighting the influence our thought-heart connection has on us but giving us tools to counteract the negative and build up the positive, getting our thoughts more aligned with the good, healthy, productive, and holy thoughts of God.

In *Daily Wisdom for Women 2023*, we dig into the idea that as we think in our hearts, so we will be (Proverbs 23:7). Join us as we embark this yearlong journey of training our mind and guarding our heart from which everything we do flows (Proverbs 4:23).

Whatever is true, whatever is noble, whatever is right, whatever is pure, whatever is lovely, whatever is admirable—if anything is excellent or praiseworthy—think about such things.

PHILIPPIANS 4:8 NIV

A NEW BEGINNING

*The earth was without form and an empty waste, and darkness
was upon the face of the very great deep. The Spirit of God
was moving (hovering, brooding) over the face of the waters.
And God said, Let there be light; and there was light. And
God saw that the light was good (suitable, pleasant) and He
approved it; and God separated the light from the darkness.*

GENESIS 1:2–4 AMPC*

. . . .

In the very beginning, our planet was dark and empty. But the Spirit of
God was moving, hovering over the surface of its waters. And then God
spoke: "Let there be light." And there was light. And God saw it was good.

Just as God was hovering over that first day, He hovers over yours.
His Spirit is continually moving, ready, willing, and able to shine His
light into your day, to separate you from darkness.

To aid in this endeavor, God initially brought His people the law,
hoping humankind would find their blessings by following His Word
(Psalm 1:1). When that proved too difficult, God sent His very own
Son into our world, requesting He be called "Emmanuel—which, when
translated, means, God with us" (Matthew 1:23 AMPC).

Today is a new day, a new year, a new beginning. Make it good
by training your mind to look for God's light, to seek out His Word,
remembering He's with you, every step of the way.

Lord, fix my eyes and mind on Your good light. Amen.

*A Read thru the Bible in a Year Plan that follows each devotion can be found at the back of this book.

CONTINUAL REFUGE

Kiss the Son [pay homage to Him in purity]. . . .
O blessed (happy, fortunate, and to be envied) are
all those who seek refuge and put their trust in Him!
PSALM 2:12 AMPC

. . . .

In the Garden of Eden, Eve fell under the influence of the father of lies. Then Adam was persuaded to join her in his untruths. Next thing they knew, they realized they were naked and so hid from God.

Yet God, who knows all and sees all, quickly surmised what had happened. Of course, there were consequences to His children's actions. But He did not desert them in their time of need. Instead, He tenderly clothed them.

God is there for you in the same way. No matter what you do, where you are, or how you mess up, God will not desert you. Of course, when you err, there will be consequences. But keep in mind that God will always stick with you. When you seek out His refuge, He will open His arms to you and pull you close. When you need a shoulder to cry on, He will offer His. When you need direction, He will be there to listen to and counsel you. And when you are in danger, He will help you find a way out. For He never fails to bless those who trust in Him.

Help me to always remember, Lord, that You are
there for me—always have been, always will be.

HABITUAL FELLOWSHIP

Noah was a just and righteous man, blameless in his [evil]
generation; Noah walked [in habitual fellowship] with God.
GENESIS 6:9 AMPC

· ·

God had created humans in His image (Genesis 5:1–2). But as the years
went on, He regretted doing so. Why? Because He "saw that the wickedness
of man was great in the earth, and that every imagination *and* intention of
all human thinking was only evil continually" (Genesis 6:5 AMPC, emphasis
added). So God decided to wipe man off the face of the earth. But then. . .
He noticed Noah, "a just and righteous man, blameless in his [evil]
generation" (Genesis 6:9 AMPC).

How did Noah get to be such a good man? Like his great-grandfather
Enoch, Noah "walked [in habitual fellowship] with God" (Genesis 5:22,
24; 6:9 AMPC). In other words, Noah made it a habit to spend time with
God. And because he did so, his thinking changed. It became more
aligned with God's thoughts than his fellow human's. Because Noah's
thoughts, heart, and actions were in sync with God's, he was not only
saved but able to rescue others.

When you habitually spend time with God, you too will begin the
process of realigning yourself with Him, beginning with your thoughts.
Doing so will not only save you but aid you in saving others.

Thank You, Lord, for giving me the hope and strength I need
to trust in You. For You are the Doer of the impossible. Amen.

BREAKFAST OF CHAMPIONS

But He answered, "It is written: Man must not live on bread alone but on every word that comes from the mouth of God."
MATTHEW 4:4 HCSB

. . . .

God has not created you, then left you to fend for yourself.

Just as a good mother can never forget the baby who nurses at her breast (Isaiah 49:15), God will never forget you. Just as He remembered Noah and his family (Genesis 8:1), God remembers you and yours. Your Abba longs to be a part of your life, to build you up and keep you safe. And the best way He can do that is through His Word—the nourishment that will make your spirit strong and your soul sublime.

Today and every day, live on God's Word, all that comes from His mouth. Allow His voice—laced with encouragement, peace, strength, and light—to override thoughts of fear, anxiety, weakness, and darkness that swirl around in your mind. Then, in the evening, when you are lying upon your bed, present your petitions, remembering that God listens when you call to Him (Psalm 4:3). Afterward, as you begin to nod off, you can pray, "In peace I will both lie down and sleep, for You, Lord, alone make me dwell in safety and confident trust" (Psalm 4:8 AMPC).

Remind me each day, Lord, to feed on Your Word, eating the breakfast of champions. In Jesus' name I pray, amen.

"I WILL"

The LORD had said to Abram, "Leave your native country, your relatives, and your father's family, and go to the land that I will show you. I will make you into a great nation. I will bless you and make you famous, and you will be a blessing to others. I will bless those who bless you and curse those who treat you with contempt."

GENESIS 12:1–3 NLT

. . . .

Count how many "I will" statements God speaks into the life of Abram in the verses above. Then observe how all those promises, all those "I wills," hinged on Abram leaving behind his home, his country, and his relatives. How bit by bit, Abram would separate himself from the things of the earth that would claim his attention until, step by faithful step, nothing of the world stood between him and his Lord.

God asks you to do the same. Through Jesus, God asks you to leave all behind to follow Him (Luke 18:28–30). In doing so, you too will be rewarded, led to the land of promises, a place of blessings and holy companionship.

God has a better plan for you than the one the world daily tries to sell you. His provides you with the blessings of eternal love, light, and life—here and beyond—blessings that will never fade or wear away.

Help me, Lord, to not get sucked into the idea that I need material things to give me joy. All I really need is You!

ABOVE AND BEYOND

*"You have heard the law that says, 'Love your neighbor'
and hate your enemy. But I say, love your enemies! Pray
for those who persecute you! In that way, you will be
acting as true children of your Father in heaven."*

MATTHEW 5:43–45 NLT

. . . .

Jesus has you on a mission. You, the daughter of the King, are to eschew
the ways of the world and embrace the ways of God. That means going
above and beyond what the average person would do. It means not just
tolerating your enemies but *loving* them! But that's not all. You're also to
pray for those who, because of your faith, give you a hard time! For only
then will you be acting as God wants His daughters to act.

Living God's way here on earth is bound to be a challenge. But it's
one He has prepared and equipped you for. Simply call up whatever faith
you need to do His will, what He would have you do, remembering *His*
way is the only true way. When you do, you will "be perfect [growing into
complete maturity of godliness in mind and character, having reached the
proper height of virtue and integrity], as your heavenly Father is perfect"
(Matthew 5:48 AMPC).

*Help grow me, Lord, into the woman You want me
to be. Give me the strength, power, determination,
and mindset, to walk in Your will and way.*

ANYTHING IS POSSIBLE

Sarah laughed to herself, saying, "After I am worn out, and my lord is old, shall I have pleasure?" The LORD said to Abraham, "Why did Sarah laugh and say, 'Shall I indeed bear a child, now that I am old?' Is anything too hard for the LORD?"

GENESIS 18:12–14 ESV

• •

When the Lord visited Abraham's tent, Sarah was standing just inside the tent door, listening to their conversation. She overheard God telling her elderly husband, "I will return to you about this time next year, and your wife, Sarah, will have a son!" (Genesis 18:10 NLT).

Hearing this news, Sarah started laughing to herself. Why? Because the Lord was promising what, in her mind, was the impossible! She was already way past childbearing age and could not imagine anyone being able to pull off such an amazing feat! Yet God did.

God can make a way when there seems to be no way. With Him on your side, actively working in your life, walls are torn down, mountains moved, threats silenced, waves walked on. Today and every day, live in the knowledge that you belong to a God who is able to do anything in and through you. He can even help an elderly couple give birth to a baby.

Help me keep in mind, Lord, that nothing is too hard for You. In Jesus' name I pray. Amen.

LOT'S WIFE

[The angels] said, Escape for your life! Do not look behind you,
or stop anywhere in the whole valley. . . . But [Lot's] wife
looked back from behind him, and she became a pillar of salt.
GENESIS 19:17, 26 AMPC

. . . .

The story of Lot's wife never gets old. Why? Because it begs us to remember, time and time again, three essential points in our walk with God.

The first is that we're to always obey God. He is like any good mother. He doesn't give us rules to try to trip us up (which we do constantly) or to make our lives difficult. He gives us rules so that we'll learn to trust and obey Him, knowing they (and He) will keep us safe!

The second is that we're to cling to God alone. The earthly possessions we crave, the ones we don't want to part with, are fleeting. They will neither save us nor help us get into heaven.

The third is that we're to never look back. For by continually looking to what we once had keeps us from moving forward.

Use Lot's wife as an example of what *not* to do. Rather than walk in her footsteps, make it your intent to live a life of obedience to God, clinging to Him alone, and never looking back.

Lord, help me to become an obedient
daughter with her eyes on You alone.

AS PROMISED

The LORD kept his word and did for Sarah exactly what he had promised. She became pregnant, and she gave birth to a son for Abraham in his old age. This happened at just the time God had said it would.

GENESIS 21:1–2 NLT

. . . .

Etch the words "The LORD kept his word and did. . .exactly what he had promised" upon your mind. Write them upon your heart. Store them so deeply inside you that when you are challenged, depressed, in trouble or doubt, harassed, distraught, and anxious, you can find your way out of it and into a place where you are assured, joyful, secure, certain, at peace, calm, and composed.

Steep yourself in God's promises when you feel the ground shaking beneath your feet. Allow His promises to give you firm footing. Begin with the ones that speak most to your heart, the ones that are medicine to your mind and a salve to your soul. Look up verses about His never-ending guidance, faithfulness, love, grace, blessings, wisdom, peace, joy, provision, power, etc. Then read the stories of the promises that God came through on in scripture.

Live your life knowing that God always keeps His Word. That what He promised will come to fruition, in exactly the way He said it would. Doing so will change your life from one of pain to promise!

Lord of love, lead me to the promise You would have me claim as I read Your Word today. Amen.

PRAISE AND JOY

*I will praise you, LORD, with all my heart; I will tell of all
the marvelous things you have done. I will be filled with joy
because of you. I will sing praises to your name, O Most High.*

PSALM 9:1–2 NLT

. . . .

There is a myriad of reasons to praise the Lord with every fiber of your being. And those reasons can be found throughout God's Word.

As Abraham and Sarah, Ruth and Naomi, Hannah and Samuel, and billions of other God-followers have discovered, you can trust in God's name because He does not and will not abandoned those who seek Him (Psalm 9:10).

The Lord God who sees that you, like Abraham, have left all—hearth, home, and family—to follow Him will send His angel *before* you, scoping out the situation before you take one step. Then, as you continue walking in step with God, He "will send His angel *with* you and make your journey a success" (Genesis 24:40 HCSB, emphasis added).

Yet that's just the beginning! For while you're on this journey with God, before you even finish praying your petitions, God is working out His answer in your life (Genesis 24:15)!

These are just three examples of what God does in your life, why He is more than worthy of praise. Need more? Read the Word—then praise!

Lord, I raise my eyes to You, my mouth full of praise, my heart of joy!

THE WHY QUESTIONS

Isaac prayed to the LORD on behalf of his wife because she was childless.
The LORD heard his prayer, and his wife Rebekah conceived. But the
children inside her struggled with each other, and she said, "Why
is this happening to me?" So she went to inquire of the LORD.
GENESIS 25:21–23 HCSB

• •

When things don't seem to be going as planned, why-questions begin creeping into our minds. And if we don't take those why-questions to God, doubts begin to develop, darkening our hopes and joys.

Rebekah's seeking out God to put her question before Him is the first recorded instance we have of a woman pursuing Him in prayer. Rebekah is a great example to follow in this regard. For she reminds us that God alone holds all the answers, that He alone is the ultimate source of wisdom, and that He alone can and will answer our specific questions.

When you have a question or concern about anything in your life, go directly to God. Do not pass go. Do not collect $200. Head straight to the ultimate Source, knowing He will give you whatever guidance you need just when you need it.

Lord, You are the source of all wisdom. So I come to You now,
asking why this is happening to me—knowing that You will
answer, You will give me whatever guidance I need. Amen.

PERFECT PEACEFULNESS

He got up and rebuked the winds and the sea, and there was a
great and wonderful calm (a perfect peaceableness). And the men
were stunned with bewildered wonder and marveled, saying, What
kind of Man is this, that even the winds and the sea obey Him!
MATTHEW 8:26–27 AMPC

. . . .

Wanting to get a break from the crowds of people surrounding Him, Jesus got into a boat. The disciples followed Him and headed out across the lake.

Suddenly a storm came upon them. The wind and waves became so violent that the boat began filling with water. But Jesus was in the stern, sleeping. In a panic, His disciples woke Jesus, pleading for Him to save them.

After admonishing His followers for having so little faith and so much fear, Jesus arose and scolded the wind and waves. At once, there was a great calm. A "perfect peaceableness."

Your Lord Jesus has power over the storms within and without. Making this a certainty in your mind should help your fear from overcoming your faith. Simply take it as a fact that with Jesus in the stern of your boat, there's no place for panic. That all you need to do is stay calm, for He won't let anything harm you, no matter how big the waves, how strong the current, how violent the wind.

Thank You, Lord, for stilling the storms within and outside of me!

WHEREVER YOU GO

The LORD. . .said. . ."I am with you, and I will protect you wherever you go. . . . I will not leave you until I have finished giving you everything I have promised you." Then Jacob awoke from his sleep and said, "Surely the LORD is in this place, and I wasn't even aware of it!"

GENESIS 28:13, 15–16 NLT

. . . .

God has a habit of showing up in the strangest places. In this instance, He was part of a dream that Jacob had—a very real dream—in which angels were going up and down a ladder that reached from earth into heaven. Then he heard God speaking to him.

Upon waking, Jacob said he'd never realized God would be there, in that place, appearing to him when he was on the run from an angry brother, a dismal place where, at sunset, Jacob used a rock for a pillow and fell asleep where he lay.

This promise that God made to Jacob—to be with you and protect you no matter where you are—He makes to you. *And* He'll never leave you until all the promises He made come to fruition.

As a God-follower, a believer, a woman of the Way, keep these facts, these truths in mind. God is everywhere you are. The more you are aware of it, the more you will be aware of Him!

Thank You, Lord, for being with me wherever I go—protecting, providing, loving!

GLINTS OF SUNSHINE

*Then God remembered Rachel and answered her pleading
and made it possible for her to have children. And [now
for the first time] she became pregnant and bore a son.*

GENESIS 30:22–23 AMPC

. . . .

Rachel had birthed no children to Jacob. Meanwhile her sister had already given him four sons! Jealous, Rachel said to Jacob, "Give me children, or I shall die!" (Genesis 30:1 ESV). In anger, Jacob said to her, "Am I in God's place, who has withheld children from you?" (Genesis 30:2 HCSB).

The turmoil in Rachel's heart then led to her sincerely plying her prayers to God. Eventually, in His time, God remembered Rachel's petitions and opened her womb, allowing her to conceive and give birth to Joseph.

There are times in our lives when we have to wait on God—and must do so faithfully, knowing that in His time, He will remember us and our prayers, He will provide His answer, and we will praise Him.

F. B. Meyers wrote, "There are more compensations in life than we think. If Rachel had her husband's love, Leah had a large family of boys. In the saddest lives there are glints of sunshine." Today, as you wait on God, look for the glints of sunshine in your own life—and praise God for every one of them!

*Thank You, Lord, for remembering me,
for providing me with sparkling glints of sunshine!*

LOVED AND VALUED

Then Jacob went on his way, and God's angels met him.
Genesis 32:1 ampc

. . . .

You may not be a patriarch, a male, a father, a big name in the annals of history. But you are just as important in God's eyes as Jacob was. So it stands to reason that as you go on your way with God, there are angels surrounding you, reassuring you of God's presence and theirs, protecting you from dangers seen and unseen.

In fact, the Bible says that very thing! Because you have made God your refuge, He commands His angels to guard you (Psalm 91:9–12).

Jesus makes a point in telling His followers that not one little sparrow falls to the ground without God knowing about it. In fact, says He, every hair on each believer's head is numbered. "So don't be afraid; you are more valuable to God than a whole flock of sparrows" (Matthew 10:31 nlt).

That's how much God is aware of you. That's how much He loves you. That's how much He values you.

So the next time you find yourself overwhelmed with thoughts of worry and worthlessness, when your fear threatens to override your faith, remember all those angels and the Lord of Light with you—loving you, guarding you, looking out for you. And soon you and your mind will be set back on the right light-filled course.

You, Lord, are my refuge, my love, my life, and light!

THE SEEKING GOD

*When John in prison heard about the activities of Christ, he sent
a message by his disciples and asked Him, Are You the One Who
was to come, or should we keep on expecting a different one?*
MATTHEW 11:2–3 AMPC

• •

In the days of King David, some fools said in their hearts that there is
no God. Such thoughts prompted God to look "down from heaven upon
the children of men to see if there were any who understood, dealt wisely,
and sought after God, inquiring for and of Him and requiring Him [of
vital necessity]" (Psalm 14:2 AMPC).

In Jesus' day, not even John the Baptist was sure his Cousin was the
Messiah. When asked if He was the one, Jesus simply told the people to
open their eyes to what He was doing in their lives: fulfilling the words
of the prophets by giving sight to the blind, working legs to the lame,
clear skin to the lepers, hearing to the deaf, and life to the dead.

When uncertainty begins to creep into your thoughts, don't walk the
fool's road. Instead, tap into the Word. Read about what God promised
in the Old Testament and what Jesus did in the New. Consider what
the Spirit does in your life today. Act with wisdom; seek the God who
seeks you.

Blessed God, Saving Shepherd, Holy Spirit, it is You I seek.

NEVER LOST

Jacob told everyone in his household, "Get rid of all your pagan idols, purify yourselves, and put on clean clothing. We are now going to Bethel, where I will build an altar to the God who answered my prayers when I was in distress. He has been with me wherever I have gone."

GENESIS 35:2–3 NLT

. . . .

When you're feeling discouraged, when you need to get your heart and head back into God, retrace your steps. Go back to the place—physically, mentally, emotionally, or spiritually—where you first encountered God. A place where your spirit soared, where you had your first very real sense of God's presence.

Shake off all that has proved to be a false idol, a hindrance to the relationship between you and God. Physically dedicate a space in your home to God that would remind you of that first magical encounter with the Lord of all Creation. Make it a place where you can and will spend time with Him—alone and uninterrupted.

Remember how God comforted you in the past, when He answered your prayers during troubled times, where He unstintingly gave you all the love, courage, and strength you needed, just when you needed it. Consider how He has been with you everywhere you have gone.

Woman of the Way, never forget that those who honor Him, those who walk His way, who follow His light will never get lost.

Lord, I'm back.

THE PATH

"Come to me, all who labor and are heavy laden, and I will give you rest. Take my yoke upon you, and learn from me, for I am gentle and lowly in heart, and you will find rest for your souls."

MATTHEW 11:28–29 ESV

. . . .

Jesus shows you His path of life by giving you the formula in how to live it.

The first step is to go to Jesus, to enter into His presence—not when you're in a rush nor with the attitude that spending time with Him is just one more thing to check off your list. He wants you to truly seek Him out with all your heart.

The second step is to learn to live as Jesus lived, walk as He walked, do as He did. As you do so, you will become as gentle and humble in your heart as He. Following His pathway, taking those steps, will bring rest, renewal, and peace to your soul.

As you live in and walk closer to Jesus, as you model His mode of living, you'll find yourself saying, "I will bless the LORD who guides me; even at night my heart instructs me. I know the LORD is always with me. I will not be shaken, for he is right beside me" (Psalm 16:7–8 NLT).

Lord, "You make known to me the path of life; in your presence there is fullness of joy. . .pleasures forevermore" (Psalm 16:11 ESV).

JOSEPH MOMENTS

O Lord, hear my plea for justice. Listen to my cry for help. Pay attention to my prayer, for it comes from honest lips. . . . You have tested my thoughts and examined my heart in the night. You have scrutinized me and found nothing wrong. . . . My steps have stayed on your path.

Psalm 17:1, 3, 5 nlt

. . . .

Every woman will, at some point in her life, experience a string of Joseph moments (Genesis 39–40), times when she just can't seem to get a break, when she believes herself a wretched victim of circumstance. These may be moments when her friends or family disappoint her. When she's forced to move into an unpleasant situation. When dungeon-like darkness threatens to overwhelm her. When people she has helped, are restored, then leave her behind.

Yet even during the darkest of days, the worst of circumstances, it would behoove a woman to remember God is with her. And because He's with her, there's hope. There's light. There's love. There's comfort. And because of those things, she will find favor. She will be raised up, succeed, and prosper—because through it all, she stuck with the God who stuck with her!

Dear Lord, "I am praying to you because I know you will answer, O God. Bend down and listen as I pray. Show me your unfailing love in wonderful ways. . . . Guard me as you would guard your own eyes" (Psalm 17:6–8 nlt).

A GOOD HEART

"Whatever is in your heart determines what you say. A good person produces good things from the treasury of a good heart, and an evil person produces evil things from the treasury of an evil heart."

MATTHEW 12:34–35 NLT

. . . .

Today's verses put forth a powerful message: Whatever you have in your heart will determine what comes out of your mouth! Just as a contaminated well will bring forth contaminated water, so will a corrupted heart bring forth corrupted words.

So how does a woman make sure her words are pure and uplifting? By guarding her mind and heart in Christ: "Whatever is true, whatever is honorable, whatever is just, whatever is pure, whatever is lovely, whatever is commendable, if there is any excellence, if there is anything worthy of praise, think about these things" (Philippians 4:8 ESV).

To keep your heart and mind pure, be *intentional* every day about what you allow into your mind and heart. Turn away from whatever TV, radio, online program, podcast, pundit, politician, parasite, pariah, party, or social media outlet is leading you away from humility, calm, and love, and turn toward the words and lessons of Jesus. Then you'll be heading the right way—God's Way.

Lord, help me to truly follow You by not just loving and caring for others more than myself but by thinking only of things worthy of You and praise.

TENDER OF THE HEART

"When anyone hears the word of the kingdom and does not understand it, the evil one comes and snatches away what has been sown in his heart. This is what was sown along the path."

MATTHEW 13:19 ESV

. . . .

Are you heart smart?

Jesus tells a parable about a sower (God), His seed (the Word), and the receiver of the sower's seed (you).

The seed that fell on the roadside represents the woman who heard the Word but didn't understand it in her heart. So, the evil one came along and grabbed what had fallen but not been absorbed.

The seed that fell on the rocky soil represents the woman who heard the Word, was thrilled about it, but didn't stick with it. Because of her shallow roots, she caved at the first sign of trouble.

The seed that fell amid thorns is the woman who heard the Word but because of the troubles of this world and her runaway worries, the Word got choked out and produced nothing.

The seed that fell on good soil. This is the woman who not only understood the Word but reaped a harvest beyond her imagination!

Look into your heart today. Consider how you have been receiving God's Word. What fruit it has borne in your heart.

Lord of the harvest, Sower of the Word, make me a better tender of my heart. May I take in Your message and reap a harvest beyond my wildest hopes and dreams.

GOD SENT

*"Don't be upset, and don't be angry with yourselves for selling
me to this place. It was God who sent me here ahead of you
to preserve your lives. . . . God has sent me ahead of you
to keep you and your families alive and to preserve many
survivors. So it was God who sent me here, not you!"*

GENESIS 45:5, 7, 8 NLT

· ·

Sometimes we may find ourselves in hard places because of the
manipulations or machinations of those who wish us ill. Yet while we
are going through such difficulties, we can be assured that we're still in
God's hands. That He's the sovereign ruler over all. That He'll make sure
to use whatever happens to us for good.

To stay on the right track, we must trust that God not only knows
what He's doing, even when we can in no way fathom how, but (1) He
will ever find a way to make good come of our situation or (2) He will
get us out, around, or through it.

So when the hard times come, when others plot against you, when
it seems as if there is only darkness and despair surrounding you, when
through no fault of your own you are in a mess, remain firm in both faith
and hope, remembering God has a plan and all will someday be well.

I'm trusting myself to You, Lord, for You are my light and hope.

THE COMPLETE PATHWAY

"The words you speak come from the heart—that's what defiles you.
For from the heart come evil thoughts, murder, adultery, all sexual
immorality, theft, lying, and slander. These are what defile you."

MATTHEW 15:18–20 NLT

. . . .

God's Word repeatedly reminds us that our heart's content and condition determine what comes out of our mouths. His continually reiterating the importance of keeping our hearts pure reflects His determination that we get this truth through our sometimes-thick skulls.

When God wants us to walk a certain road, He provides plenty of direction in how to get there. So too in the case of ensuring the words of our mouths and the thoughts in our hearts are pleasing to Him. To get from here to there, God directs us *through* His Word *to* His Word in which we discover:

- His instructions are perfect, renewing our lives
- His testimony is trustworthy, making the naive wise
- His precepts are right, making our heart glad
- His command is radiant, giving us insights to living right (Psalm 19:7–9)

So, ladies, dive into the Word. Immerse yourself within it. Then you will find the complete pathway to good words and a good heart.

"May the words of my mouth and the meditation of my heart be
pleasing to you, O LORD, my rock and my redeemer" (Psalm 19:14 NLT).

A POINT OF TRUST

God [Himself]. . .has [been my Shepherd and has led and] fed me from the time I came into being until this day, the redeeming Angel [that is, the Angel the Redeemer—not a created being but the Lord Himself]. . .has redeemed me continually from every evil.

GENESIS 48:15–16 AMPC

. . . .

When Jesus was ministering in His hometown, "He did not do many works of power there, because of their unbelief" (Matthew 13:58 AMPC). Imagine what those people missed out on!

Yet how often are we ourselves so engrossed in the material world, so far away from and doubting of the influence of the supernatural on the natural, that we too miss out on all that God can do in our lives.

The Old Testament patriarch Jacob knew the power, protection, and provision of his God. Because of his great faith, he understood and saw with his spiritual eye that the Lord had been his personal Shepherd, leading and feeding him from the beginning of his existence all the way to the end. He knew with a certainty that the Lord was his redeeming Angel, continually rescuing him from evil.

How about you? How's your faith? Who or what do you trust to save you—your horses and chariots, your common sense, or Yahweh (Psalm 20:7)?

Put your mind, heart, and money on God. He's the only sure thing in this life—and the next!

It's You I trust, Yahweh! You I believe in!

THAT SINKING FEELING

"Come," Jesus said. So Peter went over the side of the boat and walked on the water toward Jesus. But when he saw the strong wind and the waves, he was terrified and began to sink. "Save me, Lord!" he shouted. Jesus immediately reached out and grabbed him.

MATTHEW 14:29–31 NLT

. . . .

How do you ward off the sinking feeling of fear? You focus your eyes and mind on Jesus.

It can take a lot of courage to ask God to command you step out of your comfort zone. To lift your leg over the side of a familiar vessel and suddenly stand on an unfamiliar, undulating terrain. But there you are!

And then you take your eyes off Him—just for a second. The next thing you know, you realize the challenges you face, you take in the threatening wind and waves, and fear bubbles up from the bowels of doubt. You get that sinking feeling, then begin to do just that. In desperation, you cry out, "Lord, save me!" And immediately He does, wondering at your lack of faith.

To avoid the sinking feeling of fear, keep your eyes and thoughts on Jesus. And before you know it, you'll be walking on water.

Lord, help me to train my eyes and thoughts to remain on You and Your power—not my fears, obstacles, or challenges!

THE COURAGE OF FAITHFUL WOMEN

The midwives feared God and did not do as the king of Egypt
commanded them. . . . So God dealt well with the midwives.
EXODUS 1:17, 20 ESV

· ·

The Hebrews had once prospered in Egypt when they lived under Joseph, the man second only to Pharoah. But years after his death, they became enslaved by their adopted country. Yet even then, during immense hardship, two midwives named Shiphrah and Puah, remained faithful to God, not the Egyptian king. And because of their faith and courage, they were rewarded.

Jochebed, the mother of Moses, also showed her faith and courage when she hid her baby boy, then launched him in a little ark on the Nile. Miriam, her daughter, watched and waited to see what would happen (Exodus 2). The reward for efforts of these women was the saving of Moses' life and love, leading to his eventual leadership.

Just as those four women of faith seemed "out of place" in time and faith, so did the Canaanite woman who persistently requested Jesus heal her daughter. In the end, Jesus said to her, " 'Woman, your faith is great. Let it be done for you as you want.' And from that moment her daughter was cured" (Matthew 15:28 HCSB).

You are never out of place when you are with God, living a life of faith and courage.

Lord, help me be as brave and faithful as my many ancestresses.

THEREFORE GO

"Now therefore go, and I will be with your mouth and teach you what you shall speak." But he said, "Oh, my Lord, please send someone else."
EXODUS 4:12–13 ESV

. . . .

Moses was shepherding sheep in the wilderness when he saw a burning bush and heard God's voice. The Lord told him about the trouble His people were in. That He'd heard their prayers. That He'd answer them by sending Moses to lead the Jews out of Egypt.

Moses kept imagining what would happen once he tried to fulfill a seemingly impossible calling. So he reminded the Lord whom He was enlisting. After all, he was a murderer, an outcast who spoke with a lisp. He was a nobody. Finally, Moses suggested God send someone else!

Like Moses, there are times when we too are plagued with distorted thoughts. When we too, when presented with a challenge of faith, imagine what might happen if we step out of our comfort zone. And we come up with a mountain of excuses as to why we shouldn't go where we're called.

The thing is, we're neither fortune-tellers nor mind readers. We're women of the Way. And if we keep our faith in God and our focus on Him, if we remind ourselves how He tends to do the impossible through mortal vessels, we'll end up saying, "Lord, send me!" instead of asking Him to send someone else.

Lord, help me keep my mind on You, to go wherever You call me to go.

THE BALM OF A PSALM

The LORD is my shepherd; I have all that I need. He lets me rest in green meadows; he leads me beside peaceful streams. He renews my strength. He guides me along right paths, bringing honor to his name.

PSALM 23:1–3 NLT

. . . .

Psalm 23 is the most well-known and beloved psalm in the Bible, a balm to many souls—and there's a good reason for that.

When you feel lost, alone, and afraid, David's psalm assures you that God, your Shepherd, is with you. And because He is, you will not lack. For He will lead you to rest in fresh green pastures, guide you to soothing still water. He'll restore your strength and lead you down the right road.

Psalm 23 reminds you that when you walk through the dark valleys, you need have no thought of fear because God is with you, carrying a rod to protect you and a staff to guide you. He'll prepare a feast for you in the presence of your enemies, revive your sagging head, and fill your cup full of blessings.

Because God is with you and will always be with you, His goodness and love will follow you wherever you go.

When your mind is on overload, your heart trembling, your spirit drooping, sink yourself into this psalm, the balm for your soul.

Lord, You are my Shepherd. . . .

CLOSER THAN BREATHING

"This time I will spare the region of Goshen, where my people live. No flies will be found there. Then you will know that I am the LORD and that I am present even in the heart of your land. I will make a clear distinction between my people and your people."

EXODUS 8:22–23 NLT

. . . .

God brought the ten plagues upon Pharaoh and his people so that they would know that He is the God of all gods, even those the Egyptians worshipped. That He was present, even in the heart of their land.

God continues to go to great lengths to let His people know not just who He is but *where* He is. He once inspired the poet Alfred Lord Tennyson to write these insightful words about Him: "Closer is He than breathing and nearer than hands and feet." The apostle Paul agreed, saying, "He is actually not far from each one of us, for 'In him we live and move and have our being'" (Acts 17:27–28 ESV).

God wants you to know the same thing. He sees you rushing through life, stranded at a crossroad, or very alone, longing for love and companionship. And He wants you to realize that He—as well as His wisdom, help, and strength—lives in the very heart of you.

Know, believe, live a full life knowing God is closer than your breathing.

Lord, my breath and hope, thank You for being so near.

MOUNTAIN-MOVING
MUSTARD-SEED FAITH

*Truly I say to you, if you have faith [that is living] like a grain
of mustard seed, you can say to this mountain, Move from here to
yonder place, and it will move; and nothing will be impossible to you.*
MATTHEW 17:20 AMPC

. . . .

Throughout Psalm 25, David asks God to make His ways known to him, to teach him how to follow Him, to guide him in truth. When Jesus came, He did just that, making His followers, including us, students of God, people who crave learning how to live and walk God's Way.

Among His many lessons, Jesus teaches us not only how to pray but how to live a life of faith. In today's verse, He explains that if we have faith, a living faith, even as small as a mustard seed, we can move mountains. That for us nothing will be impossible.

When an obstacle comes before you, when you are faced with a seemingly immovable barrier, dig deep into the power of God and the truth of Jesus. Know that you can move that wall. That because you belong to God, because you follow Jesus, because you have invited the Spirit to live within you, for you nothing is impossible. All you need to do is simply believe.

Jesus, Lord of my life, I believe—in the impossible!

LIKE A CHILD

*He called a little child to Himself and put him in the midst of
them, and said, Truly I say to you, unless you repent (change, turn
about) and become like little children [trusting, lowly, loving,
forgiving], you can never enter the kingdom of heaven [at all].*
MATTHEW 18:2–3 AMPC

. . . .

Jesus definitely knows how to turn things around. . . .

When the disciples asked Him who is the greatest in the kingdom
of heaven, Jesus answered that unless His followers change and become
like little children, they will not even enter heaven. Then He presented
an even more radical idea: The one who is the greatest in heaven is one
who becomes like a little child—"trusting, lowly, loving, and forgiving."

How many of those descriptors fit you? Do you trust God like a
small child trusts her good and loving mother? Do you consider yourself
humble? Are you loving? And, even more of a challenge, are you forgiving?

Let's remember that in no way does Jesus want us to be child*ish*—
just child*like*. If you need help in this regard, find a friend who can help
keep you accountable in this goal. Even better, pray with her about it,
remembering that where two or three are gathered, Jesus is there in the
midst of them.

---

*Help me, Lord, to become like a little child, humbly looking
up to You with loving eyes, full of trust, and fully forgiving.*

FORGIVENESS

Then Peter came to Jesus and asked, "Lord, how many times shall I forgive my brother or sister who sins against me? Up to seven times?" Jesus answered, "I tell you, not seven times, but seventy-seven times."

MATTHEW 18:21–22 NIV

. . . .

We often think of forgiveness as an emotion or an attitude we have to somehow work up within our hearts. Again and again, however, the Bible links our hearts to our actions; neither one can stand alone because they're intertwined, our actions growing from the emotions and attitudes we hold in our hearts—and vice versa: our actions can also shape our hearts.

When Matthew wrote these verses, the Greek word he used for "forgive" is *aphiémi*, which means, literally, "send away." The same word is used for "divorce." Jesus isn't saying we should send our brother or sister away, of course, or divorce ourselves from them in any way. Instead, what He means is that we should separate our emotions and our actions from whatever offense was committed against us. When we truly forgive someone, we send away those feelings; we step back from them and no longer allow them to influence our actions.

Jesus, thank You that You have sent all my offenses far away, so they no longer come between You and me. Help me to do the same for others.

BURSTING OUT IN SONG

The LORD is my strength and shield. I trust him with all my heart. He helps me, and my heart is filled with joy. I burst out in songs of thanksgiving. The LORD gives his people strength.
PSALM 28:7–8 NLT

. . . .

Notice how the psalmist in these verses connects our inner self with external action.

We trust with our heart, that private center of our being no one can see but ourselves and God—and God responds with help and protection that fill us with joy. That joy doesn't remain inside of us, though, where no one else can see it, but instead bursts out of us in song everyone can hear. That doesn't necessarily mean we're literally singing at the top of our lungs (although we might); our "song" could be expressed on our faces or in words or in other actions that tell the world God has done great things for us. And then God continues to help us, giving us more strength, emotionally, spiritually, and physically, so we can serve Him with our hearts, souls, and bodies.

Lord, I thank You for all the ways You help me. May the love and joy You give me flow out from me and touch everyone with whom I come in contact today.

THE VOICE OF THE LORD

The voice of the Lord is upon the waters; the God of glory thunders; the Lord is upon many (great) waters. The voice of the Lord is powerful; the voice of the Lord is full of majesty.

PSALM 29:3–4 AMPC

. . . .

The Hebrew word used for "voice" in these verses has several shades of meaning. It can mean a roar, a scream, a growl, or a thunderbolt. It can also be a gentle jingle or the sweet sound of birds twittering.

We hear God in many ways. Sometimes He uses events in our lives that thunder like wild waves breaking on the shore—and sometimes He speaks to us in the still, small voice only we can hear. Either way, we need to be paying attention or we may miss what He is trying to tell us. This means listening for God's voice as we interact with the circumstances of our lives. It also means taking time to hear Him speaking to our hearts. As we learn to recognize God's voice, we can allow His Spirit to lead us into the actions He wants us to take.

Lord, make me sensitive, I pray, to Your voice. Help me never to be so busy that I forget to listen for what You are telling me. Then, having heard Your message to me, give me the strength and courage to act in ways that please You. Amen.

FALSE GODS

Then God gave the people all these instructions: "I am the LORD your God, who rescued you from the land of Egypt, the place of your slavery. You must not have any other god but me."

EXODUS 20:1–3 NLT

. . . .

When we read the Ten Commandments, we might think this particular passage has no real meaning for us today. After all, most of us don't fall down and worship idols. But a god doesn't have to be a statue or have the name of a deity. Our "gods" are anything that takes God's place in our lives.

We often may not realize we're putting something ahead of God, but if we look at our hearts, thoughts, and actions, we may see how much time and energy we spend focused on things other than God. It could be social media or television; it might be our jobs or even our families. None of these things are evil in and of themselves, of course, but we need to be sure God is always at the center of our hearts and minds. For when He has His place there, our actions will also fall into line, reflecting the fact that God is our priority.

God, thank You for rescuing me from all the things in my life that held me captive. Teach me to always make You the central focus of my thoughts. Be my number-one priority.

TRAPS

Keep me free from the trap that is set for me, for you are my refuge.
Into your hands I commit my spirit; deliver me, LORD, my faithful God.
PSALM 31:4–5 NIV

. . . .

When David wrote these verses, the "trap" he was talking about probably had to do with external circumstances. As the king of Israel, David had many political enemies, and at times he was in physical danger. But David also faced a different kind of trap—the "trap" of temptation, of lust, of fear.

David knew that whether the trap was external and physical or internal and emotional, God could protect him. But first, David committed his spirit—his inner being—into God's hands. Now, with his spirit in the right place, he was confident God would deliver him from whatever danger he faced.

Faithful God, remind me at the start of each day to commit my inner being to You. Then remind me to recommit my spirit to You over and over, throughout this day and the days to come. For it's so easy for me to find myself repeatedly trapped by my emotions and circumstances.

Thank You, Lord, for being so patient with me. And help me be patient with myself when I stumble, then quickly recommit myself to You, no matter how many times I need to do it.

LIKE CHILDREN AND BABIES

*From the lips of children and infants you,
Lord, have called forth your praise.*
MATTHEW 21:16 NIV

. . . .

Verses like this one make clear that we don't have to have a degree in theology to praise God. We don't even need to be emotionally or spiritually mature. Just as children and babies by their very nature give glory to God, so can we. There's no standard we have to achieve first, no particular set of behaviors we need to follow. Instead, as simple as breathing, we can allow God to call forth His praise from our hearts. And then like children absorbed in their play, our actions will naturally reflect the presence of the Lord in our lives. His presence will help us grow, emotionally and spiritually, and lead us forward as we journey through the circumstances of our lives.

Call forth Your praise from my heart, Lord. I want my life to be constantly connected to You, both on the inside and on the outside.

SPIRITUALLY ROOTED

Praise be to the LORD, for he showed me the wonders of his love when I was in a city under siege. In my alarm I said, "I am cut off from your sight!" Yet you heard my cry for mercy when I called to you for help.

PSALM 31:21–22 NIV

. . . .

As human beings, we're accustomed to judge reality based on what our five senses tell us. When circumstances seem frightening or hopeless, we often feel we've somehow lost God's presence in our lives. We may blame ourselves—or we may blame God. Either way, that feeling of abandonment doesn't reflect reality, for we are never cut off from God.

The Lord is always with us, no matter what our physical senses or our emotional perceptions tell us. We may feel depressed, scared, frustrated, or angry; we might not be able to see where God is present in our lives; but God is always listening, always watching, always loving us, and always ready to help.

Lord, when my eyes and ears can't see You in the circumstances of my life, when my heart feels lonely and afraid, give me the spiritual confidence that You are always present, even when I can't see or hear You. Remind me that Your reality can't always be seen with physical senses or experienced at an emotional level. Keep me spiritually rooted in You, no matter what happens in my external life.

THE BIBLE IN A NUTSHELL

" 'You must love the LORD your God with all your heart, all
your soul, and all your mind.' This is the first and greatest
commandment. A second is equally important: 'Love your
neighbor as yourself.' The entire law and all the demands
of the prophets are based on these two commandments."

MATTHEW 22:37–40 NLT

. . . .

In these verses, Jesus is telling us we can boil down everything the Bible has to say into two simple sentences: Love God with all your being. Love others as much as you love yourself. Every decision we face, every action we take, and every thought we think should be judged by these two requirements.

The love Jesus is talking about is more than an emotion; it's something that's actively expressed in the way we live our lives and in the thoughts that occupy our minds. The emotional feeling of love may be present, as well, but even when we don't *feel* loving, we can continue to choose to give ourselves to God and others through every circumstance of our lives.

Remind me, Jesus, that following You comes down to those
two commandments You spelled out for us. May my actions,
my thoughts, my entire being be shaped by love.

LIFE-GIVER

Then I will live among the people of Israel and be their God, and they will know that I am the LORD their God. I am the one who brought them out of the land of Egypt so that I could live among them.

EXODUS 29:45–46 NLT

. . . .

The word most Bibles translate as "Lord" is actually *Yahweh*, God's proper name. This name was considered so holy that when scribes copied the Bible, they substituted the word "Lord" instead of writing out God's mysterious name.

Bible scholars still don't completely understand what *Yahweh* means, but they know the meaning has to do with life itself. Some of the possible translations are "Life-Giver," "the Ever-Living One," "Being," and finally, simply "I AM."

These verses from Exodus tell us of the Life-Giver whose Being contains our entire lives. We can't separate our lives into the two categories of "spiritual" and "not spiritual," because God is in *all* of life. He is present when we come to Him in prayer, but He is equally present when we're in our cars, sitting at our desks, washing dishes, or talking with a friend. He will lead us out from the "Egypts" in our lives, the places where we are trapped and held back, so that we can experience the true fullness of life in Him.

Living-One, I thank You that You are in me and around me. I am so glad Your life is present everywhere.

WARHORSES

*Don't count on your warhorse to give you victory—
for all its strength, it cannot save you. But the LORD
watches over those who fear him, those who rely on his
unfailing love. He rescues them from death and keeps
them alive in times of famine. . . . Let your unfailing
love surround us, LORD, for our hope is in you alone.*

PSALM 33:17–19, 22 NLT

• •

The psalmist who wrote these lines lived in a very different external reality from ours today. In his world, finely bred horses were sources of confidence and strength. In our world today, we might rely instead on our cars or our computers, our wardrobes or our houses to give us strength, to help us overcome.

One thing that hasn't changed, though, is that physical sources of security can never truly keep us safe. All created things have limitations; even our closest friends or our spouses will fail us sometimes. God, who is the source of all life, is the only One who will never let us down. His love alone never fails. When we put our sense of security in Him, then we can confidently face whatever life brings.

Lord, I am grateful for all the physical blessings You have given me—but remind me that none of those things can be the true source of life and happiness. In You alone I am always spiritually safe, no matter what is happening in the circumstances of my life.

GOD'S PRESENCE

I pray You, if I have found favor in Your sight, show me now Your way, that I may know You [progressively become more deeply and intimately acquainted with You, perceiving and recognizing and understanding more strongly and clearly] and that I may find favor in Your sight. . . . And the Lord said, My presence shall go with you, and I will give you rest. . .for you have found favor, loving-kindness, and mercy in My sight and I know you personally and by name.

EXODUS 33:13,14,17 AMPC

. . . .

Yet again, the Bible indicates to us that external circumstances are interwoven with both our spiritual and emotional lives. As we learn to experience God internally, we will begin to see His presence more clearly in what's going on around us. And as we experience God's activity in the external world, we will also come to know Him more intimately at the spiritual and emotional levels. God is present in it all—and He knows us each by name.

Loving Lord, teach me to recognize Your ways in the world around me. Fill my inner being with the knowledge of Your presence. Help me to rest in You.

OPEN TO GOD

Open your mouth and taste, open your eyes and see—how good GOD is.
PSALM 34:8 MSG

. . . .

Today's verse tells us that God wants us to experience Him with our physical senses. As we see the beauty of the world, as we taste a good meal, as we listen to the voices of our family members, as we feel the warmth of blankets on a frosty winter night, and as we breathe in the scent of a flower, we are experiencing the goodness of God.

"Open your mouths!" God tells us. "Listen! Keep your eyes open! I'm everywhere around you, waiting for you to experience Me." As we learn to perceive God with our bodies, we'll find our emotions tend to be more joyful and our spirits growing closer to Him.

The Living One is all around us, longing for us to experience His very Being with every level of our own being. "Open your mouth and taste, open your eyes and see—how good GOD is"!

*Today, God, I ask that You remind me to see You, to hear You,
to taste You, to touch You, and even to smell You. As my body's
senses are filled with You, fill also my heart and soul with Yourself.*

BLESSINGS UPON BLESSINGS

*For to everyone who has will more be given, and he will be furnished
richly so that he will have an abundance; but from the one who
does not have, even what he does have will be taken away.*

MATTHEW 25:29 AMPC

. . . .

This verse above doesn't seem quite fair, at least not when we think about it within the context of worldly possessions; it sounds as though God takes from the poor and gives to the rich. But once again, the Bible wants us to understand the connection between our inner thoughts and our outer reality.

When we focus on our blessings, our thoughts dwelling on them, we'll not only adopt a grateful and positive attitude but find more and more blessings coming into our lives. On the other hand, if we focus only on what we lack, we're not only going to become discouraged and develop a hopeless outlook but will find more and more reasons to be discontent. Our perceptions shape our realities and attitudes.

*Jesus, help me to look at life with Your eyes. Teach me
to see the many blessings You have given me, so that
my eyes will be open to all You have in store for me.*

TRUE LOVE

"Then the King will say to those on his right, 'Come, you who are blessed by my Father; take your inheritance, the kingdom prepared for you since the creation of the world. For I was hungry and you gave me something to eat, I was thirsty and you gave me something to drink, I was a stranger and you invited me in, I needed clothes and you clothed me, I was sick and you looked after me, I was in prison and you came to visit me.' Then the righteous will answer him, 'Lord, when did we see you hungry and feed you, or thirsty and give you something to drink? When did we see you a stranger and invite you in, or needing clothes and clothe you? When did we see you sick or in prison and go to visit you?' The King will reply, 'Truly I tell you, whatever you did for one of the least of these brothers and sisters of mine, you did for me.'"

MATTHEW 25:34–40 NIV

· ·

Here Jesus describes what true love looks like. He's explaining that the way to love God with all our hearts, minds, and bodies is by loving others in practical ways. This kind of love isn't made up of moonlight and roses but constantly looks for opportunities to be of service to others.

Remind me, Jesus, to see You in the faces of everyone I meet. May I show You my love by loving others.

BEING HONEST WITH GOD

O LORD, you know all about this. Do not stay silent.
Do not abandon me now, O Lord. Wake up! Rise to
my defense! Take up my case, my God and my Lord.
PSALM 35:22–23 NLT

. . . .

Some situations we encounter in life just don't seem fair. We're working hard to serve God, we're doing our best to follow His Spirit's leading in our lives—and still, things go wrong. We get sick, or a loved one does. We lose a job, and the bills pile up. We find out people have been gossiping about us, spreading rumors behind our backs. A relationship falls apart. Plans we've made come to nothing. When things like that happen, it's easy to feel God has abandoned us.

In reality, of course, the Lord knows all about each situation in our life. The psalmist knew this too, but he wasn't afraid to be honest with God and say, "Hey, I need to *see* what You're doing, Lord. I need to *feel* Your active presence in my life. Show me Your love at work in each situation. Defend my uncertain heart."

Defender Lord, when my emotions tell me You've abandoned
me, I pray that I will once more experience Your presence.
Give me confidence that You are always working in my life.

GOD'S WILL, NOT MINE

*"My Father, if there is any way, get me out of this.
But please, not what I want. You, what do you want?"*
MATTHEW 26:39 MSG

. . . .

These were the words Jesus spoke as He prayed in the Garden of Gethsemane on the night before His death. When we read Matthew's account, we can see that although Jesus was God, He was also very human. He was in anguish, not desiring to endure the horror, the terror of hanging on a cross when He breathed His last. But from the midst of His humanity, He still said to His Father, "Not what I want, but what You want."

Jesus showed us that we too can stand firm—even when our emotions tell us there's no way we can possibly endure what lies ahead. We don't have to pretend to God that we're not afraid or sad or reluctant; we can be completely honest about those feelings—and still say to God, "I'm not going to let my emotions have the final say here. I choose what *You* want for my life, Lord. No matter what."

I'm so grateful, Jesus, that You understand my emotions. When my emotions try to hold me back, give me the strength to not let those inner feelings shape my outer actions. Help me follow Your example.

GOD OF LIGHT

*How exquisite your love, O God! How eager we are to run
under your wings, to eat our fill at the banquet you spread
as you fill our tankards with Eden spring water. You're a
fountain of cascading light, and you open our eyes to light.*

PSALM 36:7–9 MSG

. . . .

God is not only Light, but He also helps us to perceive His Light. When
we run to Him—filling our minds with thoughts of His love, allowing
our emotions to be nourished by the Creator's refreshment, turning to
Him for help with every challenge we encounter—then God's Light spills
into both our inner and outer lives. We begin to see things differently.
We catch glimpses of Eden. Our lives are illuminated in wonderful ways
we never anticipated.

*God of Light, I want to run under Your protecting wings,
eat from Your table, and drink from Your streams
of life. Open my eyes so I can see Your Light.*

MAKING AMENDS

"When anyone sins by betraying trust with GOD by deceiving his neighbor regarding something entrusted to him, or by robbing or cheating or threatening him; or if he has found something lost and lies about it and swears falsely regarding any of these sins that people commonly commit—when he sins and is found guilty, he must return what he stole or extorted, restore what was entrusted to him, return the lost thing he found, or anything else about which he swore falsely. He must make full compensation, add twenty percent to it, and hand it over to the owner.

LEVITICUS 6:1–5 MSG

. . . .

The Old Testament's rules and regulations can seem harsh sometimes—but they make clear that God cares about outer actions as well as our inner selves.

These words God spoke to Moses teach us several things. First, when we betray others, we betray God. Second, it's not enough to *feel* sorry for or to apologize for our actions. God asks we do our best to make amends by repairing what was broken, returning what was lost, and restoring relationships that were damaged. Third, God asks that we go out of our way to give back even more than we took.

God of Justice, reveal to me any areas that require mending. I don't want to make excuses for my behavior, and I don't want to simply wallow in my guilt. Show me the specific actions I need to take to make restitution for my actions.

STILL BEFORE THE LORD

*Be still and rest in the Lord; wait for Him and patiently lean yourself
upon Him; fret not yourself because of him who prospers in his way,
because of the man who brings wicked devices to pass. Cease from anger
and forsake wrath; fret not yourself—it tends only to evildoing.*

PSALM 37:7–8 AMPC

. . . .

We often can't control our emotional reactions to life's challenges and
disappointments. We can, however, choose how we handle those emotions,
making an active effort to entrust them as well as any thoughts that spurred
them, to the Lord. One way to do this is to sit silently in God's presence,
turning each thought over to Him as it enters our minds.

By making this practice a habit, we will gradually learn to be still
before the Lord—and then, as we go through our day, instead of fretting
and worrying, we can continue this practice of releasing each negative
thought into God's care.

As Martin Luther once said, "You cannot keep birds from flying
over your head but you can keep them from building a nest in your hair."

---

*I give the details of my life to You, Lord, as well as my emotions.
Remind me not to whine and agonize over life's complications. Teach
me to catch myself when I'm doing that—and then immediately
turn my frustration, anger, and fears over to You. Help me keep
those negative emotions from building nests in my hair!*

THE AUTHORITY OF JESUS

*Jesus. . .said to them, All authority (all power of rule) in
heaven and on earth has been given to Me. Go then and
make disciples of all the nations, . . .teaching them to observe
everything that I have commanded you; and behold, I am
with you all the days (perpetually, uniformly, and on every
occasion), to the [very] close and consummation of the age.*
MATTHEW 28:18–20 AMPC

. . . .

It seems as though each day brings bad news—a new act of violence,
another natural disaster, or one more political controversy. We don't have
to be ostriches, though, burying our heads in the sand so we don't see
what's happening around us.

Jesus calls us to have confidence in His authority at work in the world,
regardless of circumstances. He asks us to participate in His mission,
helping people learn about Him and His love. As we take action for
Jesus, we can rest in the knowledge that no matter what is happening in
our world, He is with us.

*Thank You, Jesus, that You are right beside me in every situation.
Give me the strength I need to be Your hands and feet, Your smile and
touch, Your voice and ears to each person I encounter today. May I
carry with me the constant awareness of Your authority and love.*

GOD KNOWS MY HEART

All my longings lie open before you, Lord;
my sighing is not hidden from you.
PSALM 38:9 NIV

. . . .

One thing we can learn from authors of the Psalms is this: it's okay to be honest with God about our emotions. We don't have to sugarcoat our prayers or pretend to be more "spiritual" than we really are. We can tell God exactly what we feel, even when our emotions aren't very pretty.

As the psalmist in Psalm 38 understood, God already sees into our hearts. He knows our inner lives better than we know them ourselves. So not only is there no need to pretend with God but there's also no point in it! He already knows what's in our hearts, but He doesn't judge us or criticize us for our feelings.

We can bring God the whole tangled-up mess, no matter how snarled and ugly—and then we may find we can take a step back and see things more clearly. For once all is open and before Him, God's light will shine into our lives, both on the inside and the outside, bringing new clarity to our hearts.

Thank You, Lord, that You understand me better than I do myself. I want to share everything with You, even the not-so-nice feelings I sometimes experience: my anger, hatred, jealousy, selfishness, and resentment. I give my whole self to You, asking that You bring healing to my inner and my outer life.

ALONE TIME

Very early in the morning, while it was still dark, Jesus got up,
left the house and went off to a solitary place, where he prayed.
MARK 1:35 NIV

. . . .

When reading the Gospels, we can learn a lot from paying close attention to Jesus' actions. This short verse tells us that Jesus knew how important it is to find time to be alone with God. We might think that since He is the Son of God, He wouldn't need to seek out quiet prayer times when He walked the earth, since He carried God with Him everywhere He went. But Jesus was also human, and He knew that the busier we are, the more we need to make time for prayer and solitude. Otherwise, life's busyness can take all our attention, making it harder for us to sense God's presence.

During the final three years of Jesus' life, He was constantly busy, with crowds of people following Him everywhere He went—and still, He valued His prayer time so much that He was willing to get up early and find somewhere to be alone. He knew our busy days go better when they start with prayer.

Remind me, Jesus, that the busier and more active my
life is, the more I need to find alone time with You.

PATIENCE

*I waited patiently for the LORD to help me, and he turned
to me and heard my cry. He lifted me out of the pit of
despair, out of the mud and the mire. He set my feet on solid
ground and steadied me as I walked along. He has given
me a new song to sing, a hymn of praise to our God.*

PSALM 40:1–3 NLT

· ·

Following Jesus doesn't mean we have a magic get-out-of-trouble guarantee. Christians are as likely to encounter uncertain times as anyone else, and they may also experience times of depression and hopelessness. Again, the psalmist reminds us that God never condemns us for our emotions.

Even in the midst of our bleakest times, we can hold on to the promise of God's presence with us. We can be confident that light will return to our lives, and we will once more be filled with the joy of His love. All we have to do is wait.

*Teach me patience, Lord. Remind me that Your sense of timing is not
the same as mine—but that, ultimately, You will work out all the details
of my life. When I can't see You either inside my heart or in the world
outside, help me rest in the assurance that a new song is on its way.*

JUSTICE

*I have not kept the good news of your justice hidden in my heart;
I have talked about your faithfulness and saving power. I have told
everyone in the great assembly of your unfailing love and faithfulness.*
PSALM 40:10 NLT

. . . .

The Bible speaks a great deal about justice. We might assume it's talking about a purely spiritual quality, but scripture makes it clear that God's justice requires *action*; it asks that we feed the poor, welcome strangers, and reach out our hands to anyone in need.

God's justice is practical and concrete. It's visible, expressed through our lives and through our words. It's not something God wants us to keep hidden away inside our hearts. We can't tell ourselves that our spiritual beliefs are private, with no role in how we interact with others, socially and even politically. In all that we do, God calls us to speak out on behalf of His faithfulness, love, and justice.

*Spirit of God, I ask for Your guidance today. Show me
opportunities to speak Your love and justice. Give me the
words to say; show me the actions to take. Remind me
that my faith needs arms and legs and a voice.*

SEEDS AND FRUIT

"The seed planted in the good earth represents those who hear the Word, embrace it, and produce a harvest beyond their wildest dreams."

MARK 4:20 MSG

. . . .

When Jesus told the parable of the seeds, He was telling us something important about our relationship to His message.

We can easily nod along with Jesus' command to love God and others; most of us have heard it many times before, so often, in fact, that we've stopped thinking about what it really means. Jesus is telling us here, though, that it's not enough to simply hear what He tells us—we have to embrace His message with our entire lives. This means that we're to ponder Jesus' words in our minds, wrap our emotions around them, and then we live them. When we do all this, then the Word has an amazing effect on both our inner and outer lives. The Word that starts out as something relatively small and inconspicuous grows and flourishes, bearing spiritual, emotional, and practical fruit in our lives.

Thank You, Jesus, for bringing me God's message of love. I want to open my whole self to Your words, so that they take deep root in my life—and then grow out and into the world.

RULED BY LOVE

*GOD spoke to Moses: "Speak to the People of Israel. Tell them,
I am GOD, your God. Don't live like the people of Egypt where
you used to live, and don't live like the people of Canaan
where I'm bringing you. Don't do what they do. Obey my
laws and live by my decrees. I am your GOD. Keep my decrees
and laws: The person who obeys them lives by them."*
LEVITICUS 18:1–5 MSG

. . . .

When we think about the worldly behaviors God was talking about in these verses, what comes to mind might be the obvious sins, things like adultery and violence. Or we might think of other harmful behaviors, such as drug abuse or sexual immorality. But remember, Jesus told us that all the Bible's laws are wrapped up in these two commands: to love God with all our being and to love others as ourselves.

The culture in which we live does not make love a priority. Instead, it's a me-first civilization, a society built on competition and consumption. Those attitudes are all around us, in the media, in our workplaces, in our conversations with friends, and sometimes even in our churches. It takes real effort *not* to absorb those selfish attitudes into our minds, hearts, and behaviors. No one said it would be easy—but God calls us to a life ruled by love. Let's live it.

Lord God, remind me that love should always be my first priority.

THIRSTY FOR GOD

As the deer pants for streams of water, so my soul pants for
you, my God. My soul thirsts for God, for the living God.
PSALM 42:1–2 NIV

. . . .

We often think we really *should* get what we want. We believe something must be wrong with our lives if we feel an emptiness inside, a sense that something is missing. But the Bible tells us this sense of longing is actually healthy. It comes from our soul's awareness that only God will satisfy us completely.

Nothing this world has to offer—not money or possessions, not prestige or professional success, and not even friendship or romance—can truly fill the longing of our souls. Only God can. In this life, though, we are always searching for God, struggling to see Him more clearly, seeking to feel His presence more fully in our lives.

Our yearning will never be quite satisfied until we see Him face-to-face in heaven. In the meantime, that thirst for God drives us forward in our spiritual lives. It helps us stay focused, in our thoughts, emotions, and actions. It's like a compass, keeping us on course.

Living God, my soul is thirsty for You. May I seek Your living water
each day, knowing that only You can quench my desire.

CALLED TO HOLINESS

"Do what I tell you; live what I tell you. I am GOD. Don't desecrate my holy name. I insist on being treated with holy reverence among the People of Israel. I am GOD who makes you holy and brought you out of Egypt to be your God. I am GOD."

LEVITICUS 22:31–33 MSG

. . . .

In today's verses, God is reminding His people what it is He asks of them. He insists that they be "holy." In Hebrew, the word used is *qadash*, which means "to be set apart from everything else, to dedicate something or someone completely." The opposite of *qadash* is *halal*, which is sometimes translated as "common," "profane," or "worldly." The biblical concept of holiness has to do with being whole, healthy, truly alive. Meanwhile, its opposite, *halal*, describes something that is broken, dying, suffering a fatal wound.

God, the Living One, wants us to share His life—His wholeness, His well-being. We do this by actively living out His love in the world around us. We who have been set apart from death are called to life and love.

Life-Giver, show me how to be truly holy, separated from all that is broken and dying within me and around me, so that I can live and love for You alone.

STIR MY HEART

My heart is stirred by a noble theme as I recite my verses for the king.
PSALM 45:1 NIV

. . . .

A wedding theme. A love song. Written for the king. And the psalmist's heart is stirred by the words they are about to perform.

When you go to worship your heavenly King, do you let your heart be stirred by worship? Do you let your soul be moved by the power of your Creator reaching out to you as you pray, sing, listen, mourn, and celebrate?

Sometimes we can fall into a routine when we show up at church or take our seat for our time with God. We sing the songs, read the words, pray the prayers, but we don't let it affect us. We keep those feelings—good and freeing or heavy and deep—at a safe distance. We don't want God to see us get emotional, do we?

We should! God wants us to feel His presence, His work in our lives. He wants us to be moved, our hearts stirred, at the beautiful relationship we have with our Father that loves us unconditionally.

The next time you worship in church, at home, or even in the breath between tasks, let your heart and your life be changed by His involvement.

Dear God, thank You for being a heavenly King I can actually have a close relationship with. Stir my heart today into worship, into action, and into a life with You beside me. Amen.

SOFTEN MY HEART

Immediately he spoke to them and said, "Take courage! It is I. Don't be afraid." Then he climbed into the boat with them, and the wind died down. They were completely amazed, for they had not understood about the loaves; their hearts were hardened.

MARK 6:50–52 NIV

• •

Can you believe the disciples in this verse? Right before they saw their companion and Savior, Jesus, walking on water, they saw Him feed five thousand people with only five loaves of bread and two fish. But because they did not understand it, "their hearts were hardened." And these were His closest friends!

We might like to say we would never be like them, but think on this: How many times have you seen loved ones and strangers turn from God because they did not understand His ways? How many times have you hardened your heart against Him because of a circumstance or a verse you couldn't put an explanation or reason to?

We crave stability and answers. We fear what we don't know. But Jesus tells us again and again, "Don't be afraid."

When your mind can't comprehend the fullness of God, may your heart soften instead of harden. Let your questions open you up to the love He provides and the peace He promises.

Lord, I may not have all the answers right now, but instead of turning from You in frustration, I open my arms to You for comfort, understanding, and amazement.

FROM WITHIN

For from within, out of the heart of man, come evil thoughts.
MARK 7:21 ESV

. . . .

Jesus tells His followers that our words and our actions are ultimately affected by what comes from within our hearts. We can get caught up in legalism and rule-following, but Jesus assures us that what is more important is the way we treat others. We're not to be like the Pharisees, whose hearts were wrapped up in perfect practices and making themselves look good. They were too busy picking on the people around them to realize the sin in their own lives.

As true followers of Jesus, we are to look at our own hearts, what's within us, before we judge or comment on anyone else. Are we treating people with love? What's being shown in our lives?

God gave us a remedy for our ever-shifting hearts by not only sharing Jesus with us, but by offering His (God's) own presence in our lives. "I will walk among you and be your God, and you will be my people" (Leviticus 26:12 NIV). He vows this to the Israelites after He delivered them from Egypt. Jesus promises us the same, to walk within our hearts, after He delivered us from sin.

Thank You for the love that can change hearts, Lord. Thank You for Jesus and His wisdom. Change my heart from within, so I may show others the kindness and love they deserve. Amen.

THE MOST HIGH

God is within her, she will not fall;
God will help her at the break of day.
PSALM 46:5 NIV

. . . .

Psalm 46 is filled with this beautiful imagery of a city surrounded by "a river whose streams make glad the city of God" (Psalm 46:4 NIV).

How do you picture this city? High stone walls? A moat? Guards with arrows ready to attack enemies on sight? When you think of a city that cannot be defeated, you may think of the cautionary and military measure it will take to keep it safe. But the writer doesn't describe the city this way but notes only that "God is within her." No guns or tanks or armies.

The Most High dwells in that city, and because of that, it cannot be destroyed or conquered by any outside forces.

The presence of God anywhere changes everything. He has unlimited power, unending protection; He never sleeps and never falters. He is the ultimate Protector of His creation, including His daughters. When the Most High dwells in you, you cannot be defeated. When your heart is full of His love, you cannot be conquered and put down by this world. Hard times will come, you may be hurt, but you can find comfort that He is with you and fighting beside you.

Great Protector, thank You for fighting for me.
Go before me today into the battles I will face. Amen.

IN THE WILDERNESS

*And after six days Jesus took with him Peter and
James and John, and led them up a high mountain
by themselves. And he was transfigured before them.*
MARK 9:2 ESV

. . . .

If you've ever taken a hike in a deep forest or drove through the mountains, you probably know there's a small chance of cell reception once you're in the wilderness. You can lift that phone high above your head or climb a tree, but you'll find no Wi-Fi routers or cell towers out there.

Our Lord has a penchant for taking His followers into the wilderness. He brought the Israelites into the desert. Jesus led three disciples up a mountain. Of course, there was always a reason. God was fulfilling His promise to the Israelites of the Promised Land. Jesus wanted three men to witness His transfiguration. Each time the God-followers were alone and isolated from the world, but fully present with the Lord.

Sometimes God disconnects us from the world so we can fully connect with Him. He knows what's next in our life and where we've been, so He knows when we need to fill up on Him. Just like the peace you get after a day without your phone, you will find the calmness Your Father gives when you spend alone time with Him.

*Dear God, instead of worrying about connecting with
the world, I will try my best to connect with You.*

OUR GUIDE

For this God is our God for ever and ever;
he will be our guide even to the end.
PSALM 48:14 NIV

Through His words and actions, Jesus taught His disciples how to truly live out God's love in so many ways. In one instance, He said, "Anyone who wants to be first must be the very last, and the servant of all" (Mark 9:35 NIV). Jesus, who willingly and humbly served all those around Him, asks us to do the same. But how do we do that?

Although our nature is to put ourselves first, God assures us that He is our guide in this life to the very end. He wants to and will—if we let Him—show us how to care for others with the agape love He pours out upon us.

If we let God's love flow into our hearts, our actions toward others will change as His love changes us. It can be nerve-racking to step out in faith to help a stranger, to care deeply for a friend, to forgive the seemingly unforgiveable, but Jesus shows us through His life that it is so worth it to do so.

Dear Jesus, thank You for being the perfect model of how
to love and care for others. I will follow Your example
as I look to love those You have put in my life. Amen.

THE LORD'S COMMAND

According to the commandment of the Lord through Moses they were listed, each one with his task of serving or carrying. Thus they were listed by him, as the Lord commanded Moses.

Numbers 4:49 esv

. . . .

The book of Numbers is about the group of people that finally get to see the Promised Land. However, they still had work to do. The Lord gave Moses clear instructions that certain tribes had their own jobs to do for the Lord, and each able man within each tribe had a particular place where God wanted him.

Just as He did the Israelites, God has placed each one of us somewhere important with a job to do…or He would love the chance to place us there—if we would only cooperate.

We can get so caught up in our everyday routine, our distractions, that we aren't able to see God's path for us or hear His instructions. Take the time to be with the Lord, to see if you are where He wants you to be, if you are doing what He's asking of you.

Dear God, I want to be where You want me to be, to do what You have asked me to. Although stepping away from the familiar may be scary or uncomfortable, help me remember that You will be with me. Amen.

LIKE A LITTLE CHILD

*"Truly I tell you, anyone who will not receive the
kingdom of God like a little child will never enter it."*
MARK 10:15 NIV

. . . .

Some of us spend our years as children wishing we were teenagers, and then our time as teenagers craving adulthood. When we are in college, we can't wait till we get that big job. And when we are newlyweds, we are already thinking about grandkids and retirement.

To our heavenly Father, time doesn't mean a thing. We are His children no matter what age we are. He wants us to run to Him to seek His advice and comfort, to love Him with the trusting, sloppy, burden-free love of a child.

We lose that sometimes when we grow up and the world tells us other ways to live. We start relying on ourselves rather than on our Father. Jesus is our Savior, but He is also the Son of God; He approached God here on earth the way the children approached Him. Maybe Jesus even ran up to His Father's throne like a child runs up to her father's chair, believing with that wide-eyed faith that He can and will do the impossible. Let us see that as an example of how to receive the kingdom of God.

*Heavenly Father, I want to believe in You like a child believes in
the goodness and hopefulness of life. Free me from being dragged
down by my burdens. Help me live and love You like a little child!*

WORDS MATTER

*"If anyone says to this mountain, 'Go, throw yourself into
the sea,' and does not doubt in their heart but believes that
what they say will happen, it will be done for them."*

MARK 11:23 NIV

. . . .

In Mark 11, Jesus gives a very powerful example of how important our words can be to ourselves and to others. When Jesus cursed the fig tree by saying, "May no one ever eat fruit from you again" (verse 14), it actually withered and died. We know that Jesus had the power to make that fruitless fig tree bloom. So why did He do this?

When His followers pointed out what had happened to the poor tree, Jesus explained that if we believe the words we say with all our hearts, those words will impact our actions and what happens next. He means that the way we think and what we say actually do impact our circumstances. Whether that be in a good or bad way!

When you reach for a goal do you tell yourself you can make it? Or do you say that you'll never be good enough?

Our words can be positive or negative. We can look at a circumstance and choose to say what we *can't* do or we can choose to ask God what He *can* do.

*Dear God, remove negative talk from my mouth.
Help me see the world as You do—full of possibilities
for You to work in my life and move mountains. Amen!*

WE ARE HIS

*"For every animal of the forest is mine, and the
cattle on a thousand hills. I know every bird in the
mountains, and the insects in the fields are mine."*

PSALM 50:10–11 NIV

. . . .

God wants us to know that everything in this world belongs to Him. Every deer and chipmunk running across the road, every cow grazing on a hillside, every bird chomping away at your bird feeder, even the creepy-crawlies in your house you'd rather not see. God claims they are His and He is proud of them.

God has done even more for we who were made in His image. He claims His creation of people as His and takes pride in us. He created every single person to experience and live in the beautiful places He's made. He wants us to find joy in the simplest aspects of life and contentment in following and fulfilling our dreams. But above all, He created us to live in His love and goodness.

When sin entered the world and separated us from God, everything changed. Yet then He developed a plan that involved a great sacrifice on His part—all because He wanted to continue to live with us and have a relationship with us, His most beloved creation.

*Dear Lord, thank You for calling me Yours. Thank You for
finding a way for me to have a relationship with You and
a way to access Your great, perfect, unending love.*

ALL OF US

"The greatest Law is this, 'Listen, Jewish people, The Lord our God is one Lord! You must love the Lord your God with all your heart and with all your soul and with all your mind and with all your strength.'"

MARK 12:29–30 NLV

. . . .

Jesus tells the story of a widow giving all the money she had into the offering plate. Some others gave much more than she did, but the money they offered took absolutely no sacrifice on their part. Mark 12:44 (NLV) records Jesus as saying: "They all gave of that which was more than they needed for their own living. She is poor and yet she gave all she had, even what she needed for her own living." For the widow, God was her everything, so she gave her everything to Him.

Jesus is using this passage to explain that God doesn't only ask us to give Him our talents, our hearts, or our strength when it's easy, when it takes no work on our parts, but also when it's hard. Maybe even more so in the difficult times. God wants our messy hearts and untidy offerings even when we think we and what we have are not worthy. Why? Because the Lord knows that with His power, He can take our meager offering and make it bountiful.

---

*God, You want my heart, my soul, my mind, and my strength.
I offer what I can to You from where I am today. Amen.*

ALL CLEAN!

Soak me in your laundry and I'll come out clean,
scrub me and I'll have a snow-white life.
PSALM 51:7–8 MSG

· ·

Doing laundry can now be as easy as picking up your dirty clothes off the floor, tossing them into a washing machine, pressing some buttons, sticking them in the dryer, and folding them when the dryer bell dings. What used to take several days in the Middle Ages now only takes a couple hours. But as we know, some stains just won't come out, no matter how hard we scrub, clean, and bleach.

Many of us may look at our pasts the same way. No matter how hard we try, that dark splotch—that anger, hatred, and shame in hearts and our souls—just won't come out. It never will if we determine to keep trying on our own. But the Lord has an all-purpose cleaner that soaks us in forgiveness. His grace and mercy make us like new, without any blemishes of sin left over. All we have to do is accept His cleaning method, believe we truly have been given a fresh start and a snow-white life. God already views us this way. Isn't it time we do the same?

Father, thank You for Your unlimited forgiveness.
Please help see myself the way You see me. Amen.

HEALING OUR HEARTS AND SPIRITS

*My sacrifice, O God, is a broken spirit; a broken
and contrite heart you, God, will not despise.*

PSALM 51:17 NIV

. . . .

God always, always, *always* wants us to tell Him the truth. It doesn't matter if we are ashamed of what we have done or angry at what has been done to us. When we commune with the Lord, He wants us to offer up our shattered hearts and spirits. Why? Because He wants the chance to heal our brokenness with His love, to heal our hearts and spirits in His perfect and proper way.

Yet our hearts must be apologetic, humbled, and moldable when we approach His throne. We have to tell Him the truth—no matter how painful it might be for us—in order for Him to truly work in our lives.

Whatever you are feeling, God will not turn you away. He will not shy away from your questions. He will embrace and welcome you into His presence because, after all, when you approach His throne, you are returning to the glimmer of a home from whence you came and will someday return.

God, I approach You today with a heart and spirit created by You and crushed by this world. Help me to tell You the truth of my situation. Repair my humbled heart and shattered spirit. Help me live the way You intended me to live, to become the woman You created me to be. Amen.

SHINING-GREATNESS

So the Lord said, "I have forgiven them as you asked. But for sure, as I live, all the earth will be filled with the shining-greatness of the Lord.
NUMBERS 14:20–21 NLV

. . . .

Can you imagine what the "shining-greatness" of the Lord looks like? It has to be more beautiful than the pinkest, brightest, slowest sunset you have ever seen. It has to be deeper and truer than the love you feel for your friends and family. It must taste better than the first bite of your favorite food, sweet or salty or savory; smell better than a field full of your favorite flowers; and be more inspiring than the first notes of your favorite song.

Take anything you think is amazing in this life and times it by a gazillion. What God has in store for His daughters is so much more than we could ever imagine because He is so great and longs to share that shining-greatness with we who bear His image.

The Lord continually fills our lives with uncountable blessings and love. Praise the Lord for His forgiveness, grace, and mercy, for the "loving-kindness of God [that] lasts all day long" (Psalm 52:1 NLV). It never runs out. It never falters. It never fails.

Dear Lord, thank You for Your "shining-greatness" in my life. Open my eyes to all the wonderful things I have to thank You for. Amen.

SOVEREIGN

"My soul is very sorrowful, even to death. Remain here and
watch." And going a little farther, he fell on the ground and
prayed that, if it were possible, the hour might pass from him.
And he said, "Abba, Father, all things are possible for you. Remove
this cup from me. Yet not what I will, but what you will."

MARK 14:34–36 ESV

. . . .

What a heart-wrenching example of the fully human side of Jesus that He displays in this passage. Before His trial and crucifixion, Jesus shares with His Father, the fear—the sorrow—in His heart for what is about to happen. He asks that circumstances change, for God to intervene. But He still ends His prayer with, "Yet not what I will, but what you will." Jesus acknowledged that His Father not only knew what was to be but what was best.

When our hearts ache for change, for provision but we see none in sight, we can still find peace that God is with us. That He feels our pain and anguish. That He has a plan moving forward from this moment that is perfectly aligned with His will, a plan that wants only goodness for His creation.

My heavenly Father, Sovereign of all that was, is, and will be,
even though You may not change my earthly circumstances, I will
continue to trust and believe that You know what is best for me.

A GIFT ON THE ALTAR

*I will be glad to give You a gift on the altar. I will
give thanks to Your name, O Lord, for it is good.*
PSALM 54:6 NLV

. . . .

What do the words "a gift on the altar" really mean? What does that
look like? In Old Testament times, it could mean a sacrifice of an animal
or crop. Today it could mean donating a percentage of your paycheck to
your church. Or it could mean the giving of your time and talents. Yet
although God would love for you to offer to Him the things with which
He has blessed you, He wants something so much more on the altar.

You. He wants you. Your heart, your soul, all of you. He wants you
as a gift on the altar.

What an amazing feeling to be wanted.

But what a huge sacrifice to be made: our whole beings, our choices,
our very lives.

Yet we must remember that we are giving ourselves over to a Lord that
is good. A Lord that is love. A Lord that wants goodness and love for us.

Even if you are scared or you are not yet ready to give God your all,
He still wants you in His presence. He longs to show you how wonder-
filled life is when you move through this world amid His unblemished
goodness.

*Father, be with me as I endeavor to give
more and more of myself to You. Amen.*

GIVE YOUR CARES

Give all your cares to the Lord and He will give you strength.
He will never let those who are right with Him be shaken.
PSALM 55:22 NLV

. . . .

The psalmist pours out his heart to his Creator, writing, "My heart is in pain within me. The fears of death have come upon me. I have begun shaking with fear. Fear has power over me. And I say, 'If only I had wings like a dove, I would fly away and be at rest'" (Psalm 55:4–6 NLV).

How many times have you, like this psalmist, wanted to run or fly away from your problems? Yet God knows that when we flee from problems, we aren't dealing with them the way He intended us to. For He knows that although we may be physically miles away from whatever issue is plaguing us, it still lingers in our minds, our hearts, and our souls. Holding on to such things can hurt us in the long run, and maybe even lead us to hurt others.

Instead of avoiding your problems, run to God for strength and steadiness. With the biggest shoulders and the purest of hearts, God will carry all the shame, fear, anxiety, and stress that you try to bear alone. Simply align your heart with His and He'll rush in to help carry your load.

Give me strength and peace, Lord, as I turn my cares over
to You. For only then will I find the calm I crave. Amen.

WHAT CAN THEY DO?

*When I am afraid, I put my trust in you. In God,
whose word I praise—in God I trust and am not
afraid. What can mere mortals do to me?*
Psalm 56:3–4 niv

. . . .

Sometimes we're hurt by the carelessness or callousness of others. Such people may make tasks at work harder, spread rumors about us behind our back, pretend to be our friend but then continually leave us out of their plans. In our vain attempt to fit in and please them, we can become afraid to perform the tasks God has called us to do, or be our true beautiful selves, all because we're fearful of how they'll treat us, what they might do.

David knows how we're feeling. He was supposed to be king, but found himself on the run from those who wanted him dead! He asked himself the question: *What can these mere mortals do?* Except he rephrased it through the lens of his Lord. For what others can do to those who trust in Him is—nothing!

When we place our trust in God, others' actions and words cannot hurt us. Although in the moment, what they say or do may sting, in the long run and in His holy name, that pain will be washed away and replaced by God's strength and courage, allowing us to stand out the way we were meant to!

*My Strength, thank You for the courage
to trust You above all else. Amen.*

WHAT CAN HE DO?

*In God, whose word I praise, in the LORD, whose word I praise—
in God I trust and am not afraid. What can man do to me?*
PSALM 56:10–11 NIV

. . . .

God must have really thought we needed to hear these words. Because twice in the same psalm (56:4, 11), David asks, "What can they do?"

But the second time, David doesn't mention his fear. He puts full trust in his Lord and his God, whose word he praises, and he's stepping into courage. How can David do this?

Several things become apparent as we explore this psalm. We can see that David is in constant communication with the Lord. That he shares with God his troubles, his joys, every single thing. David is spending time in God's Word and is always listening for His voice. David has taken his troubles and laid them at his Lord's feet, proclaiming that God can and will come through for him. Although David may be afraid on his own, with God, he has no reason to shake with fear. For he knows what God can do.

When you look at what comes against you today, instead of asking, "What can they do?" courageously ask, "What can He do?"

My Courage, I am so excited to see what You will do in my life. Amen.

FULLY BELIEVE

*"Blessed is she who has believed that the
Lord would fulfill his promises to her!"*
LUKE 1:45 NIV

. . . .

The first day of spring bodes a promise for many people. It is the start of warmer weather, more sunlight, and longer days. Nature is given a brand-new, fresh start that springs up all around us.

With great expectations, we look forward to the changing of the seasons. The winter may be long and cold, but we know that spring will come, and with that truth we trudge onward. Oh, if we only believed God's promises like we believe in the promise of spring! For then we would find ourselves rejoicing every day.

Today's verse from Luke doesn't say Mary is blessed because the Lord fulfilled His promises to her or that the Lord fulfilled His promises because she was already blessed. Mary was considered blessed the moment she fully believed that the Lord would keep His promises to her. The belief in her heavenly Father is what took away her fear, uncertainty, and confusion and replaced it with His powerful peace and joy—even as Mary waited with great expectation for God to come through for her.

When we believe in our hearts that a long-awaited blessing will come as we faithfully wait upon Him, we can and will find ourselves already blessed.

Heavenly Father, thank You for the blessings found in the waiting. Amen.

HIS PROMISE

"He would show loving-kindness to our early fathers.
He would remember His holy promise."

LUKE 1:72 NLV

. . . .

What is a promise to you? Is it something little kids share on the playground? Is it an understanding between caring parents and obedient children? Is it a vow between lovers for forever and always?

Is a promise something that is steadfast and solid? Or is it something breakable and changeable?

When God issues a promise, He always intends on keeping it. When He was leading His beloved out of Eden because of wrongdoing and the Israelites out of Egypt toward freedom, He promised them a way out of sin. He promised that one day, He would make a way for all His children to experience a relationship with Him, a sacrifice to take on the price of the world's sin and fulfill the debt that needed to be paid.

We all know the end of that story: God did come through on that promise and we get to share in it. May God's fulfillment of that promise remind us that our *own* words are meaningful. That when we promise something to someone, we must fulfill it. May we remember the importance of our promises because we are a reflection of the One who first promised us.

Dear God, You always keep Your promises. Help me to keep mine. Amen.

OFFER HOPE AND ENCOURAGEMENT

At that time she came and gave thanks to God. She told the people in Jerusalem about Jesus. They were looking for the One to save them from the punishment of their sins and to set them free.

Luke 2:38 nlv

. . . .

Anna was a prophet during the days in which Jesus was born. While she was old and widowed, she spent her time at the temple, worshipping day and night, fasting and praying (Luke 2:36–37). When the Lord revealed to Anna that Jesus was finally here, she couldn't help but tell the whole city. These people had been waiting and searching for a savior, someone to set them free. So Anna shared with them the hope of the Gospel, of what freedom and true love will really look like.

God asks us to share that same message. He wants us to always offer hope and encouragement to everyone around us. Maybe that may simply be giving someone a cheerful smile or a listening ear. Maybe another day, it takes the form of our sharing the truth of Jesus and what that can mean to someone's life. Maybe it means letting others know what God did in our own lives. Whatever form sharing that message takes, we can be confident God will always be near to help us along.

Lord, help me find a way to share my hopeful heart and encouragement with others. Amen.

SING!

*As for me, I will sing of Your strength. Yes, I will sing with
joy of Your loving-kindness in the morning. For You have
been a strong and safe place for me in times of trouble.*

Psalm 59:16 nlv

. . . .

Have you actually tried singing without caring who was listening? Or dancing like nobody's watching? Or laughing as loudly as you can without a care? When your heart wants to praise the Lord, openly and purely, do you allow it? Do you sing as the psalmist does?

Because God certainly sings for us. He blesses us with loving-kindness every morning. He is a source of strength for us as we go through our days. When we are overwhelmed, He's a place of comfort. When we're attacked, He's our place of safety. These are blessings to celebrate!

God wants us to sing to Him, to praise Him, in any way we can, not just seek Him out when we're in trouble or need His help. Today, acknowledge your blessings, the strength and comfort and safety God extends to you. Treasure them and Him in your heart and soul.

Find some time to celebrate all the things your Lord has gifted you. So when a season comes that reminds you of the not-so-good times of this life, you can still access that ever-present well of goodness.

---

*I praise You, Lord, for everything You've done, in all the ways You have
worked in my life, how You have blessed me. To You, I sing! Amen.*

DREAMS

Jesus was about thirty years old when He began His work.
LUKE 3:23 NLV

. . . .

Many of us may have a hard time understanding God's timing. When we have a dream in our heart, we want it to be realized as soon as possible. But then as the months start ticking by, and the years slowly pass, we begin thinking it may be time to let our dream go, to set it aside. We tell ourselves we were perhaps meant to take another path.

Jesus waited until He was thirty years old to begin His ministry. He could have performed any of His miracles at any age, but He chose to wait for His Father's timing, knowing Abba's plan and purpose are perfect.

If you're holding on to a dream, dig deep into that promise that God's divine timing is always the best. Although it can be easy to rush what we want the way we want when we want it, that's not what He wants for us.

Whether you're still striving to achieve your dream or picking it up off a dusty shelf, trust that you are exactly where you're meant to be and God is with you as you give it another try.

Father, help me to not get discouraged by failure and defeat.
For with You, I know I can reach my dream. Amen.

TEMPTING

Jesus, full of the Holy Spirit, left the Jordan and was led by the Spirit into the wilderness, where for forty days he was tempted by the devil.
LUKE 4:1–2 NIV

. . . .

When we are in a time of wandering, lost in a desert, hungry, tired, or thirsty, the evil one strikes. He promises that all our problems will be fixed if we just step out of the path that God has prepared for us.

And it's so tempting to do. To live a life that's easier, calmer, more fulfilling according to worldly standards than the one God has put before us. Jesus knows what this temptation feels like, for the enemy tried Him in the literal desert.

Yet each time He was tempted, Jesus answered the devil's taunt with "It is written. . ." (Luke 4:4, 8, 12 NIV). For Jesus had God's promises stored in His heart. With them, He could repel and defeat the enemy's jabs with a single sentence.

We can do the same. Whether we're lost in the desert or on a mountain or enduring a season of sadness or joy, we too can have God's Word stored in our own hearts so when the enemy comes to tempt us, we'll know exactly what to say and what to do.

God, thank You for giving me a way out of temptations.
Help me store Your Word in my heart. Amen.

REFILL OUR HEARTS

From the ends of the earth I call to you, I call as my heart grows faint; lead me to the rock that is higher than I. For you have been my refuge, a strong tower against the foe.

PSALM 61:2–3 NIV

. . . .

"My heart grows faint." Darkness rises. A storm brews on the horizon. You're hurting. You're lost. You're lonely. Your heart, your soul, is tired.

Maybe you are in such a place. Once again, you're waiting for God to come through, to reach into your life and make you feel something other than exhaustion. Or maybe you have been through a season like this one, and while sunny days surround you now, you wait for the time when shadows may cover your life again. Either way, you dread tomorrow. You wonder, *What will it bring? Will I find my way through?*

We know life is hard. But we also know that God always offers us a refuge and a calm amid the pain. He gives us a place to recharge and refill our hearts with His presence and goodness. Our problems may not dissolve, but they will become bearable. With this new feeling in our hearts, we will be able to face the oncoming day in God's courage and strength.

My Comforter, I will find strength and comfort in Your everlasting and love-filled arms. Amen.

ONLY GOD

For God alone my soul waits in silence; from him comes
my salvation. He alone is my rock and my salvation,
my fortress; I shall not be greatly shaken.

Psalm 62:1–2 esv

. . . .

David, the author of today's psalm, knows only the Lord can save him from his enemies. He seeks rescue from nowhere, nothing, no one else. Not allies. Not his own means. From God. Only God. And He believes God will come through for him.

David explains his situation: "Surely they intend to topple me from my lofty place; they take delight in lies. With their mouths they bless but in their hearts they curse" (Psalm 62:4 niv). Rumors are being spread about him. Nasty talk that will diminish his image, damage his relationships, and weaken his kingly rule.

Yet David understood that only God is his fortress of safety. The Lord is David's only firm foundation, the only place where he can stand strong in the midst of turmoil and "not be greatly shaken."

Just as God comforted David, God comforts us. If we continue to trust Him and follow His path, God's truth will prevail. He will how those that curse us, those that spread lies—and the ones that believe them—the truth of the matter.

Father, thank You for always looking out of me. You alone are my rock,
salvation, fortress. With You in my life, I will not be shaken. Amen.

REMEMBER THE BLESSINGS

The LORD your God has blessed you in all the work of your hands. . . . The LORD your God has been with you, and you have not lacked anything.
DEUTERONOMY 2:7 NIV

. . . .

The book of Deuteronomy describes the events immediately before the Israelites—who've been wandering in the desert for forty years—enter the Promised Land. God wanted His people to remember all He'd done for them: the escape and rescue from Egypt and slavery, the parting of the Red Sea, the manna from the sky, the delivery of the Ten Commandments, etc. Moses reminds God's people that when they worked with and under Him, God swept in and multiplied their efforts, fulfilling every need.

God is still that way with His children today. He longs for us, His daughters, to remember the blessings that He has given us when we worked with Him to achieve our dreams, loved one another, met our responsibilities, and more. When we work hard in God's name, He will be there to make sure that all our time and efforts are worth it. He may not always give us what we want, but He will always provide us with whatever we need to complete the task He has laid before us.

Dear God, thank You for always blessing my work and always providing what I need. Help me see every project and task through Your eyes. Amen.

LOVE

But love your enemies, do good to them, and lend
to them without expecting to get anything back.
LUKE 6:35 NIV

• •

That driver who cut you off in traffic? Love him.

That high school "friend" who posted something mean on social media? Love her.

That church member who always has something negative to say about what you brought to the potluck? Love him.

That person from the past who has really hurt you. The one you just can't seem to forgive. Jesus asks you to forgive and love her too.

Regarding those who hurt us, Jesus' direction is always clear: Love them and do good to them. Give to them without wanting or needing anything in return.

The love you give to others will look different in each situation. But no worries. For if you reach out to God, with a truthful and forgiving heart, asking how to deal with someone who has hurt you, He will be there to help you figure out the best way to love that person.

You are loved so deeply by a God that is amazing at loving, by a God who loved you first (1 John 4:19), by a God who *is* love (1 John 4:16). When you feel like you have no more love to give, reach out to the Lord of love. He'll reach in and provide what you need.

The One who is Love and loves me, thank You.
Show me how to love those difficult to love. Amen.

THE SANCTUARY

*I have seen you in the sanctuary and beheld your power
and your glory. . . . I will praise you as long as I live.*
PSALM 63:2, 4 NIV

. . . .

As David—the shepherd, warrior, then king—continued to wander in the desert, he wasn't alone. God was with him. As David on the run, praised, wept, and wandered, he recalled the glimpse he'd had of God's glory in the tent of meeting.

In the Old Testament, God promised to be present with His people within the confines of a tabernacle. But David knew God could never truly be tied to the inside of a building. David knew the Lord was with him, as was His glorious power and strength.

Because of Jesus, God's daughters have the chance to access that divine power and strength any moment they need it. Your heart and soul are now the sanctuary where the glory of the Lord lives. God wants you to tap into that power every day by communicating with Him through prayer, by basking in His presence, by studying Him, by praising Him for as long as you live. The moment you are at your weakest, God will step from that sanctuary within you and show you His ultimate power.

*Protector, thank You for always being with me as I seek Your peace
and presence through prayer, praise, study, and silence. Amen.*

FULLY

*Love the LORD your God with all your heart and
with all your soul and with all your strength.*
DEUTERONOMY 6:5 NIV

. . . .

This was the very last command Moses gave the Israelites before they finally entered the Promised Land. And what an important command it is—one we still need to heed and practice today: "Love the LORD your God with all your heart and with all your soul and with all your strength."

When you work, your employer doesn't expect you to do only half the job with half the effort. You're paid to get the job done and done well. When you're in a relationship, you aren't expected to show love every other day of the week. Relationships need continuous love all week long.

God is the same. He wants all your dedication, your work, and your love. He doesn't want the scraps and leftovers. He doesn't want the five minutes you have left before something important starts. He will always want your first thoughts in the mornings, your first bursts of joy during worship, your first tears amid mourning. He wants you fully. Not halfway.

Try your best to want Him fully in return.

Thank You, God, for loving me so much. Help me to love You just as much as I bring You all my heart, soul, and strength. Amen.

PRAISE THE BLESSING-GIVER

"So obey the commands of the LORD your God by walking in his ways and fearing him. For the LORD your God is bringing you into a good land of flowing streams and pools of water, with fountains and springs. . . . It is a land of wheat and barley; of grapevines, fig trees, and pomegranates; of olive oil and honey. It is a land where food is plentiful. . . . When you have eaten your fill, be sure to praise the LORD your God for the good land he has given you."
DEUTERONOMY 8:6–10 NLT

. . . .

When we obey God, we're often blessed with a good life. And while our lives are not entirely free from hardship, the heavenly Father gifts us with blessings—often too numerous to count!

Though wonderful, our seasons of success and abundance should come with a warning. For during those easy times, we can become distracted from the true blessing-giver. And we might even become prideful, convinced we're deserving of it all.

Remember these words from Deuteronomy; soak them up in your mind and your heart. Life—the good life!—comes from God and God alone. He is the miracle worker, the keeper of promises, the One who saves! He is worthy to be praised!

Blessing-giver, thank You for this beautiful, full life. Help me to always remember that I could have none of these blessings without You. You are so, so good to me! Amen.

NOTHING IS BEYOND HIS FORGIVENESS

*[Jesus] said, "Do you see this woman? . . . She rained tears
on my feet and dried them with her hair. You gave me no
greeting, but from the time I arrived she hasn't quit kissing
my feet. You provided nothing for freshening up, but she has
soothed my feet with perfume. Impressive, isn't it? She was
forgiven many, many sins, and so she is very, very grateful."*

LUKE 7:44–47 MSG

. . . .

As Christ-followers, we know nothing can keep us from God's love. *Not
one single thing* is beyond His forgiveness.

However, it's easy to fall into the trap of thinking that we're better
than those whose sin is "worse" than ours. That God must surely find
it difficult to forgive *those sinners*. That somehow our sins are superior,
right? . . . Unfortunately, we don't always connect the dots from our
heads to our hearts to our actions.

Here in Luke 7, Jesus sets negative-thinking Simon straight. Simon
was focused on the weeping woman's past sins rather than her current
state of forgiveness. Jesus reminded Simon that he should instead focus
on a person's heart, a person's faith. That this woman's faith was beautiful,
her sins covered by God's amazing grace.

Ask God to help align your heart with your mind today.

*Heavenly Father, I often have head knowledge that doesn't
make its way to my heart, words, and actions. I need
You to help me connect the dots. Thank You! Amen.*

HOW DEEP IS YOUR LOVE?

The LORD your God is testing you to find out whether you love
him with all your heart and with all your soul. It is the LORD
your God you must follow, and him you must revere. Keep his
commands and obey him; serve him and hold fast to him.

DEUTERONOMY 13:3–4 NIV

. . . .

Have you ever asked yourself, "I wonder how God can tell that I love Him?" Is there a test that can measure it? Are there actions you can take to show the depth of your love for God? Are there words you can speak to prove it?

Deuteronomy 13:3–4 says we need to do several things if we love God:

> 1) Follow Him.
> 2) Revere Him.
> 3) Keep His commands.
> 4) Obey Him.
> 5) Serve Him.
> 6) Hold fast to Him.

Seems a little strange, doesn't it? Does God *really* need us to complete a checklist to prove our love for Him? Surely the omniscient God knows how we feel about Him!

Think more deeply on this, and you might have a lightbulb moment: This checklist isn't for Him; it's for us! It serves to keep us on track in our faith so we can live our very best lives. God loves us so much that He gives us step-by-step guidelines for living. Read His Word; meditate on it; then follow through!

Heavenly Father, thank You for showing
me the way to my very best life! Amen.

GOD OF ALL THE EARTH

Shout for joy to God, all the earth; sing the glory of his name;
give to him glorious praise! Say to God, "How awesome are your
deeds! So great is your power that your enemies come cringing
to you. All the earth worships you and sings praises to you."
PSALM 66:1–4 ESV

. . . .

Do you tend to reserve your songs of praise for Sunday morning? Or do you sing praises for God's goodness throughout the week too?

In the verses above, the psalmist is calling *everyone* to joyfully praise God—after all, God is the God over all the earth, not just the God of Israel. The psalmist then follows with instruction on *how* to praise God: "Say to God, 'How awesome are your deeds!'" Praise involves telling God how amazing He is. . .what wonderful things He has done in your life. . . Praise celebrates His awesome power.

If praise doesn't come easy or naturally because your mind runs amok with thoughts of doubt and fear, ask God to remind you that He's in control and will protect and care for you always. When you invite Him to take complete control, your worries will be replaced with joy—and, as thoughts of thanksgiving and hope fill your mind, praise will spill from your heart and lips!

Father God, You are God of all the earth. And I am so
thankful. I will praise You every day of my life! Amen.

ONE TOUCH

There was a woman who had had a discharge of blood for twelve
years, and though she had spent all her living on physicians, she
could not be healed. . . . She came up behind him and touched the
fringe of his garment, and immediately her discharge of blood
ceased. And Jesus said, "Who was it that touched me?" . . . She came
trembling, and. . .declared in the presence of all the people why she
had touched him, and how she had been immediately healed. And he
said to her, "Daughter, your faith has made you well; go in peace."
LUKE 8:43–48 ESV

. . . .

What a difficult life this woman had experienced! Twelve *long* years.
Twelve years of being untouchable—not a hug or shoulder squeeze from
family, friends. . .not one touch from *anyone*. She had spent everything
she had on doctors who couldn't heal her. Certainly, *before* her encounter
with Jesus, she was poor, discouraged, lonely, depressed, hopeless. Surely
her faith had taken a beating. By all accounts, she didn't have much to
live for. But. . .

But *then*. In a single moment, she gained *everything*. One touch. One
moment of pure, unfettered faith followed by the words, "Daughter, your
faith has made you well."

Have you allowed your circumstances and negative thoughts to limit
your faith? Believe. Reach out and touch Jesus today!

Father, strengthen my faith. When my faith
is big, my actions are sure to follow! Amen.

NEGATIVE TO POSITIVE

If I had not confessed the sin in my heart, the Lord would not have listened. But God did listen! He paid attention to my prayer. Praise God, who did not ignore my prayer or withdraw his unfailing love from me.
PSALM 66:18–20 NLT

. . . .

Sometimes our thoughts lie. Our mind fills to overflowing with negative messages:

> *I'm not good enough.*
> *I'm boring; I'm not talented or smart.*
> *God doesn't love me.*
> *And He certainly doesn't care about anything I have to say.*

Tune out those negative thoughts! Have a heart-to-heart with God today. Ask Him to help drown out your negative thinking. Ask Him to replace the lies with truths like:

> *Because of God's love and grace, I am good enough.*
> *God created me to be interesting, talented, and smart.*
> *God loves me in a BIG way!*
> *And He cares about every single thing I have to say!*

No matter what your brain tries to tell you, God is faithful, and He loves you more than you could ever imagine. Tell God exactly what you're thinking and feeling. Confess the sin in your heart and keep your focus wholly on Him. . .and He will be 100 percent tuned in to your prayers.

Father, I praise You! Thank You for loving me perfectly.
Thank You for listening. You are everything I'll ever need and
more. Please take control of my thoughts. Help me to let
go of the negative and focus on the positive. Amen.

GOD-CENTERED

"Anyone who intends to come with me has to let me lead. You're not in the driver's seat—I am. Don't run from suffering; embrace it. Follow me and I'll show you how. Self-help is no help at all. Self-sacrifice is the way. . .to finding yourself, your true self. What good would it do to get everything you want and lose. . .the real you? If any of you is embarrassed with me. . .know that the Son of Man will be far more embarrassed with you when he arrives in all his splendor in company with the Father and the holy angels."

LUKE 9:23–26 MSG

. . . .

Are you a true disciple of Christ? Do you know the requirements? . . .

In Luke 9, Jesus explains to His disciples about His mission, His ministry—and He describes what it means to be a tried-and-true disciple. Ask yourself:

> *Am I seeking to bring pleasure to the heavenly Father?*
> *Am I faithful in serving Him?*
> *Do I follow the commands of scripture?*
> *Do I submit—daily—to His will, forgetting my own?*
> *Do I focus more on Him and less on self?*

A God-focused life is a life of meaning and purpose. A God-focused life leads to a glorious reward. Let this truth seep from your head to your heart, deep into your soul.

Father, make me Your disciple today. Help me take the truth of Your Word and act on it—with a meaningful, purposeful, God-centered life! Amen.

URGENT!

"First things first.... Announce God's kingdom!"...
Jesus said, "No procrastination.... You can't put
God's kingdom off till tomorrow. Seize the day."
LUKE 9:60, 62 MSG

. . . .

Maybe you've heard the phrase, "Don't put off until tomorrow what you can do today." It rings true, doesn't it?

Those dishes in the sink. . .the piles of dirty laundry. . .the ever-growing grass. . .the flower beds overrun with weeds. . . Whatever you put off today will still need to be done tomorrow. So "Don't put off till tomorrow. . ." is pretty good advice, isn't it?

God's Word is also full of timeless, practical advice. And today's verses from the book of Luke are no exception. Here Jesus emphasizes the urgency of doing the most important thing first: growing God's kingdom! When we commit our lives to Christ, our priority should be Him—and that means sharing Him with others. Our commitment to Him can't be 80 percent; it needs to be 100 percent, with no distractions.

The challenge is the noisy world that tempts us away from God's calling on our lives. So what's a woman of God to do? . . . Look up! Ask the heavenly Father to keep your mind- and heart-focus on Him and Him alone. He won't let you down!

Father God, I humbly come before You, asking You
to help me keep my mind- and heart-focus on You.
I want to help grow Your kingdom, Lord! Amen.

WHOLLY FOCUSED

The Lord now chose seventy-two other disciples and sent them
ahead in pairs. . . . These were his instructions. . . "Pray to the Lord
who is in charge of the harvest; ask him to send more workers. . . .
Remember that I am sending you out as lambs among wolves.
Don't take any money with you, nor a traveler's bag, nor an extra
pair of sandals. And don't stop to greet anyone on the road."

LUKE 10:1–4 NLT

. . . .

Here in the book of Luke, the Lord is preparing His disciples to share the Gospel. He sends them in pairs—perhaps because there is strength in numbers.

The Lord then instructs them on what to do:

1.) Pray.
2.) Expect opposition.
3.) Travel lightly.
4.) Talk to no one on the road.

Why would the Lord tell the men to travel empty-handed and to not stop for conversation?

First and foremost, He is establishing Himself as the disciples' sole provider. He'd make sure they had everything they needed. And any people they'd meet on the road would likely distract them from their goal of sharing the Gospel. Stopping for polite conversation would only delay the Lord's work.

What about you? . . . Are you allowing distractions along the road to take you away from God's work? Ask God to make you bold and courageous in your heart, soul, and mind—and your actions will follow!

Father God, I want to be wholly focused on You! Amen.

SOUL, STRENGTH, AND MIND

" 'Love the Lord your God with all your heart and with
all your soul and with all your strength and with all
your mind'; and, 'Love your neighbor as yourself.'"

LUKE 10:27 NIV

. . . .

Love my neighbor as I love myself? . . . But I don't even "like" my neighbor.
Surely, I can do something else, can't I, Lord? . . . I mean, even a root canal
sounds more appealing.

Is there any other biblical command that seems more difficult than
"love your neighbor"? It's hard enough to love our families and friends
when we're having a bad day. But the truth of the matter is, if we love Jesus
with everything we have (our heart, soul, strength, and mind), then our
actions will show it! And that includes loving others well. Jesus loved. . .
loves. . .each of us even at our very worst, doesn't He? So who are we to
deny loving-kindness to others? Even those who are hardest to love?

Today, take a moment to reflect on these verses from Luke 10. Ask the
Lord to soften your heart, to strengthen your mind, and to change your
thinking toward your hard-to-love neighbors. God, the promise-keeper
will hear. He will respond. He will write love all over your heart and soul.

Father God, thank You for being the best example of
how to love others well. Change my mindset. Show me
that I can love people who seem unlovable. Amen.

CHOOSE LIFE!

*[If you obey the commandments of the Lord your God
which] I command you today, to love the Lord your God,
to walk in His ways, and to keep His commandments and
His statutes and His ordinances. . .the Lord your God
will bless you in the land into which you go to possess.*

DEUTERONOMY 30:16 AMPC

. . . .

We are bombarded every day with situations that require decisions. Some are simple: the red shoes or the black? Some require a bit more thought: the SUV or the minivan? And some are complex: stay in your current job or change career paths? . . .

If you're a living, breathing, human being, then you've probably made countless decisions throughout your life. How about making a life-altering decision right now: will you choose the good life or a miserable life? Seems simple, doesn't it? Who would make the conscious choice to be miserable?

The good news is you really *do* have a choice. And blessings abound when you choose to love God, follow His path for your life, and obey His Word. How wonderful!

When you're having an awful day, reread these truths from Deuteronomy, and let them work their way from your head to your heart. Then choose life—choose the abundant blessings of Christ!

*Heavenly Father, You are so good, so wonderful, so powerful. . .
it's impossible to have a horrible, very bad day when You're
the focus my life! I choose life! I choose You! Amen.*

WIDE-EYED WONDER

"No one lights a lamp, then hides it in a drawer. It's put on a lamp stand so those entering the room have light to see where they're going. . . . If you live wide-eyed in wonder and belief, your body fills up with light. If you live squinty eyed in greed and distrust, your body is a musty cellar. Keep your eyes open, your lamp burning, so you don't get musty and murky. Keep your life as well-lighted as your best-lighted room."

LUKE 11:33–36 MSG

. . . .

A light that remains unseen can't brighten a dark room. It can't illuminate a shadowy path. A hidden light serves no purpose.

The same is true of our faith. If we keep the light of our faith hidden, we're doing the world—our friends, neighbors, and strangers—a grave disservice.

The best way to fill yourself with God's radiant light is to open your eyes to His wonders:

I'm thanking you, GOD, from a full heart, I'm writing the book on your wonders. I'm whistling, laughing, and jumping for joy; I'm singing your song, High God.

PSALM 9:1–2 MSG

So keep your soul and mind focused on the goodness of God. . . on His unending mercy and blessings. When you stay tuned in to the positives, your light will grow a little brighter every day. And the beauty of it all is that you will draw others into the light.

God, open my eyes to Your awesome wonders. Amen.

IMPACT

God, you know every sin I've committed; my life's a wide-open book before you. Don't let those who look to you in hope be discouraged by what happens to me. . . . Don't let those out looking for you come to a dead end by following me—Please, dear God of Israel!

PSALM 69:5–6 MSG

. . . .

This is a heartfelt confession from the psalmist. He's speaking directly to God—admitting he has broken his heavenly Father's rules. He's pleading with God—asking Him to keep others from shame and discouragement. His words show genuine concern for other people. He doesn't want his actions to affect unbelievers in a negative way. And he doesn't want his sins to poorly reflect on God or other believers.

Each of us is imperfect. We're sinful and weak. And fair or not, the world often lumps all God-followers into one box. When one falls, the world tends to respond with a resounding, "Yep—that's how *all* God-followers are!"

Today, have a heartfelt conversation with God. Ask Him to help you and His people avoid sin that would bring a shadow of embarrassment and shame on the Church. Think before you act; think before you speak. People are watching, and what you say and do will have an impact—for good or bad. When you have a heart for others, sister, you will choose well!

*Lord, help me to choose my words and actions carefully.
I want to positively impact others for Your kingdom. Amen.*

SECRET OF SUCCESS

"Be strong and very courageous. Be careful to obey all the instructions Moses gave you. Do not deviate from them, turning either to the right or to the left. Then you will be successful in everything you do. Study this Book of Instruction continually. Meditate on it day and night so you will be sure to obey everything written in it. Only then will you prosper and succeed in all you do. This is my command—be strong and courageous! Do not be afraid or discouraged. For the LORD your God is with you wherever you go."

JOSHUA 1:7–9 NLT

. . . .

What makes a person truly successful? A custom-built home on a large lot? A six-figure salary? Luxury cars? A boat? Extravagant vacations? . . . We live in a materialistic world where "things" matter. Having more—*and better*—stuff makes a person happy. Or does it?

All you need to do is look around and you'll see that those who are successful by the world's standards are often quite miserable. It's because they are missing the secret of true success: wholehearted devotion to Jesus. He's the key to living our best life. And when we study and obey His Word, we will tap into a strength and courage that we can't get anywhere else.

Father God, help me tap into Your secret for a successful life. I want to obey Your Word, so I am on the receiving end of Your promises. Amen.

THE WORRY-FREE LIFE

Jesus said. . . , "Therefore I tell you, do not worry about your life, what you will eat; or about your body, what you will wear. For life is more than food, and the body more than clothes. Consider the ravens: They do not sow or reap, they have no storeroom or barn; yet God feeds them. . . . Who of you by worrying can add a single hour to your life? Since you cannot do this very little thing, why do you worry about the rest?"

Luke 12:22–26 niv

. . . .

What if someone else could handle the stresses and worries of your health, finances, relationships, work, politics—*all the things* that cause those pesky worry and frown lines to crease your forehead? No doubt you'd like to imagine what a worry-free life feels like.

Here's the beautiful thing: not only can you imagine it. . .you can actually *live* it! How? By giving every anxiety-inducing thought to Jesus.

The direction of your life will always mirror your strongest thoughts (Proverbs 4:23)—and if those thoughts are worry-filled, you'll never be able to escape overwhelming fear and anxiety. When you create new pathways of thought, fully trusting the heavenly Father with your life, then this positive way of thinking will become your default. And the worry-free life will be yours for the taking!

Jesus, help me redirect my worried thoughts and fully trust You in the process. Thank You, Lord! Amen.

ALWAYS PRAISE

I am afflicted and in pain; let your salvation, O God, set me on high! I will praise the name of God with a song; I will magnify him with thanksgiving. . . . When the humble see it they will be glad; you who seek God, let your hearts revive.

PSALM 69:29–30, 32 ESV

. . . .

When you think about the life of a king, what comes to mind? Perhaps a luxurious palace, unimaginable wealth, a bevy of servants, an endless supply of food and drink. . .every whim fulfilled. Certainly, a life of ease.

However, this wasn't the case for King David. He lived a very troubled life. He was involved in adultery, deceit, and murder. His infant son died right after birth. David had many enemies. And the list of hardships goes on. Throughout the Psalms, David pleads with God, repeatedly asking for His help and deliverance. He knew God alone could ease his pain and suffering.

Rich or poor, king or servant, we all will experience troubles and trials throughout life. And while it's tempting to take on a woe-is-me attitude, we need only look to King David's example. For even when he faced adversity, David never failed to praise God. This kind of attitude pleases our heavenly Father! And if David, who faced every imaginable hardship in life, could do it, we can too!

Father God, no matter what hardships I experience in life, let me always sing praises to You! Amen.

BECAUSE HE'S GOD!

Let those on the hunt for you sing and celebrate. Let all who love your saving way say over and over, "God is mighty!"
PSALM 70:4 MSG

· ·

David is calling all God's people to be happy in Him and to sing His praises. He doesn't put any stipulations on it: "*If* God makes your life perfect. . ." or "*If* God answers your prayers the way you'd like Him to. . ." or "*If* God blesses you financially. . ." There are no "ifs"—no requirements are attached to David's directive. God's people should be joyful solely because He's God!

Today let your thoughts rest on the character of God. He is good. He is holy. He is just. He is infinite. He is patient. He is faithful. He is Love. He is forgiving. He is creative. He is Truth. He is welcoming. . . And so much more! Spend some time in His Word, and you'll realize that God is worthy of your love and praise just because of who He is.

When you focus on how good God is (all the time!), you'll find your heart growing more grateful, more content, more joyful. And when your heart is overflowing with joy, positivity will trickle into every area of your life. Say it out loud: "God is mighty!"

God, You are mighty! You are so, so good to me. I am so grateful to have You in my heart and in my life. I praise You! Amen.

LEAN ON ME

Lord, I seek refuge in You. . . . In Your justice, rescue and deliver me; listen closely to me and save me. Be a rock of refuge for me, where I can always go. Give the command to save me. . . . Deliver me, my God, from the power of the wicked. . . . For You are my hope, Lord God, my confidence from my youth. I have leaned on You from birth. . . . My praise is always about You.
PSALM 71:1–6 HCSB

. . . .

We all need someone to lean on when life throws us a curveball. No matter how close we walk with God, He doesn't guarantee a trouble-free life (John 16:33). And when trouble comes, it's difficult to face the struggle alone.

When trouble comes in the form of a health scare. . .a financial crisis. . .a strained relationship. . .who is your go-to person? Our brains often train us to first approach a friend, family member, professional counselor, or other "expert" for help. But our first "go-to" should be the One who provides refuge, deliverance, and support through *all* life's trials. The heavenly Father is significant to our physical and mental well-being.

So when you need someone to lean on, recall this passage from the Psalms—and call out to the One who handles your heart with the very best care!

God, when life is hard, remind me that I can always lean on You! Amen.

KEEP ON. . .

*God, don't stay away. My God, please hurry to help me. Bring
disgrace and destruction on my accusers. . . . But I will keep on hoping
for your help; I will praise you more. . . . I will tell everyone about
your righteousness. All day long I will proclaim your saving power,
though I am not skilled with words. I will praise your mighty deeds,
O Sovereign LORD. I will tell everyone that you alone are just.*

PSALM 71:12–16 NLT

. . . .

"I *will*. . ." This phrasing through these verses from the Psalms indicates
that David, who has always praised God regardless of his circumstances,
will continue to praise God in the future.

"I *will* keep on hoping. . ."

"I *will* praise you. . ."

"I *will* tell. . ."

"I *will* proclaim. . ."

"I *will* praise. . ."

As life happens to us, we tend to grow comfortable and complacent
in our faith. But the truth is, as the days go by, it's more important than
ever to trust God, to love Him more, to share Him, to praise Him. As
the days, weeks, months, and years pass, can you think of anything more
wonderful than igniting your faith with such intensity that others can't
help but notice?

*Father God, I will. . .keep on growing closer to You. I will keep on
growing in my faith. Stay near me, Lord. I will praise You. Amen.*

RESTORATION

Your righteousness, God, reaches to the heavens, you who have done great things. Who is like you, God? Though you have made me see troubles, many and bitter, you will restore my life again; from the depths of the earth you will again bring me up. You will increase my honor and comfort me once more.

PSALM 71:19–21 NIV

. . . .

Ever felt like the walls are closing in around you? No matter which way you look, you can't see a way out. You feel like you're beyond all hope. Your life is a wreck. And you're left wondering if it's beyond repair.

Although it doesn't seem possible, when you feel hopeless, you are presented with a wonderful opportunity. Because the very best way to grow your faith and increase your trust in God is through your trials. Whatever hardships you encounter in life, they all present you with delightful moments to recognize and embrace God's deliverance and grace. The God who heals (Jeremiah 17:14) offers complete restoration for your heart and soul.

The more your heart and mind are tuned to the heavenly Father's deliverance, the more you'll be able to release your bitter thoughts and burdens to Him. Just try it! You'll be so glad you did. Your thoughts and your soul will thank you! Ask the heavenly Father for His healing restoration today!

Father, restore my heart. Restore my hope. Thank You for taking my broken life, giving me healing, and covering me with Your grace. Amen.

ARE YOU REALLY LISTENING?

*"Simply put, if you're not willing to take what is dearest to you,
whether plans or people, and kiss it good-bye, you can't be my
disciple. Salt is excellent. But if the salt goes flat, it's useless,
good for nothing. Are you listening to this? Really listening?"*
LUKE 14:33–35 MSG

. . . .

What are you willing to give up for Jesus? Would you be willing to walk
away from everything most important to you? . . . Your family? Your
friends? Your home? Your job? Your future plans? It might be easy to
give up some things you *like*. But those you *love*?

Jesus doesn't mince words when it comes to following Him and
being committed to Him. He is uncompromising in what He asks of His
disciples. And so, there have been many who have chosen to walk away.
But. . .those who really understand what He offers, they stay.

When you recognize that Jesus is love. . .He is life. . .He is *everything*
you'll ever need. . . When the truth of His Word sinks deep into your
heart, you can't help but follow Him wholly, with everything you have.
You'll walk away from everything to follow Him.

You can't have other priorities that the Lord has to compete
with. . .no! He alone must be your priority. Are you listening? . . . Won't
you stay?

*Jesus, I am listening. I will stay and follow You.
You alone are my priority. Amen.*

EVEN "ONE"

"If a man has a hundred sheep and one of them gets lost, what will he do? Won't he leave the ninety-nine others in the wilderness and go to search for the one that is lost until he finds it? And when he has found it, he will joyfully carry it home on his shoulders. When he arrives, he will call together his friends and neighbors, saying, 'Rejoice with me because I have found my lost sheep.' In the same way, there is more joy in heaven over one lost sinner who repents and returns to God than over ninety-nine others who are righteous and haven't strayed away!"

LUKE 15:4–7 NLT

. . . .

Rebels. Thieves. Hypocrites. Bullies. Liars. Bad people. If we're completely honest, we'd probably never choose to spend time in the presence of humanity's worst kinds of people. We probably can't imagine ever having reason to celebrate *anything* about these undesirable people either. We want to celebrate and hang out with "the good people," don't we?

Yet God's Word sets us straight with this parable of the lost sheep. He's actively searching for the lost—He's looking for sinners to join His flock. Every soul who longs to be found is welcome! Like Christ, we should join the heavenly celebration when even one lost soul says "yes" to Jesus.

Lord, let Your Word sink deep into my heart. Change my attitude and actions toward people I'd normally avoid. Help me to rejoice when even just one repents and returns to You. Amen.

EVERYTHING YOU ARE,
EVERYTHING YOU HAVE

"Be vigilant in keeping the Commandment and The Revelation
that Moses the servant of GOD laid on you: Love GOD, your
God, walk in all his ways, do what he's commanded, embrace
him, serve him with everything you are and have."

JOSHUA 22:5 MSG

. . . .

"Be vigilant. . . ," begins Joshua in his directive to the eastern tribes. They had just helped support their brother tribes, as they settled into the Promised Land. Joshua is advising them to be watchful, to be alert, as they keep the commandment of Moses. Why is this so important?

Throughout life, we tend to grow complacent. When things are going well, we become quite comfortable and often ignore God and His plans. When our selfish plans begin to garner our time and attention, that's when things usually fall apart.

When we're not loving God with all we are and all we have—when we're not in the Word—we're allowing room for the world's vision and values to seep into our heart and soul and begin to take root, crowding out God and His perfect plan for us.

The simple truth is that a life centered around God is just better. And who doesn't want to live a better life? Cling to Him today. Make Him your primary focus, and watch the blessings abound. You won't regret it—not for one minute!

Heavenly Father, with all I am, with all I have. . .I love You! Amen.

FAITHFUL IN MUCH

"One who is faithful in a very little is also faithful in much, and
one who is dishonest in a very little is also dishonest in much.
If then you have not been faithful in the unrighteous wealth,
who will entrust to you the true riches? . . . No servant can
serve two masters. . . . You cannot serve God and money."

LUKE 16:10–11, 13 ESV

. . . .

When it comes to wealth, there is no better teacher or example than Jesus. In His own words, taken from the book of Luke, "Sell your possessions, and give to the needy. Provide yourselves. . .with a treasure in the heavens that does not fail, where no thief approaches and no moth destroys. For where your treasure is, there will your heart be also" (12:33–34).

When we don't manage our money well, when we build up debt that takes months—or even years—to repay. . .then we aren't able to obey God's call to share our abundance with others. We can't be the blessing God has created us to be. Today, live as though your riches fully belong to God—because they do! And live and love as God's faithful steward. Where is your heart today?

Father God, I want my heart to be in the right place. You created
me to be a blessing to others. Help me to follow through and obey
Your Word. I want to be a "faithful in much" woman. Amen.

SERIOUS AND PERSONAL

*[Jesus said,] "Temptations to sin are sure to come, but woe to
the one through whom they come! It would be better for him if a
millstone were hung around his neck and he were cast into the sea
than that he should cause one of these little ones to sin. Pay attention
to yourselves! If your brother sins, rebuke him, and if he repents,
forgive him, and if he sins against you seven times in the day, and
turns to you seven times, saying, 'I repent,' you must forgive him."*

LUKE 17:1–4 ESV

· ·

"Pay attention to yourselves!" Jesus said.

In addition to His call to forgive, Jesus tells His disciples to pay careful attention that they don't lead others to sin. Jesus wants the disciples to realize sin is both a serious *and* personal matter.

Jesus' message still applies to us today. We are individually responsible for our own sin. However, we're also responsible "to" others—because we can easily influence them to sin as well. Need a few examples? Just take look at the "sin" stories of Adam and Eve (Genesis 3:1–19) and Cain and Abel (Genesis 4:1–18).

When you consider the consequences of your sin, think deeper. Think of your influence. Then ask the heavenly Father to help you when temptations come your way. He'll be sure to help you make the best choices—for yourself *and* others!

---

*Heavenly Father, when temptations come,
help me to think beyond myself. Amen.*

ALL I WANT!

You're all I want in heaven! You're all I want on earth! . . . GOD is rock-firm and faithful. Look! Those who left you are falling apart! . . . But I'm in the very presence of God—oh, how refreshing it is! I've made Lord GOD my home. God, I'm telling the world what you do!

PSALM 73:25–28 MSG

. . . .

There are so many things to enjoy on earth: the beauty of God's creation, fun with family and friends, our favorite foods, travel. . . Yet none compare with the glory of heaven: walls decorated with precious stones, streets of pure gold. . .no mourning, no tears, no pain—only eternal joy! (Read Revelation 21.) However, it *all* pales in comparison to experiencing the presence of God for eternity.

Asaph, the writer of Psalm 73, beautifully expressed a heart of longing—a heart that recognizes *nothing* in heaven or on earth can compare to an eternity spent in the presence of God. Can the human mind even fathom eternity? Certainly, our finite brains can't even come close!

Woman of God, what does your heart long for today? Do you crave the refreshment of eternity in heaven—*forever* in your heavenly Father's presence? Put your mind on the things of heaven today (Colossians 3:2)!

Lord, my heart longs for eternity with You, and I don't want to keep it to myself. Who needs to hear the reason for my hope today? Show me, Father. Amen.

LITTLE CHILD

People were also bringing babies to Jesus for him to place his hands on them. When the disciples saw this, they rebuked them. But Jesus called the children to him and said, "Let the little children come to me, and do not hinder them, for the kingdom of God belongs to such as these. Truly I tell you, anyone who will not receive the kingdom of God like a little child will never enter it."

LUKE 18:15–17 NIV

. . . .

How beautiful are the words of Jesus: ". . .the kingdom of God belongs to such as these"!

The disciples were disgusted that parents were bringing their babies to Jesus. Certainly, Jesus was too important to be bothered with infants! But Jesus' immediate intervention showed He welcomed even the youngest of children. He would turn none away.

These passages from the book of Luke remind us that *all* are welcome in God's Kingdom. Even when we can't fathom His welcome. . .even when it doesn't make sense. . .Jesus says, "Come!" Come and experience joy and wholeness. Come and encounter His love and grace. Approach Him with expectation and excitement. Approach Him as a child, fully dependent upon the One who gave Himself for us.

God, when I sometimes try to reason why some should be welcome in Your presence and why others shouldn't. . .remind me of Your Word. Remind me of Your salvation made available to all. Help me to approach You as a child, Lord. Amen.

WHOLEHEARTED DEVOTION

Once a religious leader asked. . . , "Good Teacher, what should I do to inherit eternal life?" . . . Jesus. . .said, "There is still one thing you haven't done. Sell all your possessions and give the money to the poor, and you will have treasure in heaven. Then come, follow me." But when the man heard this he became very sad, for he was very rich.

Luke 18:18, 22–23 NLT

. . . .

Think about the earthly things that are most important to you. Are there things you grip tightly—things you would *never* want to give up?

The religious leader in Luke 18 asks the question of Jesus, "What should I do to inherit eternal life?" This man was asking for a list of all the things he could "do" to gain entrance into heaven. When Jesus points out the one thing he would need to give up—*his riches*—the man was sad because it was a *huge* ask. This man held tightly to his wealth. He didn't want to give it up—not even for Jesus.

What about you? . . . What are you willing to give up for Jesus? Is anything worth more than the riches of eternity (Matthew 19:27–30)?

What needs to change to give Jesus your wholehearted devotion?

God, help me to recognize anything I need to let go. If something is crowding You out of my heart, help me to get rid of it! I want to live in wholehearted devotion to You! Amen.

CLIMBING TREES

Jesus [said]. . . "Zacchaeus, come down immediately. I must stay at your house today." So he came down at once and welcomed him gladly. All the people saw this and began to mutter, "He has gone to be the guest of a sinner." But Zacchaeus stood up and said to the Lord, "Look, Lord! Here and now I give half of my possessions to the poor, and if I have cheated anybody out of anything, I will pay back four times the amount."

LUKE 19:5–8 NIV

. . . .

Zacchaeus probably thought quite highly of himself. He had an important job as a tax collector, but he was hated by many because of his dishonesty. He took more than he was supposed to from the people and pocketed the extra cash for himself.

Despite Zacchaeus' flawed character, he would do *anything*—even climb a tree!—just to get a better view of Jesus. He was willing to face possible public humiliation to get a glimpse of the Lord. He was so moved by Jesus that he was even willing to pay back "four times the amount" he stole in tax money.

You'll likely never have to climb a tree to see Jesus, but what are you willing to do to spend time in His presence? Will you do *whatever* it takes?

Jesus, thank You for showing us how You warmly received the sinner, Zacchaeus. . .a beautiful reminder that You'll receive me as well. I love You, Lord. Amen.

FREE FROM DISTRACTIONS

*[Jesus] came near the path down the Mount of Olives, and
the whole crowd of the disciples began to praise God joyfully
with a loud voice for all the miracles they had seen: The
King who comes in the name of the Lord is the blessed One.
Peace in heaven and glory in the highest heaven!*

LUKE 19:37–38 HCSB

. . . .

What occupies your mind throughout the day? Are you able to stay focused
on what truly matters? Or do your thoughts dart from worry to worry?
Is your heart centered on the Savior—or on the world's distractions?

When Jesus came onto the scene, as described in these verses from the
book of Luke, the crowd was wholly focused on Him. They had nothing
but Jesus and praise on their minds. Their words and actions showed
their honor and love for Jesus. Certainly, the people in the crowd had
problems of their own—maybe a sick family member, possibly a difficult
relationship, or perhaps tight finances. Regardless, they didn't let their
human problems stand in the way of celebrating and praising Jesus. Their
focus on the One who matters most kept them free from life's distractions.

Today, keep your heart and mind focused on Jesus. What are you
praising Him for today? When your focus is heavenward, your soul will
overflow with thanksgiving!

*Father God, I praise You for all You have done in my life.
Thank You for saving me, for blessing me. I love You! Amen.*

GIFTS OF THE SOUL

They discussed it among themselves and said, "If we say, 'From heaven,' he will ask, 'Why didn't you believe him?' But if we say, 'Of human origin,' all the people will stone us, because they are persuaded that John was a prophet." So they answered, "We don't know where it was from." Jesus said, "Neither will I tell you by what authority I am doing these things."
LUKE 20:5–8 NIV

. . . .

People have been questioning the authority of God since the rebellion of the first couple in the Garden of Eden. As most folks know, that story did not go well.

In Jesus' day, He was brazenly questioned by the priests, teachers, and elders. Jesus knew how to respond to their pointed queries and sly replies, because He was God.

Today, some people still practice the same kind of defiant and sometimes sly stance against the Lord—every time they step away from His guidance.

This kind of "doing it our way" attitude will keep us from getting closer to God—to His forgiveness and freedom, and the peace and joy. All these gifts of the soul were meant for us. But only when we remember that God is God. And we are to be His faithful female followers. It's that simple, that freeing and refreshing. Oh, and that glorious!

Lord, please turn whatever stubbornness I may have into a sweet attitude of surrender that I might live a good and lovely and noble life with You by my side. Amen.

A PRAISE DAY

We give praise and thanks to You, O God, we praise and give
thanks; Your wondrous works declare that Your Name is near and
they who invoke Your Name rehearse Your wonders. . . . I will
declare and rejoice forever; I will sing praises to the God of Jacob.

PSALM 75:1, 9 AMPC

. . . .

When was the last time you took a good look around you at God's creation, at His wonders—of which you are one—and allowed their beauty, majesty, and grandeur to fill your eyes and soul?

Consider where you are sitting right now. If there's a window, take a look outside. Allow your eyes to roam over the sky, the ground, the people, the animals. They are all a reflection of the Lord who loves you like no other. The God who is closer than your breath is near, hoping you will seek Him, desire Him, draw close to Him.

Today sing praises to God. Rehearse the wonders He has worked in this world, the beauty with which He has surrounded you. Thank Him for fashioning you and your soul, spirit, heart, and body.

Lord of Light, hear my song of praise, my words of
thanksgiving, as You cradle me in your everlasting,
ever-loving arms. It is You I love, You I desire, You I seek.

MIGHTY MITES

He saw also a poor widow putting in two mites (copper coins).
And He said, Truly I say to you, this poor widow has put in
more than all of them; for they all gave out of their abundance
(their surplus); but she has contributed out of her lack and
her want, putting in all that she had on which to live.

LUKE 21:2–4 AMPC

. . . .

Heartfelt giving. That's what Jesus is looking for. That's what He's not just commending but pointing out to His followers. He wants them to see, to understand that He doesn't pay much attention to the amount that's given to God but rather what the cost of giving is to the giver. If the gift is a sacrifice, yet a selfless one given willingly, Jesus praises the heart of that giver.

If there are times when it hurts to give, don't worry what other people might consider the littleness of your contribution. Instead, remember that Jesus knows what's going on in your life. He knows the sacrifice that gift cost you. He sees your heart and commends you and your action. In His eyes, it's all good!

Lord, thank You for this lesson in giving. For the reminder
that You look at the heart of the giver, not the amount offered.
Help me be like this widow, giving up my best, my all, to You.

PERMANENCE

*"Heaven and earth will pass away,
but My words will never pass away."*
LUKE 21:33 HCSB

. . . .

Jesus makes it clear that His words, His predictions, His promises will stand against time, against darkness, against trials. And that although the things of this earth may fade and eventually pass away, His words will not.

Through the prophet Isaiah, God claimed the same truth, saying: "The grass withers, the flowers fade when the breath of the LORD blows on them; indeed, the people are grass. The grass withers, the flowers fade, but the word of our God remains forever" (Isaiah 40:7–8 HCSB).

These promises, these truths that God's words will never pass away give believers a boost in their faith. For it is a reminder that far from fading or growing weak, God's words of hope and love can continually work to impart life and strength to the weak, joy to the downtrodden, and freedom to those in chains within and without.

Today, sink your mind and heart into this idea that God's words will forever stand, will forever continue to impart their strength and wisdom into your heart and mind, spirit and soul. Take it as a fact, a certainty that God's promises will grow brighter and brighter, shining their power into your life, as you claim each and every one day by day by day.

---

*Thank You, Lord, for Your words that will forever remain,
fueling my prayers, my faith, and my life. In Jesus' name, amen.*

I WILL CHOOSE TO REMEMBER. . .

"Will the Lord reject forever? Will he never show his favor again?
Has his unfailing love vanished forever? Has his promise failed for
all time? Has God forgotten to be merciful? Has he in anger withheld
his compassion?" Then I thought, "To this I will appeal: the years
when the Most High stretched out his right hand. I will remember the
deeds of the LORD; yes, I will remember your miracles of long ago."

PSALM 77:7–11 NIV

. . . .

Today's verses give some insight into how the mind works. Thoughts sometimes creep in, suggesting God has rejected you, rescinded His love, neglected to be merciful. But then another part of you, your good angel, promptly remembers all the wonders and miracles He has performed on behalf of you and other believers, reviving your faith once more.

When doubts subtly worm their way into your thought processes, think back to the promises God clearly states in His Word. You know, where He says He will never leave, nor forsake you. Consider all the times you've felt and experienced His presence and power.

Consider writing down those times you've felt God's hand extended into your life, so that when doubts rear their ugly heads, you'll know and remember God is still in charge and still loves you dearly. Then may hope rise up in your soul like sweet incense.

Lord, help me to remember, to never doubt
Your miracles and everlasting love for me.

WHEN GOD PASSES BY

When the Red Sea saw you, O God, its waters looked and trembled! The sea quaked to its very depths. The clouds poured down rain; the thunder rumbled in the sky. Your arrows of lightning flashed. Your thunder roared from the whirlwind; the lightning lit up the world! The earth trembled and shook.

PSALM 77:16–18 NLT

. . . .

According to the Psalms, all of creation is under God's authority, and all of the elements of His world are at full attention. Imagine, even when the waters of the Red Sea saw God, the very depths of the sea quaked.

When God passes by, no part of creation should be left unmoved by His presence, His glory, and His Almighty power. His is a sovereignty like none other—and He has the power to rescue us, to redeem us through the sacrificial work of Christ, to help us walk through this life in victory, and to deliver us safely home into glory.

May we always be moved by the presence of the great I AM.

Lord, sometimes I may get too busy, and forget to talk to You and honor You with my time and my talents, and my life. May I each and every day recognize You as my God and my Deliverer— and extend to You my adoration, my full attention, and my dearest love—for that's what You extend to me. Amen.

A LIFE TURNED BEAUTIFUL

Ruth said, "Do not urge me to leave you or to return from following you. For where you go I will go, and where you lodge I will lodge. Your people shall be my people, and your God my God. Where you die I will die, and there will I be buried. May the LORD do so to me and more also if anything but death parts me from you."

RUTH 1:16–17 ESV

. . . .

When you read the book of Ruth, you will come away with not only the heartwarming story of Ruth's loyalty and love for her mother-in-law, but it may begin to stir your thoughts of God's great devotion and affection for us—for you.

Even when all seemed lost to Ruth and Naomi, it becomes obvious that God is watching out for them in ways they could not even fathom at the time. Ruth's devotion was rewarded not only in her lifetime, but for all time, in that Ruth married Boaz and then bore a son that was in the linage of our Lord, and Savior, Jesus Christ.

Just as Ruth stuck with Naomi through thick and thin, God will stick with you. So when hard times come your way, simply keep in step with God, knowing that as you remain in Him, all will be well.

Lord, thank You for Your love, loyalty, comfort, and companionship. Help me keep my thoughts focused on You, knowing You'll turn my life into something beautiful.

LET'S DO LIFE!

Then they would put their trust in God and would not forget his deeds but would keep his commands. They would not be like their ancestors—a stubborn and rebellious generation, whose hearts were not loyal to God, whose spirits were not faithful to him.

PSALM 78:7–8 NIV

. . . .

God gave people free will, and for a very good reason. Just as we do not force our children to love us, so it goes with God in His family, wanting us to love Him freely. That's the best kind of love—the only kind, really, because it's real.

As we can see in biblical times, humankind has always had the choice of either trusting and loving God or stubbornly turning their backs on Him. But how can we live the good life if we walk away and deny the very Creator who made us? Yes, we want the best for our lives. Amazingly, God wants an even better life for us. More than we could have imagined. Hope, joy, and purpose, and yes, even happiness!

It is a daily choice, no matter the generation. Choose the glory. Choose the grace. Choose to love God freely!

Lord, I choose You every day. To love You with all my mind, heart, and soul. Let's do life together! Amen.

TAKE HIM AT HIS WORD

As they were talking about these things, Jesus himself stood among
them, and said to them, "Peace to you!" But they were startled and
frightened and thought they saw a spirit. And he said to them,
"Why are you troubled, and why do doubts arise in your hearts?
See my hands and my feet, that it is I myself. Touch me, and see.
For a spirit does not have flesh and bones as you see that I have."
And when he had said this, he showed them his hands and his feet.

LUKE 24:36–40 ESV

. . . .

When Jesus rose from the dead and appeared to the disciples, they experienced excitement, but with an unsettling mixture of doubt and even fear. Jesus compassionately confronted them on the issue. Then they went from doubt and fear to joy. And from hopelessness to the greatest hope humankind has ever known.

We can use this story to remind us to ask questions about our own lives. What is illusion and what is real? Satan tells us all kinds of lies, but Jesus speaks the truth and He means for us to have a thriving Christian life. A life of growth and maturity. A life that will encourage and inspire others. A life worth living!

Let's start taking Jesus at His Word! In this moment, allow His peace to flood you from head to toe, from within and without.

Lord, help me move from doubt and fear to joy,
from hopelessness to hopefulness. Amen.

SOUL CRAVINGS

They tested God in their heart by demanding the food they craved. They spoke against God, saying, "Can God spread a table in the wilderness? He struck the rock so that water gushed out and streams overflowed. Can he also give bread or provide meat for his people?" Therefore, when the LORD heard, he was full of wrath; a fire was kindled against Jacob; his anger rose against Israel.

PSALM 78:18–21 ESV

. . . .

What if a child had the best dad ever, but what if that child grew up always questioning and berating and not trusting this father? Well, we would say that the son deserves a rebuke, because he's not treating his father with the love and respect he deserves. That's like the children of Israel in the desert. God loved them, watched over them night and day, and even gave them the bread of angels to eat, but alas, they were more concerned about their superficial cravings rather than a longing for God and His fellowship.

Today, when we attain some of the pleasures of this life, instead of a positive attitude of gratitude toward God, we crave more. But if we fine-tune our spirits, we can sense a soul tug like none other—the longing to be closer to God, to be more aligned with His thoughts, to love His ways of heaven. Ahh, yes. Can't you already feel the sweet winds of change?

Lord, teach me to be thankful! Amen.

WHAT ARE WE MADE OF?

Jesus saw Nathanael coming toward him and said of him, "Behold, an Israelite indeed, in whom there is no deceit!" Nathanael said to him, "How do you know me?" Jesus answered him, "Before Philip called you, when you were under the fig tree, I saw you."

JOHN 1:47–48 ESV

. . . .

When Jesus met up with Nathanael—who would become one of the twelve disciples—He already knew the man. Jesus knew that Nathanael was a man of honor, guileless and honest. A man He could trust with His ministry.

Jesus knows us inside and out too, regardless of whether we know Jesus or not. What does the Lord say about us? What are we made of? What are we up to when we think no one is looking, even though God sees all? What are we thinking in secret, even though we know no thought is hidden from God?

Wouldn't it be wonderful if Christ saw many of the good attributes in us that He did in His disciple, Nathanael? Wonderful indeed!

Holy Spirit, I earnestly desire to grow into a godly and guileless woman of faith. I pray You would bless me with more wisdom and maturity, and victory over negative thinking. May I be transformed daily to be more like You, and become a powerful witness to Your glory and grace! Amen.

STAND STILL, FIRST

And as they were going down to the outskirts of the city, Samuel said to Saul, Bid the servant pass on before us—and he passed on—but you stand still, first, that I may cause you to hear the word of God.

1 SAMUEL 9:27 AMPC

. . . .

We're busy women, not just at home and at work but in our church and community. Sometimes we may feel like we're being pulled in a thousand different directions, making it difficult to get our minds on God. Yet only when we're focused on Him will we be entertaining the right thoughts, speaking words of healing, and following the plan, walking the road God has set before us.

Today and every day, before you take one step, stand still. Take the time to open up your mind and heart to seek, to hear the Word of God. To pray and ask for His help in playing your part in His plan. Then you will remember who and what the Lord is in your life—your Rock, Redeemer, Comforter, Cheerleader, Peace, Joy, Love, and Light. Your reason for being.

Woman of the Way, stand still, first.

Here I am, Lord, standing before You. My mind, heart, spirit, and soul await You in stillness. Tell me what You would have me know, think, do, and say today.

HOLDING OUR PEACE

*Saul also went home to Gibeah; and there went with him a band
of valiant men whose hearts God had touched. But some worthless
fellows said, How can this man save us? And they despised him
and brought him no gift. But he held his peace and was as if deaf.*
1 SAMUEL 10:26–27 AMPC

. . . .

God's people wanted a king, just like all the other nations. Although this was their way of rejecting the Lord, He told Samuel the prophet to go ahead and appoint a king for His people.

God "revealed to Samuel in his ear" (1 Samuel 9:15 AMPC) that it was Saul he was to anoint as king. And the prophet did just that, later introducing Saul to the Israelites and letting the people know he had been chosen and appointed by God to be their king. Then Samuel sent everyone home.

When Saul went on his way, a group of men whose hearts had been touched by God went with him. But Saul, hearing the remarks of those who hated him and refused to bring him gifts, ignored the disgruntled men and their comments.

We're bound to meet some people who won't like us. And that's okay. We can't please everyone. But we can protect our thoughts and our hearts by ignoring their remarks and actions and, in doing so, hold on to our peace as well.

*Lord, help me keep my mind on Your love,
not the mean comments of others.*

RECOGNIZING GOD'S GIFTS

*Jesus answered her, If you had only known and had recognized God's
gift and Who this is that is saying to you, Give Me a drink, you would
have asked Him [instead] and He would have given you living water.*

JOHN 4:10 AMPC

. . . .

Moms deserve a tribute for all they do. After all, they carried us, bore us,
and helped to raise us. The older we get, the more clearly we can see and
understand all that they have done for us. But how often do we miss or
not recognize the gifts God has set before us, the blessings He is holding
right in front of us?

F. B. Meyer writes, "Two conditions precede our reception of God's
best gifts: we must know, and we must ask." How open are your eyes,
mind, heart, soul, and spirit to the gift Jesus has presented to you? Once
having seen that gift or known about it, how well do you know the giver?
And what have you asked of Him in regard to that precious gift that He's
just waiting for you to take out of His hand?

---

*Lord, make me fully cognizant of the gifts that You, in Your
power and graciousness, Your love and mercy, have given
me in the past and now hold in Your hands for me. Give me
the courage to ask You to release those gifts. Make me a
woman, a daughter, a mother after Your own heart.*

NEW LIFE IN CHRIST

"For you have had five husbands, and the one you now have is not your husband. What you have said is true." The woman said to him, "Sir, I perceive that you are a prophet. Our fathers worshiped on this mountain, but you say that in Jerusalem is the place where people ought to worship."

JOHN 4:18–20 ESV

. . . .

Children learn quickly that when they get caught doing something naughty, it's best to distract Mom and Dad pronto.

In the passage provided, we see that's what the woman at the well did when Jesus told her that she had had five husbands and the one she was living with was not her husband. Yikes! To be found out by Jesus, well, you too might want to distract Him. And so the Samaritan woman tried to do that very thing by changing the subject.

Don't we sometimes do something similar? We pretend our missteps didn't happen. Or we make excuses. Or maybe we rush out and make the same mistakes again and again. None of this is a good way to conduct our lives as Jesus-followers. If we want a new life in Christ, may we (with the help of the Holy Spirit) leave our mistakes behind and move forward in step with God, filled with renewed faith and courage!

Lord, I want to shake off my old ways and start anew. Please help me walk in rhythm with You, with the faith and courage to live Your way. Amen.

INDEED ATTAINABLE

Saul told his servants, "Go ahead. Find me someone who can play well and bring him to me." One of the young men spoke up, "I know someone. I've seen him myself: the son of Jesse of Bethlehem, an excellent musician. He's also courageous, of age, well-spoken, and good-looking. And GOD is with him."

1 SAMUEL 16:17–18 MSG

• •

There are many things we can hope to be in this life. Perhaps an artist who inspires viewers to think on good and lovely things. A chef who wows everyone's taste buds with her culinary skills. Or maybe a truthful and godly politician wanting sincerely to serve this country. Or any number of callings we might have in this life.

But along with fulfilling our purpose, wouldn't we love for people to say some of the things about you and me as Saul's servant said of David in the Bible? That we come highly recommended and that the Lord is with us? Might sound a bit impossible, but when our character, when our words, thoughts, and actions yield to the power of the Holy Spirit, this godly goal is indeed attainable!

Lord, make me a woman after Your own heart. Give me a spirit of courage. Help me flee from fear and cling to Your promises. And may all who meet me know that God is with me! Amen.

BEING YOU

David said to Saul, "I'm not used to them." So David took them off.
Instead, he took his staff in his hand and chose five smooth stones
from the wadi and put them in the pouch, in his shepherd's bag.
Then, with his sling in his hand, he approached the Philistine.

1 SAMUEL 17:39–40 HCSB

. . . .

David was an unlikely hero, at least in the eyes of his older brother and King Saul—but never in the eyes of God.

David's dad had asked him to go check on his brothers. When he did so, he saw the Philistines and the Israelites on opposite sides of a hill. He heard the giant Philistine Goliath taunt the living God.

When David asked what would be done for the man that faced Goliath, his brother Eliab told him to go back home. Then when Saul heard David had volunteered to face the giant, he told him he was too young to win such a battle. But once the boy convinced him otherwise, Saul attempted to dress David in the king's own armor.

But the shepherd boy insisted he approach Goliath with his usual gear. Armed only with his staff, stones, sling, and trust in God and His power, David slew the giant.

So can you. Simply be yourself, trust God, and allow no one to discourage you.

Lord, show me how I can serve You as I am,
to be the woman, the hero, You created me to be.

WHAT IS YOUR GOLIATH?

*When the Philistine arose and came and drew near to meet
David, David ran quickly toward the battle line to meet the
Philistine. And David put his hand in his bag and took out a stone
and slung it and struck the Philistine on his forehead. The stone
sank into his forehead, and he fell on his face to the ground.*

1 Samuel 17:48–49 esv

. . . .

When you read the story of David and Goliath in 1 Samuel, you may inwardly shudder as you imagine yourself facing a giant with malevolent intentions. But don't we often face monster-like problems in this life?

What do we do with those giants? Run for our lives? Tempting, yes. But we're women of God. And although the world might chuckle at our childlike trust, the slings of faith and the stones of courage really will bring us victory with our modern-day Goliaths. Maybe not always on this side of eternity, but most certainly in the life to come. With Christ's help we can overcome our night terrors and day trials and stand in victory.

So, who or what is your Goliath today? As a Christian, may you stand up with confidence and say, "Bring it on. My mountain-moving God is mightier than all the armies and giants of this world."

*Almighty God, help me remember that I can rely on
You for every problem in my life, big or small. Amen.*

REACHING THE SHORE

Jesus said to them, It is I; be not afraid! [I Am; stop being frightened!] Then they were quite willing and glad for Him to come into the boat. And now the boat went at once to the land they had steered toward. [And immediately they reached the shore toward which they had been slowly making their way.]

John 6:20–21 ampc

. . . .

Having fed the 5,000-plus crowd, Jesus desired some alone time. So He headed for a hillside. His disciples, meanwhile, decided to take the boat across the sea to Capernaum. As they headed out into the night, the sea got rough and a violent wind rose up.

The disciples had rowed a few miles when they saw Jesus strolling on the sea. They yelled out in fear, thinking He was a ghost. But Jesus told them it was only He. No worries. Then, once they let Him into their boat—willingly and gladly—they immediately reached the shore they'd been striving for.

When you're frightened, tired of getting nowhere, don't let your wild thoughts and overactive imagination get the best of you. Instead, remember Jesus—the Lord of the visible and invisible—is in your midst. Invite Him along for the ride, willingly and gladly. And be assured—mentally, emotionally, and spiritually—that He will make sure you reach the shore you've been striving for all along.

Lord, I willingly and gladly invite You into my life. Let's ride this out together!

SERVING A MIGHTY GOD

Sing aloud to God our Strength! Shout for joy to the God of Jacob!
Raise a song, sound the timbrel, the sweet lyre with the harp. Blow
the trumpet at the New Moon, at the full moon, on our feast day.
PSALM 81:1–3 AMPC

• •

Humankind can know the mighty hand of God, whether we're born in ages past or in modern-day times. Just as God rescued the Israelites from the miseries of slavery in Egypt, He has the supernatural ability to rescue us from our afflictions.

Even though the liberation the Israelites sought surely did not come in the time frame they would have chosen, God in His all-knowing sovereignty knew well the "whens and hows" of the perfect rescue.

And when God does come to our aid in times of trials, whether He takes away the travail from us completely or He walks us through the fiery times with courage—may the Lord find us faithful and prayerful and thankful. And even singing and shouting for joy! We might even want to blow a trumpet or two!

Lord God, when I face trouble, remind me of Your mighty power and Your ability to supernaturally rescue me from afflictions. Give me daily strength and a positive mindset for all that comes my way, and may You find me faithful, prayerful, and thankful! Amen.

A STRICKEN HEART

David arose [in the darkness] and stealthily cut off the skirt
of Saul's robe. Afterward, David's heart smote him because he
had cut off Saul's skirt. He said to his men, The Lord forbid that
I should do this to my master, the Lord's anointed, to put my
hand out against him, when he is the anointed of the Lord.

1 SAMUEL 24:4–6 AMPC

. . . .

You can see the logic of it, why David wanted to end the conflict Saul
had been imposing upon him for so long. Yet as soon as the tempter had,
working in the dark, prompted David to cut off the king's robe, David's
heart, his conscience had rebelled against his action. He immediately
realized that he, an anointed king himself, should never reach out in an
attempt to harm another of God's anointed.

What strength of mind David had to not only check his own behavior
with his words but that of his men, ensuring that they would not attack
Saul themselves.

When your actions prick your heart or conscience, stop. Ask God
to give you wisdom, direction, and power to back away from where you'd
been tempted to go, to change your thought pattern. You can count on
Him and His strength to help you resist what the darkness had beckoned,
as well as give you the courage to make any amends where needed.

Lord, give me the strength to stop what
I'm doing when my heart is stricken.

BUNDLED WITH THE LORD

*Though man is risen up to pursue you and to seek your life,
yet the life of my lord shall be bound in the living bundle
with the Lord your God. And the lives of your enemies—
them shall He sling out as out of the center of a sling.*

1 SAMUEL 25:29 AMPC

. . . .

When life throws you a curveball, when nothing seems to be going right, when you feel as if you can no longer ride the waves of life, stop thinking, stop worrying, stop fearing. And run, as fast as you can, to the arms of the Lord your God.

Allow the Lord of Creation to wrap His entire being around you, to bind you to Himself, to erase the margins of where you end and He begins. For in Him you will find the rest you so desperately seek. There your mind will be eased and, once calmed, filled with all the wisdom you need to live the life you were created to live. And all those things that have been hampering you, chasing you down, keeping you from doing what you've been called to do? They will be flung away from your presence.

Lord, I need to feel Your presence, to bask in Your light, to share in Your warmth, to seek Your wisdom. Bind me in a living bundle to You. Then fling all the darkness away from me as I find my calm in Your closeness.

RIVERS OF LIVING WATER

If any man is thirsty, let him come to Me and drink! He who
believes in Me [who cleaves to and trusts in and relies on
Me] as the Scripture has said, From his innermost being shall
flow [continuously] springs and rivers of living water.

JOHN 7:37–38 AMPC

. . . .

Without Jesus, life can be like a barren desert. No matter how much you try to live in your own power, your existence continues to be dry, arid, and barren.

Then you encounter Jesus. And suddenly, everything changes. For you have finally found someone you can cling to, trust in, and rely on. For the first time in your life, the barrenness within becomes filled with a continual stream of living water. As rivers begin to flow deep within the inner well of your being, you realize, beyond a shadow of a doubt, that this is the true life, the one you had been created to live.

Today and every day, allow that river of living water to wash away any doubt and fears, any wrong or shallow thoughts that may be hindering the free flow of Jesus' power and light. Then use what you have gained in the Spirit's tide for the good of others.

Thank You, Lord, for quenching my thirst, for flowing
so deeply within, for equipping me to help others
quench their thirst and be forever changed.

HOMESICK

*My soul longs, yes, faints for the courts of the LORD; my heart
and flesh sing for joy to the living God. Even the sparrow finds
a home, and the swallow a nest for herself, where she may lay her
young, at your altars, O LORD of hosts, my King and my God. . . .
For a day in your courts is better than a thousand elsewhere.*

PSALM 84:2–3,10 ESV

. . . .

There may be times when we find ourselves physically a long way from our church. In those days away, we miss the people we worship with, the pastor and his or her messages, and the time of fellowship that follows after the service. We become homesick for our house of God, longing for the intimacy we share between our fellow believers, our shepherd, and our God.

Then, when we come back to town and return to our church home, we rejoice that we are once again truly where we belong. We are back in our spiritual nest where we are trained to imitate Jesus, to walk in the Spirit, and soar as high as the eagle, forever upward toward our God.

Today praise God for giving you a church home, a place where you can meet and greet God. A place where you can become the best version of yourself, the best place you could ever be!

*Thank You, Lord, for my church home, where I can linger
in Your presence and rest under the shadow of Your wing.*

ON THE LIGHTER SIDE

For the LORD God is a sun and shield. The LORD gives grace and glory; He does not withhold the good from those who live with integrity. Happy is the person who trusts in You, LORD of Hosts!
PSALM 84:11–12 HCSB

. . . .

When you make God your home, dwelling with Him day and night, when you make Him your source of strength, and when you trust in Him, you will be blessed (Psalms 4, 5, 12). God will be your Sun in the times of darkness and your Shadow in times of scorching heat. In the present moment He will bless you with grace and in the future, glory. Nothing good will He keep from you!

Jesus confirms these wondrous promises, these truths, saying, "I am the light of the world. Anyone who follows Me will never walk in the darkness but will have the light of life" (John 8:12 HCSB).

Child of God, sister of Christ, walk in the Light of your master. Focus on these facets of your loving Father. Know that no matter what comes your way, seeds of God's goodness cannot help but grow in the Son's Light.

I cannot live without Your light, Lord. For Your grace, glory, and goodness have blessed me beyond compare. Remind me, in every moment, that You are my home, You are the place in which I dwell.

"NOW I SEE"

*Then he answered. . . . One thing I do know, that whereas I
was blind before, now I see. . . . The man replied, Well, this
is astonishing! Here a Man has opened my eyes, and yet you
do not know where He comes from. [That is amazing!]*
JOHN 9:25, 30 AMPC

. . . .

We all have our blind spots. Things we don't see or choose not to see. It
may be something we ignore because it's unpleasant or difficult. It may be
a misperception or a prejudice we have about something or someone. It
may be that we, in some area of our life, are taking someone or something
so much for granted that we no longer notice or appreciate them. The
point is, we are all a bit shortsighted—not just in our eyes or outlook
but in our thoughts, actions, words, imaginations, spirit, soul, and heart.

Although we may not always be able to pinpoint our blind spots, we
do know one thing. That Jesus is the only One who will help us regain
our sight. He is the only One who can open our eyes and help us to see
the world around us as He does. And that, sisters, is amazing!

*Thank You, Lord, for opening my eyes, for allowing me
to be a part of Your plan, for changing my outlook.
Show me today what You would have me see.*

A BEAUTIFUL WAY TO LIVE

Steadfast love and faithfulness meet; righteousness and peace kiss each other. Faithfulness springs up from the ground, and righteousness looks down from the sky. Yes, the LORD will give what is good, and our land will yield its increase.

PSALM 85:10–12 ESV

. . . .

This passage in Psalms is one of the most beautiful in the Bible, offering us by far the loveliest way to live. How wonderful to know that the Lord wants to give us what is good and that our land will yield its increase. But for that glorious living to happen, steadfast love and faithfulness should meet up with one another in our hearts. And peace will then follow so closely behind righteousness that it will almost seem that they are kissing.

That deep trust in God is so pleasing to Him, He looks down from the heavens and calls it righteousness. Just as He did in the days of Abraham. Ahhh, yes.

May we be swept away from the old way of living, and may this beautiful way of life be ours.

Lord, I want to trust in You fully. Please push away my old habits that are trapping me in a way of life that is neither healthy, positive, nor victorious. Help me to live a new way. Your way. In You. Amen.

NO SKIN IN THE GAME

"I am the good shepherd. The good shepherd lays down his life for the sheep. He who is a hired hand and not a shepherd, who does not own the sheep, sees the wolf coming and leaves the sheep and flees, and the wolf snatches them and scatters them. He flees because he is a hired hand and cares nothing for the sheep. I am the good shepherd. I know my own and my own know me."

JOHN 10:11–14 ESV

. . . .

If a babysitter is watching a young child and that child is in an accident, it will be the mother who will prayerfully stay by that child's side when a doctor is sought, a remedy given, and a recovery dealt with. Not the babysitter. Why? As the saying goes, "Because she has no skin in the game." She did not conceive the child, birth, nurse, know, and love the child like its mother has. After all, that little child is her treasure!

As we read today's verses, we begin to understand Jesus' commitment to us, that only He has *all* the skin in the game. The Lord created us and He loves us. We are His treasures! And in that extravagant love, Jesus laid down His life so we could be offered forgiveness and eternal life with Him. Let's thank the Good Shepherd today!

Oh Lord, thank You for being my Good Shepherd. Show me how to tell others of Your amazing sacrifice and love. Amen.

ALL KINDS OF PRAYERS

But you, O Lord, are a God of compassion and mercy, slow to get
angry and filled with unfailing love and faithfulness. Look down
and have mercy on me. Give your strength to your servant; save me,
the son of your servant. Send me a sign of your favor. Then those who
hate me will be put to shame, for you, O LORD, help and comfort me.
PSALM 86:15–17 NLT

. . . .

There are all kinds of prayers. Those that are filled with praise and
thanksgiving. Or perhaps we offer our song or dance or written words
as a kind of prayer. There are supplications, asking for various needs to
be met. There are appeals for forgiveness, or we might simply bask in the
Lord's presence and listen for Him to speak to us. Or we might remind
the Lord how much we love Him! Then sometimes, there are pleas that
come from the depths of our being.

Psalms is full of those lamenting kinds of petitions, and always, God
is there. When those deepest cries of our souls rise up, when enemies
threaten us, and when all seems lost, may we remember and reach out
to the One who's known throughout all time for His divine compassion
and mercy, His love and His faithfulness.

Thank You, Lord, for Your mercy and compassion.
Please hear my prayer. Amen.

A NEW MINDSET

Then Jesus, deeply moved again, came to the tomb. It was a cave, and a stone lay against it. Jesus said, "Take away the stone." Martha, the sister of the dead man, said to him, "Lord, by this time there will be an odor, for he has been dead four days." Jesus said to her, "Did I not tell you that if you believed you would see the glory of God?"

JOHN 11:38–40 ESV

. . . .

To read this passage in John may make you sad. It might even make you sigh or cringe. Jesus' friend Martha is being lovingly rebuked by Jesus for her disbelief, and the correction probably stung a bit. Being disciplined is never easy.

Yet this is such a good biblical lesson, because it's so easy for us to be stuck in the same skeptical mindset. How many times have we prayed for our dearest aunt to be healed and then the Lord hears us say to a friend, "Do you think my aunt will ever recover?" Or perhaps we do pray, then immediately make travel plans to attend her funeral. God hears us speak, and He knows our thoughts, so we are hiding nothing from Him. Ever.

May our faith grow stronger every day, and may we speak words and think thoughts that reflect that trust!

Lord, please grow my faith in You, and may I live that faith in words and deeds and with a new mindset. Amen.

RISE UP WITH COURAGE

*LORD, you are the God who saves me; day and night I
cry out to you. May my prayer come before you; turn your
ear to my cry. I am overwhelmed with troubles and my
life draws near to death. I am counted among those who
go down to the pit; I am like one without strength.*

PSALM 88:1–4 NIV

. . . .

Let's face it, sometimes life is painful and harsh and sometimes it might even feel unbearable. We can see in Psalms that God's people are not exempt from the sorrows of this broken world. In fact, our Lord knew our painful life firsthand. Jesus was called the man of sorrows, and we know from His Word that when faced with the death of His friend Lazarus, He wept.

Today, as Christians, we may sometimes feel a deep groaning sorrow in our souls for the lost sheep of this world. Or we may feel sorrow for other various reasons. Sometimes people will ridicule and hate us and threaten us because of who we are, what we believe, and who we follow. Yes, there will be times of sorrow and even more as Christ's return gets closer. Yet even in the midst of our lament we can have peace no matter what humankind throws at us. We can know joy rather than be disabled by fear.

We can rise up with courage. And that courage can be ours. We need only ask.

Lord, grant me courage! Amen.

IN GOD'S HANDS

"Carry the ark of God back into the city. If I find favor in the eyes of the LORD, he will bring me back and let me see both it and his dwelling place. But if he says, 'I have no pleasure in you,' behold, here I am, let him do to me what seems good to him."

2 Samuel 15:25–26 esv

. . . .

When King David's son Absalom attempted to claim his father's throne for his own, David and his entourage fled Jerusalem. Noting that the Levites had brought the ark with them, he told the priest Zadok to take it back to Jerusalem. David was humble enough to realize his situation was in God's hands, *and* he was willing to go along with whatever seemed good to God.

Later, Shimei, a Benjamite, cursed David as he was heading into the wilderness. David's nephew Abishai said to the king, "Let me go over and take off his head" (2 Samuel 16:9 ampc). But David resisted, telling those with him to leave the man alone. For Shimei's curses could have been a part of God's plan—or perhaps God would notice these bad things that were happening and bless David because of them.

When you're afflicted with trouble, take this tip from David: leave all that's out of your hands in God's hands, knowing He will do as He deems best!

Lord, I leave myself and my situation in Your hands.

A HUMBLE HEROINE

Absalom's servants came to the woman at the house and asked,
"Where are Ahimaaz and Jonathan?" "They passed by toward
the water," the woman replied to them. The men searched
but did not find them, so they returned to Jerusalem.

2 SAMUEL 17:20 HCSB

. . . .

Even though David trusted God to work in his situation, he still did his part in helping things to go his way. One of his crafty ploys was to send his trusted advisor, Hushai, back to Jerusalem to serve Absalom. Hushai was then to pass all he'd heard to priests Zadok and Abiathar. The priests would relay the inside information to a servant girl, who would then pass it on to Jonathan and Ahimaaz, who would then relay the information to David.

One day a young man realized what was happening and told Absalom. Fearing for their lives, Jonathan and Ahimaaz fled to a house in Bahurim. There they hid in a well. The woman then "spread a covering over the well's mouth and spread ground corn on it, and the thing was not discovered" (2 Samuel 17:19 AMPC).

When Absalom's servants came to find the men, the woman admitted they'd been there but said they'd gone off already, saving both David's spies and his kingdom!

Just as God used a nameless maid and housewife, He can use you. Never let anyone tell you otherwise!

Lord, give me the faith, humility, intelligence, and courage
to do whatever You call this humble heroine to do!

THE LOVE FACTOR

"Now I am giving you a new commandment: Love each other.
Just as I have loved you, you should love each other. Your love for
one another will prove to the world that you are my disciples."

JOHN 13:34–35 NLT

. . . .

Let's face it. It can be very difficult to love some people, even though they, like we, are Christians. Yet that is just what Jesus calls us to do. And this love for others isn't to be a mere surface kind of love; it's one that's to go deep—as deep as Jesus' love is for us.

Perhaps you're thinking that those who have betrayed you or deserted you are no longer worthy of your love. But didn't Jesus continue to love those followers who'd betrayed Him, those who'd deserted Him, those who'd claimed they didn't even know Him?

Today, consider those you find difficult to love. Ask Jesus to give you the humility and forgiveness you need to love them in spite of what they may have said or done to you or others. Ask Him to pour so much love down upon you that you cannot help but use what has spilled over to touch them, to reach them, to love them.

Thank You, Lord, for Your love and light. Help me to love
and forgive others just as You love and forgive me. Amen.

PEACE OF HEART—AND MIND

Do not let your hearts be troubled (distressed, agitated).
JOHN 14:1 AMPC

. . . .

Jesus not only tells you to not let your heart be troubled. He gives you reasons why you can stay calm, cool, and collected no matter what or who comes your way.

- Jesus says He's gone ahead of you to prepare a place for you in Father God's house. No need to ask for directions—you'll know how to get there (John 14:2–7).
- Jesus says that if you believe in Him, you will be able to do "even greater things" (John 14:12 AMPC).
- Jesus says He will do whatever you ask in His name (John 14:14).
- Jesus has asked God to send you the Holy Spirit, "another Comforter (Counselor, Helper, Intercessor, Advocate, Strengthener, and Standby), that He may remain with you forever" who live "with you [constantly] and will be in you" (John 14:16, 17 AMPC).

No matter how rough life may seem, remember Jesus' calming words:

Peace I leave with you; My [own] peace I now give and bequeath to you. Not as the world gives do I give to you. Do not let your hearts be troubled, neither let them be afraid. [Stop allowing yourselves to be agitated and disturbed; and do not permit yourselves to be fearful and intimidated and cowardly and unsettled.]
JOHN 14:27 AMPC

Lord of peace, live in me. Keep my heart and mind—calm, cool, and collected—in You.

WISDOM AND COURAGE

"There used to be a saying, 'If you want to settle an argument, ask advice at the town of Abel.' I am one who is peace loving and faithful in Israel. But you are destroying an important town in Israel. Why do you want to devour what belongs to the LORD?"

2 SAMUEL 20:18–19 NLT

. . . .

King David's commander-in-chief Joab had tracked Sheba—a man who'd led a revolt against David—to the city of Abel. When Joab's forces started battering down the town wall, a wise woman called out to Joab's officers, wanting to talk to David's commander.

As Joab approached the woman, she explained that she lived in a town known for its wisdom and peace, a town faithful to their king and God. So why destroy what belongs to Him?

Joab explained the situation, how he and his men were looking for Sheba, a rebel against King David. If the townspeople could give him that one man, Joab promised to leave in peace. "Then the woman went to all the people with her wise advice, and they cut off Sheba's head and threw it out to Joab. So he. . .called his troops back from the attack" (2 Samuel 20:22 NLT).

If you ask, God will give you, as He did this woman, whatever wisdom and courage you need, just when you need it. That's His command *and* promise (Joshua 1:9; James 1:5)!

Thank You, Lord, for Your dual gifts of courage and wisdom!

GAIN IN LOSS

*"I am going away to the one who sent me, and not one of you is asking
where I am going. Instead, you grieve because of what I've told you.
But in fact, it is best for you that I go away, because if I don't, the
Advocate won't come. If I do go away, then I will send him to you."*
JOHN 16:5–7 NLT

. . . .

We gain by our losses.

In today's verses, Jesus tells His disciples He has to go away. For if He doesn't, the Holy Spirit won't come into their lives. If He does go away, He will send the Spirit to them, to fill the role of being their "Comforter (Counselor, Helper, Intercessor, Advocate, Strengthener, and Standby)" (John 14:16 AMPC).

Then, Jesus tells them that although they might be sad when He departs, especially when they see what happens to Him, their grief will turn to joy when He sees them again! To help them understand what this means, Jesus likens their experience to that of a woman who during childbirth is in anguish and pain. But once her labor is over, she forgets what she has endured for the joy of holding that baby in her arms (John 16:21).

Whenever you suffer pain or a loss in your life, look for the gain from Jesus!

*Lord, give me Your perspective when I face a challenge or grief.
Help me realize what I have gained from whatever I lose!*

JESUS' ETERNAL GIFTS

*"An hour is coming, and has come, when each of you will be
scattered to his own home, and you will leave Me alone. Yet I am
not alone, because the Father is with Me. I have told you these
things so that in Me you may have peace. You will have suffering
in this world. Be courageous! I have conquered the world."*

JOHN 16:32–33 HCSB

• •

No matter what happens in your life, no matter how many people may
desert you, you will never be left alone, bereft of friend, guidance, or
unfathomable love. Why? Because wherever you go, however long you live,
God is with you, standing by Your side, holding your hand, guiding, loving,
protecting, and equipping you with whatever you need to live this life.

Yet that's not all! For in Jesus, you can and will find the peace you
need. Although you'll have trials, troubles, and frustrations in this material
world, you need not be discouraged. Because Jesus has overcome this
world. He has "deprived it of power to harm you" (John 16:33 AMPC).

Sit with these truths for a while today. Allow them to sink into your
consciousness, become written upon your heart, etched deep into your
mind. And you will find all the companionship and peace you desire!

---

*Lord, take my hand as I reach out for You. Fill me
with Your constant presence and conquering peace!*

HOME SAFE

"Keep them safe from the evil one. They do not belong to this world any more than I do. . . . I am praying not only for these disciples but also for all who will ever believe in me through their message."

JOHN 17:15–16, 20 NLT

. . . .

Imagine this. The One who did only good in this world, the One who suffered, who died so that you could be in a relationship with God, this loving Son of God prayed to His Father *for you*, you who are reading this book, this page, these words.

Jesus had *you* in mind, prayed for *you*, over two thousand years ago. He asked that God keep *you* from the evil one. To protect *you* by the power of God's name, all so that *you* and believers such as yourself, would be as one, as God and Jesus are one (John 17:11).

When dark thoughts begin to creep into your mind, shadowing your heart for God, making you believe you're not important—to anyone—remember these words of Jesus. Remember that you do not belong to this world. Remember that Jesus has prayed for you, asking for God to protect you, keep you, guide you.

All because you believe in the message, the Word, the One who came to save you.

You, Jesus, are my home. You are my place of safety, companionship, love, and light. Thank You for praying for me!

A WISE REQUEST

*"I am but a lad [in wisdom and experience]; I know not
how to go out (begin) or come in (finish). . . . So give Your
servant an understanding mind and a hearing heart to judge
Your people, that I may discern between good and bad."*

1 KINGS 3:7, 9 AMPC

· ·

When Solomon asked God for wisdom to rule His people, God was
very pleased with His request. For Solomon could have asked for a long
life, wealth, or the death of his enemies. But he, a king, was humble
enough to ask the Lord solely for wisdom. And because of this young
king's request, God granted him not only unsurpassable wisdom but
those things Solomon had not asked for, namely, "both riches and honor"
(1 Kings 3:13 AMPC).

In Matthew 20:32, Jesus asked some blind men what they wanted
Him to do for them—just as God, appearing here to Solomon in a vision,
says, "Ask. What should I give you?" (1 Kings 3:5 HCSB).

How would you respond if God came to you and asked, "What may
I give you?" Why not ask for wisdom only? For then you too may find you
have all you need to lead a life in and with the One who rules the world.

Lord, the one thing I seek and ask for is Your wisdom. Grant it, I pray.

THAT SECRET PLACE: PART 1

He who dwells in the secret place of the Most High shall remain stable and fixed under the shadow of the Almighty [Whose power no foe can withstand]. I will say of the Lord, He is my Refuge and my Fortress, my God; on Him I lean and rely, and in Him I [confidently] trust!

PSALM 91:1–2 AMPC

. . . .

When you need a cleansing of the mind and a reinforcing of power, calm, and courage from God, immerse yourself—your *entire* self—in Psalm 91. For the psalmist emphasizes that if you would merely dwell in that secret place of God, sheltering in His shadow, you will forever be unshaken, for in that place you are under the protection of the mightiest power in heaven or on earth. If you unequivocally declare that God alone is your Refuge and Fortress, the One on whom you will always rely and in whom you will always trust, all the promises the psalmist proceeds to list will be yours!

What are those promises? That God will deliver you—an abider in that "secret place"—from traps and plagues. He'll cover you with His wings. There you'll find refuge and shielding. With and in Him, you'll have no terror of the night or be nicked by arrows flying in the day. No harm will come to you.

Today, in this moment, meet God in that secret place.

Lord, my Refuge, I seek that secret place in You.

THAT SECRET PLACE: PART 2

Only a spectator shall you be [yourself inaccessible in the secret place of the Most High] as you witness the reward of the wicked. Because you have made the Lord your refuge, and the Most High your dwelling place, there shall no evil befall you, nor any plague or calamity come near your tent.

PSALM 91:8–10 AMPC

· ·

When you make the secret place of the Most High your dwelling place, says Psalm 91:1–2, when you make God your sole refuge, trusting Him alone, you will then be entitled to the rich promises that follow in the rest of that chapter!

The previous day's devotion covered the first of those promises. Today we're focused on the rest, which include the fact that because you abide in the secret place of God, He will assign angels to watch over you, to stay with you, defend and preserve you as you obey and serve God. They will bear you up so that you won't even stub your toe on a stone.

Because you love God, He will protect you. When you call on Him, He promises to answer you, to be with you in trouble, to rescue and honor you. And in the end, He will reward you with long life and His salvation.

Lord, thank You for all the rich promises that will be mine as I abide in the secret place in You. You alone are my refuge, my one and only God.

LEAD IN LOVE

*When Jesus saw his mother and the disciple whom he loved
standing nearby, he said to his mother, "Woman, behold,
your son!" Then he said to the disciple, "Behold, your mother!"
And from that hour the disciple took her to his own home.*

JOHN 19:26–27 ESV

. . . .

In the last moments of His life, Jesus allowed His love and compassion
to lead Him when He saw His mother standing by the cross upon which
His body hung. Although Jesus must have been suffering extreme pain
and torture, He gifted His mother to the care of His disciple John who
welcomed her in love. Jesus died soon after, finishing His life in human form.

Later that day, it was love that prompted Joseph of Arimathea to
approach Pilate. Joseph had kept his discipleship of Jesus a secret for
he feared what the Jews might do to him. But now love motivated him
to put his fears aside and ask Pilate's permission to remove Jesus' body.

Then came Nicodemus, the one who had previously come to Jesus
under cover of night. Love motivated him to bring the spices needed to
bury His Savior. Together, Joseph and Nicodemus prepared Jesus' body
and placed it in a tomb.

Allow love of Jesus to lead you, motivate you, prompt you, and give
you the courage to walk His Way.

*Lord, may Your love lead me wherever I go,
in whatever I encounter, whoever and whatever I face.*

CLOSE AT HAND

*Mary Magdalene came to the tomb early, while it was
still dark, and saw that the stone had been taken away
from the tomb. . . . Mary stood weeping outside the
tomb, and as she wept she stooped to look into the tomb.*

JOHN 20:1, 11 ESV

. . . .

A distraught Mary Magdalene had come seeking Jesus' body, wanting to
complete the needed preparation for His burial. But, horror of horrors,
she discovered His body missing!

Mary took to tears. Two tomb-dwelling angels asked why she was
crying. She explained, "Because they've taken away my Lord. . .and I don't
know where they've put Him" (John 20:13 HCSB). After saying this, she
turned around and saw Jesus, mistaking Him for the gardener. He too
asked why she was weeping, who she was looking for.

Mary asked Him where they had taken her beloved Jesus, not knowing
it was He until He spoke her name.

About this touching scene, F. B. Meyer writes:

*It is because we know so little of the inner meaning of events which are
happening around us, under the hand of God, that we weep so bitterly. What
we suppose we have lost is really close at hand, and what we count disastrous
is part of the process designed to irradiate our lives forevermore.*

Lord, help me understand that no matter what happens in my life,
You are close at hand, enlightening me with every step I take.

"PEACE BE WITH YOU"

*The doors being locked where the disciples were for fear of the
Jews, Jesus came and stood among them and said to them,
"Peace be with you." When he had said this, he showed them
his hands and his side. Then the disciples were glad when they
saw the Lord. Jesus said to them again, "Peace be with you."*

JOHN 20:19–21 ESV

. . . .

No matter where you are, no matter what you are hiding from, no matter
how many entrances are locked, Jesus will find a way to reach you.

And when He does reach you, He brings the peace of His presence.
As He does so, whatever fears you may have been harboring are eased.
Whatever doubts are plaguing you are erased (John 20:26–29). Because
you believe in Jesus, even though you've never seen Him, you are blessed.

Today, rejoice in this knowledge. Absorb these truths as gospel. Add
them to the firm foundation of your faith. Regardless of what comes
your way or what fears may be riddling you, whatever doubts may be
entangling you, know the peace and love of Jesus, the courage and trust
His presence exudes, when you believe.

*Lord, enter into my life. Ease through the walls that separate
You from me. Then make Your peace and presence my
perpetual guide this day and every day to come.*

JESUS STANDING ON THE SHORE

Jesus said to them, "Children, do you have any fish?" They answered him, "No." He said to them, "Cast the net on the right side of the boat, and you will find some." So they cast it, and now they were not able to haul it in, because of the quantity of fish.

JOHN 21:5–6 ESV

. . . .

Simon Peter told his fellow believers he was going fishing. They agreed to go with him. But that night caught nothing.

At the break of dawn, Jesus was standing on the shore, looking out at them. Not yet recognized by His followers, Jesus asked if they'd caught anything. They said no. So He told them where to cast and they did so, netting so many fish they struggled to haul them in!

That's when John recognized Jesus, saying, "It is the Lord!" (John 21:7 ESV). Peter dove into the water and swam to shore while the rest came in the boat, dragging their net full of fish behind them.

Jesus awaited them with a fire and bread.

Just as He did then, Jesus stands on the shore to comfort your heart when you're discouraged, telling you where to cast your net, helping before He's asked, providing warmth and nourishment for body and soul.

Today, keep your eyes open for Jesus, knowing He's standing on the shore, looking out for you, ready to help and guide, comfort and nourish.

Lord, You are so precious, so loving, so mine.

CALM, COMFORT, AND CHEERS

*The Lord knows the thoughts of man, that they are
vain (empty and futile—only a breath). Blessed
(happy, fortunate, to be envied) is the man whom You
discipline and instruct, O Lord, and teach out of Your law.*
PSALM 94:11–12 AMPC

. . . .

It's difficult to admit that compared to God's thoughts, ours are so fleeting and futile. Yet when we read through God's Word and compare our thoughts with His, we cannot but concede it's true!

Fortunately, we can learn about God, learn to think what He thinks by studying His Word and following it. When we do so, a strange and wonderful thing happens: God gives us the power to keep ourselves "calm in the days of adversity" (Psalm 94:13 AMPC).

By soaking our minds in God's Word and following His will and way, we can find the calm we need to face anything that comes. But that's not all! We also begin to recognize our thoughts. When we think we're slipping, we can tap into His steadfast love and stay upright (verse 18). When we're filled with anxiety and turn to Him, we can be sure His comfort will cheer us (verse 19). And when we're joyful in Him, we'll find He's delighted in us!

*You, Lord, are my refuge, my stronghold,
and my rock—my calm, comfort, and cheer!*

WAITING ROOM

He commanded them not to leave Jerusalem but to wait for what the Father had promised, of which [He said] you have heard Me speak. For John baptized with water, but not many days from now you shall be baptized with (placed in, introduced into) the Holy Spirit.

Acts 1:4–5 ampc

. . . .

Many of us are immersed in a culture of instant gratification. We want immediate pleasure, reward, or satisfaction. And we want it when we want it.

Yet that's not how God works. Consider Abraham and Sarah. They were promised a child when Abraham was 75 years old. But his son by Sarah didn't arrive until Abraham was 100 years old and Sarah 90! Chances are, their period of waiting made the manifestation of God's promise even more precious.

Both Jesus and God encouraged people to wait on God's timing to receive the promised blessing. For some things to come to fruition—such as Jesus' return—we're told not to worry about it. It's not for us to know all the details of God's plan. We're just to have faith.

So sit tight. And wait. Remember that "the Lord isn't really being slow about his promise, as some people think. No, he is being patient for your sake. He does not want anyone to be destroyed, but wants everyone to repent" (2 Peter 3:9 nlt).

Help me, Lord, to not rush ahead of You but to be patient and sit with faith in Your waiting room.

WELL MET

The LORD came to him: "Depart from here and turn eastward and hide yourself by the brook Cherith, which is east of the Jordan. You shall drink from the brook, and I have commanded the ravens to feed you there." So he went and did according to the word of the LORD.

1 KINGS 17:2–5 ESV

. . . .

When a drought entered the land, God the Father told Elijah the prophet to go to Cherith where he would have water to drink. There God arranged for some ravens to bring him bread and meat each morning and evening.

When the brook dried up, God directed Elijah to go to Zarephath where a widow would provide for him. Elijah did so. He met the widow, but she said she had only a little of oil and flour left. She was going to use it to prepare a cake for herself and her son, which would be their last meal.

Elijah told her not to be afraid but to make him a little bread first, then use what's left to prepare a meal for her and her son. He told her God would make sure she'd have enough flour and oil left in their containers until God sent rain again. And that's just what happened.

Be assured that no matter where you are in life, God the Father will provide what you, His servant, require. All you need is faith. He'll do the rest.

Thank You, Lord, for always meeting my needs!

YOUR JOURNEY

*"I saw the Lord always before me, for he is at my right hand
that I may not be shaken; therefore my heart was glad, and
my tongue rejoiced; my flesh also will dwell in hope."*

Acts 2:25–26 esv

. . . .

Queen Jezebel threatened the life of Elijah. Filled with fear, he ran for
his life. Once he reached the wilderness, he journeyed for a day, then sat
under a broom tree and prayed that he would die, saying, "I have had
enough, Lord. . . . Take my life, for I am no better than my ancestors who
have already died" (1 Kings 19:4 nlt). He then fell asleep.

God sent angels to wake Elijah and give him something to eat and
drink. He slept again, and an angel came back and gave him more food
and drink, saying, "Get up and eat, or the journey will be too much for
you" (1 Kings 19:7 hcsb). On the strength gleaned from that angel food,
Elijah journeyed for forty more days and nights, stopping when he got
to the mountain of God. There God pointed out the error in Elijah's
thoughts and sent him back from whence he'd come (1 Kings 19:13–18).

When you're soul weary, pour your heart out to God. When you do,
He'll care for you, correct your thinking, and get you back on the right track.

*Lord, meet me where I am when I've had enough.
Then help me find the right road back.*

GREAT EXPECTATIONS

Peter, along with John, looked at him intently and said, "Look at us." So he turned to them, expecting to get something from them. But Peter said, "I don't have silver or gold, but what I have, I give you: In the name of Jesus Christ the Nazarene, get up and walk!"

ACTS 3:4–6 HCSB

. . . .

A man who'd been lame since birth would be carried each day to the temple complex. There, at the gate, he would beg from people who were entering the temple. So, when he saw Peter and John, about to go into the temple, he asked them for some sort of tangible gift.

Peter and John stopped in their tracks. Peter asked the man to look at them. So the man did so, eagerly expecting to receive some money from them. Peter corrected that misconception immediately, saying, "I have no money to give you but what I can give you is the healing power of Jesus Christ. Get up and walk!" And the man did!

Perhaps you have something in mind that you want from God. Perhaps you're looking up at Him with great expectations of material gain. If so, try taking another tack. Consider simply telling God your need without telling Him how to fill it, yet knowing He will give you something better than you could ever imagine.

Here is my need, Lord. I'll leave it up to You how to fulfill it—to my profound joy!

CONSCIOUS OF GOD

*Light is sown for the [uncompromisingly] righteous and strewn
along their pathway, and joy for the upright in heart [the
irrepressible joy which comes from consciousness of His favor
and protection]. Rejoice in the Lord, you [consistently] righteous
(upright and in right standing with God), and give thanks.*
PSALM 97:11–12 AMPC

. . . .

When you're walking God's way, loving, forgiving, and putting others
before yourself, and using your talents to further His kingdom, light will
be sown on your path. And you'll experience the greatest joy as you live
your life conscious of God's favor and protection!

Yet so many of us allow the darkness of the present time to cloud
that joy. We let the woes of the world, the troubles of these days drag us
into the shadows. In the darkness, we forget that we are women of the
Way, ones who walk in God's favor, safe under His shield of protection.

Resolve to live your life knowing God is continually shedding His
light upon your path. Make it a point to live each day conscious of His
protection and in His favor. When troubles come your way, remember
He plans all things for your good—and although you might not see that
good today, you will see it tomorrow.

Look to the Lord who keeps you His, loves you, protects you, and
enlightens you. And joy will be yours!

*Help me, Lord, to each day live conscious of Your continual
light, favor, and protection, in this life and the next!*

THE FREEDOM WALK

*The high priest rose up, and all who were with him (that is, the
party of the Sadducees), and filled with jealousy they arrested the
apostles and put them in the public prison. But during the night an
angel of the Lord opened the prison doors and brought them out.*

ACTS 5:17–19 ESV

. . . .

The apostles had been healing people, both the sick and those afflicted
with unclean spirits. More and more people were coming to the Lord,
both men and women.

Those against the apostles, the high priest and the Sadducees, were
so jealous that they had the believers jailed. But the Sadducees' efforts
couldn't keep the message from being spread. For that night an angel of
God came and freed Jesus' followers, telling them, "Go and stand in the
temple and speak to the people all the words of this Life" (Acts 5:20 ESV).

When you think all is lost, remember the power of your God.
Remember He has a plan for your life—and He will do anything He
needs to do to help you along your way.

Your Lord is a God of miracles. He can free you from whatever
hinders your walk with Him. He can deliver you from any illness—mental,
emotional, physical, or spiritual. Believe that nothing can hinder Him
from rescuing you. His purpose will prevail! His message will be spread!

Thank You, Lord, for freeing me from whatever hinders my walk with You.

"ALL IS WELL"

*She called to her husband and said, "Send me one of the servants
and one of the donkeys, that I may quickly go to the man of God
and come back again." And he said, "Why will you go to him today?
It is neither new moon nor Sabbath." She said, "All is well."*

2 KINGS 4:22–23 ESV

. . . .

Elisha the prophet used to frequent Shunem. There he met a woman
who not only insisted on feeding him but eventually had a room built
for him in her home.

In return for this nameless woman's kindness, God gifted her with
a child, a son. But one day that son suffered heat stroke while out in the
fields with his father. A servant brought him into the Shunammite woman
who held her child until he died. She then laid him down on the bed in
the room she had had built for Elisha.

She then called to her husband, saying she'd be going to find Elisha.
When he questioned her motives, she simply said, "All is well." She gave
the same response to Elisha's servant who ran ahead of his master to
see how things were with her. So great was her confident faith that she
dared to believe and say all would be well. And God did not disappoint.

Might you have that same confident faith.

*Lord, help me be confident that with You in
my life, all is and always will be well! Amen.*

GOD'S PLAN PREVAILS

"If this plan or this undertaking is of man, it will fail;
but if it is of God, you will not be able to overthrow
them. You might even be found opposing God!"

ACTS 5:38–39 ESV

. . . .

The apostles had been preaching the good word of Jesus and healing many people when the high priest's council had them arrested and thrown into jail. Yet that night an angel of God opened the prison doors and told them to go the temple and preach about Jesus and His message. So they did.

When the religious leaders sent for the apostles to be brought before them, an officer reported, "We found the prison securely locked and the guards standing at the doors, but when we opened them we found no one inside" (Acts 5:23 ESV). The apostles were eventually retrieved from the temple and brought before the officials. When they were asked why they had continued to teach in Jesus' name after the council told them not to, Peter replied, "We must obey God rather than men" (Acts 5:29 ESV).

That's when one of the Sadducees advised his fellow council members that if what was happening was of God, they would not be able to stop it.

When you remember that God's plan cannot be thwarted, you'll find the courage and confidence to continue walking in His will, moving with God instead of against Him.

It's You and Your Word alone that I obey. For You are Lord of all!

GOD'S LITTLE SERVANT

*Now the Syrians on one of their raids had carried off a little girl
from the land of Israel, and she worked in the service of Naaman's
wife. She said to her mistress, "Would that my lord were with the
prophet who is in Samaria! He would cure him of his leprosy."*

2 Kings 5:2–3 esv

• •

Naaman, the commander of the army of the king of Syria, was a great
and mighty man of valor. He was also a leper.

On one of the Syrian raids against Israel, a child had been taken
captive and brought to Syria. She became a maid to Naaman's wife. Yet
this nameless child rose above her troubles and sorrows of losing her
home and family. Out of this dark place, the girl looked for and lived in
God's light. She continued in her faith, to the point where she looked
to her mistress's husband's welfare, suggesting he see the man of God in
Samaria, for he would heal him of his leprosy.

Eventually Naaman did go to see Elisha. And he was not only
cured but vowed to worship from the heart no one other than the Lord
(2 Kings 5:17–19).

Would that we would have the same heart and mind of the little
servant girl, following and keeping faith in her God no matter how hard
the circumstances.

Put within me, Lord, the heart and faith of this little servant girl.

SPIRITUAL EYES

"Do not be afraid, for those who are with us are more than those who are with them." Then Elisha prayed and said, "O LORD, please open his eyes that he may see." So the LORD opened the eyes of the young man, and he saw, and behold, the mountain was full of horses and chariots of fire all around Elisha.

2 KINGS 6:16–17 ESV

. . . .

Some days it seems like trouble follows us wherever we go, even though we are following the Lord of lords. Yet we need not ever be shaken or alarmed when the trouble against us seems not only swift but overwhelming. We need not be like Elisha's servant, who rose early one morning, went outside, saw the Syrian army with its horses and chariots surrounding the city, and panicked, asking his master what they were to do.

Instead, may we remember that as God's children, we need not be afraid of anything in this world. For although at times unseen, God has more of His agents surrounding us, shielding us, than any earthly enemy. All we need to do is open the spiritual eyes of our faith to see the truth of the matter.

Lord God, You who are my Sun and Shield, when trouble comes my way, remind me to open my spiritual eyes and see Your agents surrounding me, a force bigger, stronger, and more powerful than any other that may seek my harm. Amen.

UNLIKELY HEROES

It was this very Moses whom they had denied (disowned and rejected),
saying, Who made you our ruler (referee) and judge? whom God sent to
be a ruler and deliverer and redeemer, by and with the [protecting and
helping] hand of the Angel that appeared to him in the bramblebush.

ACTS 7:35 AMPC

. . . .

God has a penchant for raising up unlikely heroes.

He raised up Rahab, a prostitute, who saved the lives of Joshua's spies, and later married Salmon of Judah and became the mother of Boaz. He raised up Jael, identified only as the wife of Heber, who killed army commander Sisera with a hammer and a tent peg, thereby delivering Israel from King Jabin of Canaan.

Then there was Ruth, a Moabitess and widow, who refused to leave her widowed mother-in-law's side. She married Boaz, becoming the great-grandmother of David and an ancestress of Jesus. Consider Esther, a Jewess who became a queen in the country that had destroyed her own. Why? So that she could save His people.

Consider Mary Magdalene, a woman from whom Jesus exorcised demons and who later became the first evangelist, spreading the news of Jesus' resurrection.

God can use anyone to further His means, to work out His plan. So put away those doubts about not being hero material or worthy enough to be used by God. Instead, open up your mind, heart, and soul and allow Him to spirit you where He wills.

Here I am, Lord. Use me where You will.

COURAGE AND FAITH

When Athaliah, Ahaziah's mother, saw that her son was dead,
she proceeded to annihilate all the royal heirs. Jehosheba, who was
King Jehoram's daughter and Ahaziah's sister, secretly rescued Joash
son of Ahaziah from the king's sons who were being killed.

2 KINGS 11:1–2 HCSB

. . . .

Athaliah was pure evil. When her son King Ahaziah died, she was so greedy for power that she killed all who stood in her way. But, unbeknownst to Athaliah, she missed one: Joash. He'd been spirited away by his aunt Jehosheba, the half-sister of Ahaziah.

Jehosheba hid Joash and his nurse in a bedroom. Later, he was moved to the temple of the Lord where he stayed for six years while the now-queen Athaliah ruled Judah.

In the seventh year of Athaliah's reign, Jehosheba's husband, the priest Jehoiada, presented Joash to some of Judah's mighty men and had them swear allegiance to the king's son. The seven-year-old Joash was soon declared king and Athaliah met her demise.

Just as Jochebed and Miriam hid Moses, Jehosheba hid Joash, all for the benefit of God's people and His Word. Never allow the fact that you are an ordinary woman keep you from performing extraordinary feats of courage. Maintain the faith that God can and will use you, to do what He calls you to do, including overturning evil.

Give me the confidence, Lord, to know that with You working
through me, I can do anything You call me to do!

BENEFITS AND BLESSINGS

Bless (affectionately, gratefully praise) the Lord, O my soul; and all that is [deepest] within me, bless His holy name! Bless (affectionately, gratefully praise) the Lord, O my soul, and forget not [one of] all His benefits.

PSALM 103:1–2 AMPC

. . . .

When you're having a rough day, when your faith needs a boost, when you need to get your head in a better place, remember all the good things with which God blesses you.

God not only forgives but forgets all your misdeeds; and He heals all your maladies. He pulls you up from the pit of corruption and crowns you with not just favor but compassion. He fills your life with goodness and renews your youth like the eagles'. God brings justice to those who are treated unfairly and reveals Himself and His power.

Then, He really hits the heartstrings by being so full of mercy and grace toward you, slow in becoming angry, and filled with plenty of love and kindness. He won't stay angry nor hold a grudge. But the most amazing part of all this is that your Abba, your Father, doesn't punish you for all your sins, not as you deserve. Why? Because your God is all about love, which is more vast than you can imagine and which will never fail.

Today count all those benefits. Then tonight, fall asleep, counting all your blessings.

Lord, You overwhelm me with Your love—and so much more. Let me count Your many blessings.

NO ONE IRREDEEMABLE

*"The Lord Jesus who appeared to you on the road by which
you came has sent me so that you may regain your sight and
be filled with the Holy Spirit." And immediately something
like scales fell from his eyes, and he regained his sight.*

ACTS 9:17–18 ESV

. . . .

Saul (who later became Paul) was persecuting people who belonged to
the Way. He stood by when Stephen was stoned to death (Acts 7:58).
Yet even Saul—who called himself the worst of sinners (1 Timothy
1:15–16)—received mercy from Jesus Christ.

If there is someone in your life who you believe is irredeemable,
remember Saul. Remember the light with which Jesus struck him blind.
Remember how Jesus' booming voice instructed him. How Saul rose from
the ground, now completely sightless. How he was led by the hand into
Damascus. How for three days he neither ate nor drank. How a man of
the Way, the courageous Ananias, came to Saul on day three, placed his
hands upon Saul's face, and prayed that "Brother Saul" (Acts 9:17 HCSB)
would regain his sight and be filled with the Holy Spirit. How something
like scales then fell from Saul's eyes, and he was baptized.

If God can redeem Saul, he can redeem anyone. Do not doubt.

*In Your eyes, Lord, no one is irredeemable. That gives me hope
for _____, I pray, Lord, that You would remove
the scales from his/her eyes as I lift him/her up to You.*

TURNING AWAY FROM EVIL

*GOD had taken a stand against Israel and Judah, speaking clearly
through countless holy prophets and seers time and time again,
"Turn away from your evil way of life. Do what I tell you and
have been telling you in The Revelation I gave your ancestors and
of which I've kept reminding you ever since through my servants
the prophets." But they wouldn't listen. If anything, they were even
more bullheaded than their stubborn ancestors, if that's possible.*

2 KINGS 17:13–14 MSG

. . . .

God's desire is for His children to turn away from evil ways of living.
He wants them to say no to gossip, lying, unforgiveness, jealousy, and
selfishness. It's not always the easiest choice, but it's the right choice.

We often become stubborn because our flesh wants to be the boss
and make our own decisions in the moment. But when we keep our
thoughts focused on following God's commands, they will manifest in
our actions. Every time we get to a crossroads and chose His way over
our own, blessings will come as rewards for standing firm in our belief.

Today do the right thing—the thing that glorifies God.

*Lord, give me the strength to turn away from evil in my thoughts and
actions. Help me make the faithful decision to follow Your perfect ways
over mine. I confess my stubbornness and ask for help to focus on You.*

THE NEED TO BELIEVE

*But Peter put them all outside, and knelt down and
prayed; and turning to the body he said, "Tabitha, arise."
And she opened her eyes, and when she saw Peter she sat
up. And he gave her his hand and raised her up. Then,
calling the saints and widows, he presented her alive.*

ACTS 9:40–41 ESV

. . . .

Not only did Peter have a divine infusion of power to perform miracles
in the name of Jesus, but he also had a strong belief in who Jesus was.
He believed what the Lord said would come to be in his own life. And
so when the opportunity to bring Tabitha back to life came to him, Peter
activated his faith.

Did you catch that amazing detail? Before he acted, he believed? His
thoughts had to align with Jesus' promises before he was able to perform
the Lord's work. Peter embraced His words fully and completely, asked
for power, and his belief was transformed into a miracle.

You can find strength in the same way. When you choose to believe
God is who He says He is and will do what He says He will do, you will
live your life through the lens of steadfast faith.

*Lord, help me believe Your words and promises, and let
them infuse my life with Your power. I know the powerful
connection between my mind and my actions, so I pray
You would align them to benefit me and glorify You.*

HONESTY IN PRAYER

*Hezekiah became terminally ill. The prophet Isaiah son of Amoz came
and said to him, "This is what the LORD says: 'Put your affairs in
order, for you are about to die; you will not recover.'" Then Hezekiah
turned his face to the wall and prayed to the LORD, "Please LORD,
remember how I have walked before You faithfully and wholeheartedly
and have done what pleases You." And Hezekiah wept bitterly.*

2 KINGS 20:1–3 HCSB

. . . .

Sometimes we struggle to embrace what we believe God is telling us.
It may feel too scary. It may be miles out of our comfort zone or trigger
deep insecurities. It might remind us of other times we've tried and failed.
Perhaps we wonder if it's really God's voice we're hearing.

When Hezekiah received a distressing word from God through the
prophet Isaiah, he immediately prayed. In that moment, his faith took
over and Hezekiah went right to the throne room. Through his tears, this
righteous king of Judah took his pain and angst to the only One who
could bring comfort. He was vulnerable in his pleading with his Creator.

When you hear a word from God, will prayer be your immediate
response? Have you invested in your relationship with God to where you
can be honest with Him?

---

*Lord, mature my trust in You and Your Word so that I will
feel confident in being vulnerable before You, even honest
about my feelings about Your plans for my life. Amen.*

EXPECTANT LIVING

All the creatures look expectantly to you to give them their meals on
time. You come, and they gather around; you open your hand and
they eat from it. If you turned your back, they'd die in a minute—
Take back your Spirit and they die, revert to original mud.

PSALM 104:27–29 MSG

. . . .

What a beautiful reminder that we can look expectantly for God's provision. Think of how He meets the needs of nature and animals, so much so it's an automatic assumption. The birds aren't stressed out. The grass isn't complaining. The deer don't worry about their next meal. They just know provision will come in one form or another. They embrace the ebbs and flows life brings their way with seasons.

Let your faith in God be so strong that your actions display it. Let the promises throughout His Word sink so deep into the marrow of your bones that you live expectantly for His goodness. Let it be your automatic assumption when struggles arise.

Friend, the Lord's love for you is unending and unshakable. It's forever trustworthy. And when this truth becomes your operating system, it will affect the way you live your life. It'll guide you through every up and down.

Lord, thank You for seeing my every need and meeting each
in meaningful ways. Give me the kind of faith that expects
Your goodness to come to pass. Help me live without worry
or fear no matter what comes—or doesn't come—my way.

THE POWER OF PRAISE

*Oh, let me sing to GOD all my life long, sing hymns to my God
as long as I live! Oh, let my song please him; I'm so pleased
to be singing to GOD. But clear the ground of sinners—no
more godless men and women! O my soul, bless GOD!*

PSALM 104:33–35 MSG

. . . .

If you're busy singing praises to God, it's a sure-fire way to keep your thoughts on the right things. Rather than obsessing over what disrespectful words she said to you, or wondering if you looked silly at the event, or trying to puzzle out the fight you had with your spouse before work, train your mind to focus on God's goodness.

Thanking Him has a unique way of changing our mood. It brings a hopeful perspective when we need it the most. It shifts our negative thoughts to positive ones as we remember His faithfulness in the hard moments. And it keeps our eyes on the prize—eternity with God.

Be intentional to fill your mind with the joys of the Lord. Don't let anything in this world pull you from meditating on the Lord's magnificence. Because when your thoughts are full of Him, your choices will follow.

*Lord, when my heart is heavy with the worries of the world,
help me remember all the times You've come through for
me. Lead me to praise and thank You. Help me focus on
Your provision, healing, and kindness so I can find peace.*

A MIND OVERHAUL

Seek the LORD and his strength; seek his presence continually!
Remember the wondrous works that he has done, his
miracles, and the judgments he uttered, O offspring of
Abraham, his servant, children of Jacob, his chosen ones!
PSALM 105:4–6 ESV

. . . .

When we realize that our strength comes from God, we won't step out in faith without being prayed up. We'll understand how flawed and limited we are in our flesh, and we'll seek His presence as we go through our day. Yes… the more we embrace faith, the more we will understand how very much we need God.

Where do you need to seek the Lord and His strength today? Where do you need to meditate on His goodness in your life? What promises has He kept that you need to revisit? How do your thoughts about God affect how you approach your day?

There's a direct connection between what you think and how you act. If you don't think you need God, you won't ask for His help. If you don't think His presence is necessary, you won't seek it. Let God overhaul your mind so you can live righteously.

Lord, overhaul my thoughts so they settle on the truth of how much I need You. Let me look to only You to meet my needs so I can live an empowered life. Focus my eyes on Your goodness.

AFTER HIS OWN HEART

And when he had removed him, he raised up David to be their king, of whom he testified and said, "I have found in David the son of Jesse a man after my heart, who will do all my will." Of this man's offspring God has brought to Israel a Savior, Jesus, as he promised.

ACTS 13:22–23 ESV

. . . .

What an honor for David to have God say he's a man after His heart. Can the Lord say that you're a woman after His heart?

What's required is a desire to do what's right in the eyes of God. It's a longing to follow His commands day in and day out. It's a craving to learn more about your Creator through time spent in the Word and prayer. It's a choice to follow Him above anything the world offers. It's a yearning to glorify His name through the words you speak and the ways you live your life.

Consider how much it would delight God's heart to watch you purpose to live righteously. Every day, ask Him to help you find the desire to do His will. And at the same time, ask God to give you the strength and wisdom to walk it out in real time.

Lord, I want my life to bring You joy. I want You to see a woman full of faith and love for her Father. I want You to see my heart for You.

RIPE FOR GOD'S WORK

There was a man in Lystra who couldn't walk. He sat there,
crippled since the day of his birth. He heard Paul talking, and
Paul, looking him in the eye, saw that he was ripe for God's
work, ready to believe. So he said, loud enough for everyone to
hear, "Up on your feet!" The man was up in a flash—jumped
up and walked around as if he'd been walking all his life.

Acts 14:8–10 MSG

. . . .

Let us always be ready to believe. Just like the man from today's passage of scripture, let us always be ripe for God's work.

It took hearing the Good News of Jesus for this crippled man to open his heart to the truth. At that moment, his thoughts shifted from the bondage of his condition to the possible freedom from it. He began to believe life could be different. Hope began to rise up from deep within. And when Paul commanded him to stand, his belief in the Lord manifested in his actions. He was healed.

For you to be effective in your faith, you must believe God's Word to be Truth. You have to accept His love and receive His promises. And once those are anchored in your heart, you'll experience heavenly power to walk out each day with confidence and courage. You'll find yourself ripe for God's work.

Lord, I'm ready to believe in my heart so my life will reflect my faith.

STANDING FIRM IN FAITH

When they had preached the good news (Gospel) to that town and made disciples of many of the people, they went back to Lystra and Iconium and Antioch, establishing and strengthening the souls and the hearts of the disciples, urging and warning and encouraging them to stand firm in the faith, and [telling them] that it is through many hardships and tribulations we must enter the kingdom of God.

ACTS 14:21–22 AMPC

. . . .

Do you see the connection? Today's passage of scripture is confirming that for us to get to the other side of hardships and tribulations, we must stand firm in our faith. It's when we settle the truth of God's goodness and protection in our mind, it will strengthen our resolve for the fight.

There is a direct connection, an important connection, between what we think and how we act. God's Word has a powerful way of infiltrating our thoughts. It helps us focus on the right things. And because it transforms our mind, it also transforms the way we interact with the world.

Open your Bible daily and let it establish your heart on the things of God. Let it empower you to live and love others well. And let it encourage you in the battles you're facing.

Lord, help me settle the truth of Your love and goodness in my mind because I know it's what will empower me to walk out the plan You have for my life in meaningful ways. Amen.

NOTICING THE BLESSINGS

So he brought his people out of Egypt with joy, his chosen ones with rejoicing. He gave his people the lands of pagan nations, and they harvested crops that others had planted. All this happened so they would follow his decrees and obey his instructions. Praise the LORD!

PSALM 105:43–45 NLT

. . . .

When you begin to notice the blessings God brings into your life, it will turn your heart toward the Lord. The hardness in your spirit will soften and become tender for Him.

So often we forget every good thing comes from Him. We keep our eyes down as we plow through life, forgetting to look up and see the beautiful things coming to fruition in our circumstances. And it affects how we face the world.

The Lord has done amazing things for you, friend. Take time today to think through the times He has intervened on your behalf or restored something broken or met an unspoken need. And let it be the fuel you need to glorify His name in all the world. Let it be what drives you to share hope and love.

Lord, open my eyes to see the ways You have brought beautiful things into my life. Let those blessings penetrate any hardness in my heart so I am freed up to live a life that glorifies Your name. Let my life always point to You and Your goodness.

FAITHFUL TO BELIEVE GOD IS GOOD

Hallelujah! Thank GOD! And why? Because he's good, because his love lasts. But who on earth can do it—declaim GOD's mighty acts, broadcast all his praises? You're one happy man when you do what's right, one happy woman when you form the habit of justice.

PSALM 106:1–3 MSG

. . . .

Let's always remember that God is good, and His love lasts forever. Meditate on that truth day and night. Look for examples in your life that prove it as fact. Be willing to share your testimony that supports the truth that God is good and His love eternal.

If you can stay faithful to this belief, it will trickle out through your actions. You'll love others better when you understand God's love is unfailing. You'll be kinder and more generous when you believe all good things come from above. When you live with the intention to do the right thing, your days will be filled with happiness regardless of the ups and downs that come your way.

The deepest desire of your heart should be to share God with your community. And often the most powerful way to walk it out is by how you live. Be the kind of woman who invests time in her relationship with the Lord, evident by how she blesses others.

Lord, thank You for being good. Thank You for Your everlasting love. Let those beautiful blessings infiltrate my heart and powerfully affect my actions toward others.

A FAITHFUL RESPONSE

*And a vision appeared to Paul in the night: a man of Macedonia
was standing there, urging him and saying, "Come over to
Macedonia and help us." And when Paul had seen the vision,
immediately we sought to go on into Macedonia, concluding
that God had called us to preach the gospel to them.*

ACTS 16:9–10 ESV

. . . .

God called and Paul responded. His faith was so strong and his belief so firm, that he wasted no time in obeying what God was asking.

Sometimes we need confirmation because we're not sure it's God's voice we're hearing. Sometimes we don't feel worthy of the call at all, so we doubt we've actually heard Him. But Paul was saturated in the Lord, and it allowed him to move forward in his faith and obey.

Your ticket to living an exemplary life is knowing God. It's investing your heart in eternal things and letting them guide your choices and decisions. And as you align your thoughts with the Lord's, your actions will follow. Then when you feel God calling you into something new, your heart will have already been primed to not only hear His voice but to obey.

*Lord, I want to know Your voice so distinctly that I act without
question. Let Your Word ring true in my thoughts, helping
me discern the difference between Your will and mine.*

A DIRECT ANSWER

And when the Philistines heard that David was anointed king over
all Israel, [they] all went up to seek David. And [he] heard of it
and went out before them. Now the Philistines had come and made
a raid in the Valley of Rephaim. David asked God, Shall I go up
against the Philistines? And will You deliver them into my hand?
And the Lord said, Go up, and I will deliver them into your hand.
1 Chronicles 14:8–10 ampc

. . . .

David asked God a direct question and got a direct answer. He wasn't
afraid. Instead, he boldly went to God, confident he'd get a response.

Think how it changed David's battle mindset, recognizing he would
be the victor. Maybe it gave him freedom to be more courageous. Maybe
it provided strategy to try new things. Maybe it made him creative in
how he approached it. But, friend, understand that his thoughts directed
his actions.

Even when we don't get a direct answer, we can look at the Bible as
a guide. It can give us confidence to take the next step because we know
certain things about God. We know He is loving. We know He will
protect us. We know He is our salvation. And we know God will provide
us with the tools necessary to do His will. If we let it, that knowledge
alone will give us confidence to move forward in courage.

Lord, I trust You.

FEARING GOD ABOVE ALL

*For great is the LORD, and greatly to be praised, and he is
to be feared above all gods. For all the gods of the peoples are
worthless idols, but the LORD made the heavens. Splendor and
majesty are before him; strength and joy are in his place.*

1 CHRONICLES 16:25–27 ESV

. . . .

Every time the Bible says to fear God, it means we are to respect Him. It's a call to show reverence to the Creator of heaven and earth, not be afraid of who He is or what He will do. And fearing Him helps us remember our position in reference to His.

When we truly understand we're to esteem the Lord above everything else we deem important, it creates a priority for our life. Think about what matters the most to you. How much of your time does it get? How much of your heart? How much of your money? What tops that list?

If anything on your list is above God, ask Him to help you change it. Let the Lord be top of mind because your faith will help set the tone for your day. When you fear Him above all other gods, you will walk in His strength and power. You will find peace and joy regardless of your circumstances. And in return, you will know how "great is the LORD."

*Lord, You are my favorite. You top my list.
Help me live every day with this as my reality!*

BOLD FAITH

While Paul was waiting for them in Athens, he was deeply troubled by all the idols he saw everywhere in the city. He went to the synagogue to reason with the Jews and the God-fearing Gentiles, and he spoke daily in the public square to all who happened to be there.

ACTS 17:16–17 NLT

. . . .

Paul was not afraid to stand up for what was right. He was bold in his faith and willing to do the hard things when necessary. He never shied away from calling people out as he was calling them higher.

What gave him the grit? It was his steadfast faith in God. Simply put, his belief was unshakable. Paul's conviction and God's authority drove Paul's passion for both Jews and Gentiles to follow the Lord's commands. His love and dedication informed his actions.

We can be just as purposeful as Paul. We can have the confidence he had. And we can settle in our minds right here and now—just like Paul—that there's no one above God. Make a habit of spending time in the Word every day, meditating on His goodness and sovereignty. Then ask God to give you the ability to live in that conviction yourself, pointing to the path of righteousness with your words and actions.

Lord, let me be bold enough to encourage those around me to follow Your ways. And help my heart and motivation be recognized as pure. Amen.

TELL THE WORLD

Oh, thank GOD—he's so good! His love never runs out. All
of you set free by GOD, tell the world! Tell how he freed
you from oppression, then rounded you up from all over
the place, from the four winds, from the seven seas.

PSALM 107:1–3 MSG

. . . .

Today's scripture issues a challenge to share your God-moments with the world. Others need encouragement from someone who has walked a mile in their shoes. They need to know God is alive and active even today. They need reminders that He is sovereign and able to meet every need.

Why? Because when we have that hope to hold on to, it will dramatically change how we live. It will reassure us that God is relevant. It will inspire us to wait with expectation for the Lord to show up in meaningful ways. It will boost our mood, allowing us to find peace in the middle of our mess.

Ask God to open your eyes so you can see every opportunity to tell the world of His goodness. Let your testimony of freedom be cued up and ready to share at a moment's notice. And know that your God-moments will help others align their thoughts and actions with His.

Lord, You have freed me from the bondage of my sin, and
I want the world to know they can experience it too. Help
my words and actions lead others to Your goodness.

KNOWING HE'S WILLING AND ABLE

Then you called out to GOD in your desperate condition; he got you out in the nick of time. He led you out of your dark, dark cell, broke open the jail and led you out. So thank GOD for his marvelous love, for his miracle mercy to the children he loves.

PSALM 107:13–15 MSG

. . . .

The psalmist in today's passage of scripture recognized something extraordinary. When you press into the Lord in the hard moments—in those desperate conditions—He will be there to help you. It's God who will lead you out of darkness. He's the One to free you from the chains of sin.

Friend, here's the gold nugget to grab onto today. For us to find the courage to ask for the Lord's intervention, we have to know in our heart He is willing and able. Our faith has to activate our belief that He is sovereign. And there must be a history of us trusting the promises of God, even if it's a brief history.

It's from that understanding we cry out to our heavenly Father for help. It's our thoughts that fuel our actions, which is why spending time with the Lord is vital. Every moment you invest in growing your faith is time well spent.

Lord, mature my faith so that doubting Your ability and willingness to help me doesn't rule in my heart. Help me believe You in all things.

KEEPING TRACK OF GOD'S GOODNESS

*He quieted the wind down to a whisper, put a muzzle on all the
big waves. And you were so glad when the storm died down, and he
led you safely back to harbor. So thank GOD for his marvelous love,
for his miracle mercy to the children he loves. Lift high your praises
when the people assemble, shout Hallelujah when the elders meet!*

PSALM 107:29–32 MSG

. . . .

Every time God does something wonderful in your life, write it down.
Maybe you make a note in your Bible or write in a journal but find a
way to memorialize the moments where God has showed up in your life
in meaningful ways.

Why is this important? Because we will need to revisit these moments
again and again. When we're facing a situation that seems hopeless or a
circumstance that feels overwhelming, we will need to remember the times
God intervened. We will need to remember that He is good all the time.

Nothing breeds hope more than a positive past experience. So be quick
to write down the times He quieted the wind or calmed the tumultuous
waters in your life. And keep track of the powerful ways God has shown
His unconditional love.

*Lord, I see You moving in my life and I'm grateful You've
chosen to love me the way You do. Help me remember
Your goodness so I'm encouraged to look for it again.*

A GENERATIONAL BLESSING

And you, Solomon my son, know the God of your father and serve him with a whole heart and with a willing mind, for the LORD searches all hearts and understands every plan and thought. If you seek him, he will be found by you, but if you forsake him, he will cast you off forever.

1 CHRONICLES 28:9 ESV

. . . .

Do you recognize the generational blessing in today's passage of scripture? The fact that Solomon knew his father's God proves the authenticity of King David's faith. And that Solomon chose to serve the Lord shows the faith he grew up watching and learning about became real and true in his own heart.

Let this be encouragement that how you live your life matters because others are watching. They're looking to see how you handle both joyful times and difficult ones. They're watching how God manifests in your mess and how you respond. They are looking at the ways you manage stress and anxiety and fear.

Solomon didn't see perfection in his father's faith, but instead saw a man who lived with purpose and passion for God. He recognized the strong connection between his father's thought life and actions. And it helped secure his own faith in God, which is a blessing we all hope to pass down to the next generation.

Lord, let me live my faith out loud in honest and transparent ways. And let it positively affect the hearts of others for You.

GOD SEES YOUR HEART

God answered Solomon, "Because this was in your heart, and you have
not asked for possessions, wealth, honor, or the life of those who hate
you, and have not even asked for long life, but have asked for wisdom
and knowledge for yourself that you may govern my people over whom
I have made you king, wisdom and knowledge are granted to you.

2 CHRONICLES 1:11–12 ESV

. . . .

This is such a beautiful story about the heart of Solomon. And it's the perfect example of the truth that God has the ability to see the depth of who we are.

Given the chance, what would you ask God for today? Maybe you need His provision. Maybe you need a change of heart. Maybe you need for something broken to be restored. Maybe it's a fear that needs to be extinguished. Maybe you need hope or peace or the ability to love someone completely unlovable. Maybe you need the right words for a difficult conversation.

God will recognize and honor those requests made through faith. He will hear your heart through your prayers. So be thoughtful in what you ask for, and let it be an appeal that demonstrates your steadfast trust in the One you know can make a difference.

Lord, give me a pure heart like Solomon, and help me petition
You through unshakable faith in Your love and compassion.
Let my requests be examples of how much I trust in You.

STARTING WITH PRAISE

I'm thanking you, GOD, out in the streets, singing your praises in town and country. The deeper your love, the higher it goes; every cloud's a flag to your faithfulness. Soar high in the skies, O GOD! Cover the whole earth with your glory! And for the sake of the one you love so much, reach down and help me—answer me!

PSALM 108:3–6 MSG

• •

Just like the psalmist began his prayer with praise, let us follow suit. When we have a heart of gratitude as we go before the Lord in prayer, it changes the way we talk to Him. It solidifies healthy expectations. And it builds our faith to ask boldly and humbly.

What are the things you appreciate about God? Where have you seen His hand move in your life recently? What unexpected blessings have come your way? What impossibilities have you watched come into fruition? Friend, these are the kinds of things that fuel your gratitude, and giving thanks should always be how you start your prayers.

When your heart is full and you see His goodness all over your life, nothing will stop words of thanksgiving flowing from your lips as you praise God for all He has done.

Lord, thank You for moving in my life in such meaningful ways! I'm grateful beyond words. Help me always see where You are active in my circumstances, and give me unshakable gratitude.

WHEN YOU NEED TO SEE

*When all the people of Israel saw the fire come down and the glory
of the LORD on the temple, they bowed down with their faces to the
ground on the pavement and worshiped and gave thanks to the
LORD, saying, "For he is good, for his steadfast love endures forever."*

2 CHRONICLES 7:3 ESV

. . . .

There are times we need our eyes to witness something so we can believe.
Before we can move forward, we need visual confirmation. Amen? And
it seems God understands this about His people.

While faith is defined as trusting in someone or something we can't
see, there are times God gives us a glimpse of who He is and what He
is doing in our life. Just like when the Israelites saw the glory of God on
the temple, those are the times that move us to reverence. They are what
help shape our next step.

When your faith feels shaky and you need help with your unbelief,
ask the Lord to show His glory. Ask for signs and wonders. And then ask
God to give you the eyes to see His heavenly fingerprints and footprints
leaving their mark in your life.

*Lord, I believe, but sometimes I need help with my unbelief. Sometimes
I just need to see Your work in my circumstances or feel Your presence
surrounding me. Thank You for understanding what I need when I need it.*

THE POWERFUL COMBINATION

When I shut up the heavens so that there is no rain, or command
the locust to devour the land, or send pestilence among my people,
if my people who are called by my name humble themselves, and
pray and seek my face and turn from their wicked ways, then I will
hear from heaven and will forgive their sin and heal their land.

2 CHRONICLES 7:13–14 ESV

. . . .

When we are steeped in sin and unwilling to walk in righteousness, God sees it. And based on today's scripture, one could make the argument there are consequences for our sin—consequences that are divinely distributed.

Yet when we change how we think and what we entertain in our mind, God responds in powerful ways. Reread today's verse and let it encourage you to change how you may be living today. Make note of His requests.

God is telling us to humble ourselves, setting aside our prideful tendencies. He is asking us to seek Him through intentional prayer. And the Lord is telling us to turn away from our wretched and sinful ways. It's this powerful combination that prompts God to hear us, forgive us, and bring healing.

Lord, thank You for Your Word that guides how we should be living. Help me humble myself, pray and seek Your face, and live righteously. I don't want anything to interfere with our relationship.

A DIVINE TRANSFORMATION

"As I was on the road, approaching Damascus about noon, a very
bright light from heaven suddenly shone down around me. I fell
to the ground and heard a voice saying to me, 'Saul, Saul, why are
you persecuting me?' 'Who are you, lord?' I asked. And the voice
replied, 'I am Jesus the Nazarene, the one you are persecuting.'"

ACTS 22:6–8 NLT

. . . .

Right then and there, Paul's transformation took place. His thought process shifted. His heart softened. And the Lord rearranged his life, calling him up and into the ministry.

It's important to remember Paul was on his way to harass and persecute Christians. He was going to round them up for harm's purpose. He held great disdain for them, and his actions proved it. But God had other plans.

Sometimes we need the Lord to shine a bright light on our thought life. We form judgments against certain people. We adopt a critical spirit that hardens our heart toward others, because what we think is how we act. But God has the power to change what your mind focuses on regarding those around you, so you're able to love the unlovable and forgive the unforgivable. He can transform your heart in a divine moment.

Lord, work Your wonders on my thought life so I live with
compassion and care for others. Transform my heart so I can
love unhindered. Change me to live with righteous pursuit.

THOUGHTS INFLUENCE ACTIONS

*They swore an oath to the LORD with a loud voice and with
shouting and with trumpets and with horns. And all Judah
rejoiced over the oath, for they had sworn with all their heart
and had sought him with their whole desire, and he was
found by them, and the LORD gave them rest all around.*

2 CHRONICLES 15:14–15 ESV

. . . .

Notice the order in today's passage of scripture. They made a decision in their mind to commit themselves to the Lord, and then their voices erupted with rejoicing and praise. It's important to recognize how the mind influences actions.

If you focus your thoughts on the goodness of God, you will live in that belief. If you decide the Lord is for you, you will find patience to wait. If you choose to believe He's your provision, you'll live without worry. If you see God as your comfort, He will be your first stop when things get hard. In the same way, if you decide the Lord is weak and uninterested and unable, the struggles in life will eat you up.

Decide today to set your mind on God's sovereignty. Look through His Word for times He came through for those who believed. And ask for an extra measure of faith so your heart is full of expectation for His work in your life.

*Lord, help my mind stay steady on Your
magnificence so I live in Your resurrection power.*

THE GIFT OF WISDOM

He sent redemption to his people; he has commanded his
covenant forever. Holy and awesome is his name! The fear of
the LORD is the beginning of wisdom; all those who practice
it have a good understanding. His praise endures forever!
PSALM 111:9–10 ESV

. . . .

What an awesome reminder that when we respect God, it's our first smart move. The Bible says it's the beginning of wisdom. And the more we dig into the Word and seek His discernment for our life, the more wisdom will become part of what we do.

The truth is that every day we get to decide whether we will make good choices or bad ones. It's up to us whether we follow His commands or embrace what the world offers. And every time we're wise, it's credited to our account. God sees every hard decision we make.

Even more, wisdom will eventually become a habit. Once we see the blessings that come from it, we won't want to live any other way. We won't want to compromise the good gifts we receive from purposeful living. And we will be encouraged to seek God more and more throughout our life, asking and listening for His guidance for each choice that comes our way.

Lord, I am seeking the wisdom that comes from You alone.
Open my eyes to see Your way and Your will for me to follow.

THE POWER OF TRUSTING

*He is not afraid of bad news; his heart is firm, trusting
in the LORD. His heart is steady; he will not be afraid,
until he looks in triumph on his adversaries.*

PSALM 112:7–8 ESV

. . . .

Trust is a big deal, and many of us struggle with it because of things we've dealt with in our past. We are often timid and nervous to give up the control that's required so we can put our faith in someone else. And it's especially challenging when we can't see that person with our own eyes.

Yet if we believe God is who He says He is, and if we believe He will do what He says He will do, then our actions should reflect that belief. We won't be afraid of bad news because we have chosen time and time again to trust the Lord. Our heart can be firm and steady because we are thoroughly convinced of God's sovereignty.

Be the kind of woman who is full of faith no matter what. Trust Him in the small things. Trust Him in the big things. And watch how consistently you're able to walk out that faith as life ebbs and flows.

*Lord, give me a faithful heart that is unshakable. Let
me walk in confidence every day. And help me trust
You with each part of my life, all the time.*

WHAT IS YOUR RESPONSE TO THE BATTLE?

*"You will not need to fight in this battle. Stand firm, hold your
position, and see the salvation of the LORD on your behalf, O
Judah and Jerusalem. Do not be afraid and do not be dismayed.
Tomorrow go out against them, and the LORD will be with you."*

2 CHRONICLES 20:17 ESV

. . . .

There are times the battle is ours to fight in His strength and there are
situations where we must advocate for ourselves. The truth is we'll often be
in circumstances that require us to engage so we can get to the other side.
But there are other times our job is to stand firm and watch God engage.

It's important we know our role in each battle. We simply can't allow
ourselves to be tossed about in the choppy water of our mess. And the
only way we'll know what part to play is by asking God for guidance.
We need Him to tell us how to respond.

What battles are you facing? Today, take inventory, making sure
you're doing what God is asking in each situation. It's vital we wrap our
minds around His expectations of us so we can be part of the process
and not part of the problem.

*Lord, show me where You want me as I discern my role in
the battles I face. Help me be bold when necessary and
still when You are the One fighting on my behalf.*

WORKING TOGETHER

*And Jehoiada made a covenant between himself and all the
people and the king that they should be the LORD's people.
Then all the people went to the house of Baal and tore it
down; his altars and his images they broke in pieces, and
they killed Mattan the priest of Baal before the altars.*

2 CHRONICLES 23:16–17 ESV

• •

There is nothing like the power of community to help us walk out our
faith in meaningful ways. The priest Jehoiada harnessed the power of
togetherness and made a pact that all the people were to be God's people.
As a team, they worked together to remove evil.

While community can often be messy and frustrating, the truth is
we need it. It's necessary. And God designed us to be part of a group of
like-minded people. Think about the disciples. Think about the Israelites.
Think about David's men. All throughout the Bible you see remarkable
examples of community.

There is beauty in working together for a common good. Who are
the people in your life offering support and guidance and wisdom? Take
a moment to thank God for them. Let Him know why they matter.

*Lord, I've never really considered the value that community brings
to my life, but I see it now. Help me be an effective team player
and respecter of those You put in my life. And thank You for
choosing the right group of people for me at the right time.*

ONLY ONE TRUE GOD

Our God is in heaven doing whatever he wants to do. Their gods are metal and wood, handmade in a basement shop: Carved mouths that can't talk, painted eyes that can't see, tin ears that can't hear, molded noses that can't smell, hands that can't grasp, feet that can't walk or run, throats that never utter a sound. Those who make them have become just like them, have become just like the gods they trust.

PSALM 115:3–8 MSG

Never doubt the magnificence of God. Don't entertain thoughts that He is unable or unwilling. Don't believe people who tell you the Lord isn't the supreme authority. There are none as powerful and wonderful as your Father in heaven.

The Bible warns us to not create or adore false gods who are powerless. They are nothing more than a distraction—a tool from the enemy to separate us from God. They take our time and our treasure, leaving us feeling empty in the end.

What consumes your thought life? What do you think about most? Chances are, whatever it is can be categorized as a false god because you're putting it above the One and Only. Settle in your mind today that the Lord is the only true God. Let that be your firm foundation.

Lord, I confess I have put other people and other things before You. They have held more importance. But from today forward, You will be the only true God in my life!

RIGHT IN THE EYES OF THE LORD

*And he did what was right in the eyes of the LORD, according to
all that his father Amaziah had done. He set himself to seek God
in the days of Zechariah, who instructed him in the fear of God,
and as long as he sought the LORD, God made him prosper.*

2 CHRONICLES 26:4–5 ESV

. . . .

Righteous living delights the Lord. While we can't do it perfectly, we
can be full of passion and purpose. We can be intentional to do what we
know is right. Setting our mind to it and asking God for wisdom and
strength is a powerful combination. It's a deliberate decision to do what's
right in the eyes of the Lord.

Are your thoughts focused on faithful living or worldly distractions?
Are you caught up in your social events or climbing the corporate ladder?
Do family and friends get the best of you every day? Are you obsessing
over things you can't have?

Spend time in the Word and in prayer so you will truly know what's
right in the eyes of the Lord. And then ask for the courage and the
confidence to walk it out in faith.

*Lord, I want to live Your plans for my life. I want Your will to be my
pursuit. Help me seek Your face and follow Your ways every day.*

OVERWHELMED

*The cords of death entangled me, the anguish of the
grave came over me; I was overcome by distress and
sorrow. Then I called on the name of the LORD.*
PSALM 116:3–4 NIV

. . . .

Everyone feels overwhelmed at times. Perhaps we spill our morning coffee
or we're late for work or we're facing a daunting task with seemingly no
resolution or we've been betrayed by a close friend. Sometimes it feels
as if Murphy's law is the order of the day: "Anything that can go wrong,
will go wrong." What we need to remember is we're not alone.

Even David had bad days, times when he experienced seemingly
unbearable hardships. But when the chips were down, he did not lose
faith. In Psalm 63:1–2, he writes, "You, God, are my God, earnestly I seek
you; I thirst for you, my whole being longs for you, in a dry and parched
land where there is no water. I have seen you in the sanctuary and beheld
your power and your glory" (NIV).

Just as God cared for and protected David, He will care for and
protect you too. David, just like you, faced many hardships but rather
than feel defeated, he used those struggles to make himself stronger. You
too can emerge victorious in any difficulty by merely keeping the faith
and calling on the name of the Lord.

*Dear God, guide me through difficult times, strengthen
me and help me to learn from every experience.*

DO YOU BELIEVE?

For in the gospel the righteousness of God is revealed—
a righteousness that is by faith from first to last, just as
it is written: "The righteous will live by faith."
ROMANS 1:17 NIV

. . . .

So many venues and products are introduced with an unveiling. We look forward to these events with anticipation, pantingly awaiting the coveted arrival. Perhaps the latest version of the iPhone or the latest new-fangled car, equipped with cutting-edge technology. Even museums, stores, and concert halls have grand openings. We long for the latest revelation in our ever-changing world. Yet all are empty of real meaning.

In Romans 1:17, Paul tells us the greatest revelation ever shown to mankind—the righteousness of God through the Gospel! While all other grand openings and unveilings come at a monetary cost, this one requires no money! Just faith. It's that simple. The first and last step of that revelation is faith, believing that Jesus Christ gave His life so you could be saved.

Do you believe? Do you accept that Jesus dying on your behalf is true, that it happened—even without any visible proof?

Remember Jesus said, "Blessed are those who have not seen and yet have believed" (John 20:29 NIV).

Dear God, help me believe in Your perfect
righteousness and to live and grow in faith.

NOTHING TO FEAR

"Be strong and courageous. Do not be afraid or discouraged because of the king of Assyria and the vast army with him, for there is a greater power with us than with him. With him is only the arm of flesh, but with us is the LORD our God to help us and to fight our battles." And the people gained confidence from what Hezekiah the king of Judah said.

2 CHRONICLES 32:7–8 NIV

. . . .

King Hezekiah and the nation of Judah were certainly up against it. The powerful Assyrian army was closing in fast, set to invade, and things looked bleak. While King Hezekiah instructed his army to take precautions such as bolstering the city's walls and cutting off water supply, he knew his biggest defense did not lie in his military might. So he instructed his army to *not* be afraid, claiming there was a greater power protecting them. His faith-filled words gave the people confidence. In the end, God not only protected Judah but soundly defeated the Assyrian army.

This dire situation helped an entire city learn to trust God, to have faith that He'd always lead them down the right path. Have you ever felt desperate, full of fear, convinced that you were facing defeat? Consider the people of Judah, and take a page from their book. The Good Book. Know that with God, you've nothing to fear.

Dear God, with You leading me, I know I've nothing to fear. I trust You will protect me.

A MATTER OF TRUST

It is better to take refuge in the LORD than to trust in humans.
It is better to take refuge in the LORD than to trust in princes.
PSALM 118:8–9 NIV

. . . .

These days, it's becoming increasingly difficult to know what information sources to trust. News outlets and political parties seem to have vastly different takes on the issues of the day. Medical science has different suggestions for keeping optimum health. And they all seem to be prefacing their advice with the same words, "Trust me."

So who can we trust? God. Trust in the one true Source. No matter the status or position of the people seeking your trust, He is the only one that is steadfast and reliable. According to Isaiah 12:2, "Surely God is my salvation; I will trust and not be afraid. The LORD, the LORD himself, is my strength and my defense; he has become my salvation" (NIV).

It's easy to become disheartened by being led in so many different directions these days by human entities and talking heads. So do yourself a favor and seek your answers in God's Word and through prayer. Soak yourself in His teachings and His love for you. Take refuge in Him alone and He will guide you down the right road in the right way.

Dear God, these days it is easy to feel lost or alone. Please lead me down the path that is right, down a road paved with Your love. Guide me in these difficult times, and bring me peace.

THE BUILDING OF YOUR LIFE

The stone the builders rejected has become the cornerstone.

PSALM 118:22 NIV

. . . .

Have you ever watched the process of an old building being deconstructed? Once the old structure is razed, the ground is prepared for the construction of a new building. And it begins with the assembly of a cornerstone on which the new building will stand. Slowly the progress spreads out from there, all resting on that strong, dependable, ever-reliable cornerstone that started it all.

In a similar way, you too have a cornerstone for the building of your life. You may have days when you feel the building is crumbling around you or perhaps some repairs are necessary. But if Jesus is your cornerstone, your building will *never* crumble. Sometimes a little renovation may be necessary to make your life the best it can be, but your base, your cornerstone, will remain forever constant.

No matter what challenges come your way, remember that God is the architect of a masterpiece. And that masterpiece is *you*.

Dear God, help me remember that You are the cornerstone, upon which I can safely and confidently build my life, my world. It's comforting to know that no matter what, my base cannot be shaken, and that in You I can and will remain immovable when facing adversity. Thank You, Lord, for always holding me up.

MISSTEPS AND MISTAKES

"Blessed are those whose transgressions
are forgiven, whose sins are covered."
ROMANS 4:7 NIV

. . . .

Everyone makes mistakes or at times suffers from lapses in judgment. It's a human trait. The good news is, no matter what, we are forgiven!

The apostle Paul reminds his readers that it's faith, *not* works or deeds, that makes Christ-followers righteous in the eyes of God (Romans 4:4–6). Though this letter was written to the Romans, in verses 7–8, Paul is quoting David from the Psalms, reminding us that those whose sins are forgiven and will never be counted against them are blessed. This message is repeated many times.

Hard as we may try to be perfect, mistakes do happen. Everyone makes them. The best thing to do is learn from them and move on, knowing and believing that we are righteous in God's eyes.

Have the faith of Abraham who "believed God, and it was credited to him as righteousness" (Romans 4:3 NIV). Never allow your faith to waver. Never doubt God's Word. Rest assured that His promises have got you covered. Keep the faith!

Dear God, I know that as a human being, I will mess up. I will do the wrong thing or fail those around me. But I am relieved to know that through Your promise, I am forgiven and that through my faith, You see me as righteous.

I THINK I CAN

Not only so, but we also glory in our sufferings,
because we know that suffering produces perseverance;
perseverance, character; and character, hope.

Romans 5:3–4 NIV

. . . .

The great football coach Vince Lombardi once said, "It's not whether you get knocked down. It's whether you get up." Chances are, you have been knocked down more than once. Yet although you cannot control the challenges and adversities that come into your life, you can choose how you react to them. You can choose to let a difficult circumstance defeat you or you can choose to get up, dust yourself off, and face the situation head-on.

According to today's verses, adversity produces perseverance, and perseverance builds character, and character builds hope. Hope can be defined as the confidence that God will take care of you. Think back to Deborah of the Judges, Esther of the exiles in Persia, or Ruth of the Moabites—the deck was most definitely stacked against them. But they persevered, they did not let adversity get to them, and in the end, they triumphed. Each of these biblical heroes had faith, and in the end, because of their faith, the rewards were great.

Remember when you face struggles, eventually there will be a silver lining. You just have to push through, difficult as doing so may be. In the end, you will be rewarded.

God, thank You for Your message of hope. Help me persevere in
difficult times, knowing that because of my faith, I will be rewarded.

THE GREATEST GIFT

Now since you have been set free from sin and have become the slaves of God, you have your present reward in holiness and its end is eternal life. For the wages which sin pays is death, but the [bountiful] free gift of God is eternal life through (in union with) Jesus Christ our Lord.

ROMANS 6:22–23 AMPC

. . . .

You've probably gotten many gifts in your lifetime, on birthdays, Christmases, graduations, Mother's Day, anniversaries—all occasions worthy of gift-giving. But all those gifts pale in comparison to "eternal life," which the apostle Paul describes as "the gift of God," a gift that truly stands alone, above and beyond all others.

Try as we humans might to live our lives right, there will always be obstacles in our way, challenges that may cause us to go down the path of sin. But the beauty of God's gift is that it's irrevocable. No matter what we have done, the gift of eternal life is ours. We've done nothing to earn it. It was not based on merit or works. It comes from trusting in Jesus, melding our lives with Him who died for us. By joining ranks with Him, we are no longer slaves to sin. Instead, we choose to serve God.

Remember John's words in his Gospel, verse 3:16: "God so loved the world that he gave his one and only Son, that whoever believes in him shall not perish but have eternal life." (NIV). This "whoever" includes *you*. The recipient of God's greatest gift.

Dear God, thank You for the greatest gift of all—eternal life. Though I did nothing to earn it, I cherish it. I stand in awe of Your mercy!

LAID LOW

I am laid low in the dust; preserve my life according to your word. . . .
My soul is weary with sorrow; strengthen me according to your word.
PSALM 119:25, 28 NIV

. . . .

We all have bad days, times when we feel beaten down, defeated. To feel lowly and unworthy, "laid low in the dust" is a sad feeling indeed.

How can we rise up from the dust? The answer is God's Word. Isaiah 40:8 (NIV) says, "The grass withers and the flowers fall, but the word of our God endures forever." If ever there was energy for our soul, it is the Word of God. It can bring strength to the weak, comfort to those in need, and peace to those who believe and seek His grace.

When you are feeling like you are surrounded by darkness, when you feel as if you can fall no further, when your soul and heart are weary with sorrow, when you can barely catch your breath, reach out for the Word of God. Its light will illuminate your path and direct your feet, leading you back up from the dust, giving you the strength to rise up, a new woman.

Dear God, many are the times I have been laid low, sad and lonely,
weary and despondent. I thank You for Your Word that pulls me up from
the depths. May Your light be my strength, my guide, my life preserver.

THE GREATEST FATHER

For those who are led by the Spirit of God are the children of God.
ROMANS 8:14 NIV

. . . .

Have you ever seen the classic cartoon depiction of a person struggling with a decision: on one shoulder stands a devil and on the other, an angel, and each is making its case for that individual to choose its particular course of action. While this image is amusing, there is some truth to the process.

In Romans 8:5 (NIV), the apostle Paul writes, "Those who live according to the flesh have their minds set on what the flesh desires; but those who live in accordance with the Spirit have their minds set on what the Spirit desires." When you choose to be led by God's Spirit and away from sin, you are choosing the right path—the one upon which a child of God has embarked.

When children are young, their parents give them rules to follow, allowing certain things that are considered safe, and forbidding certain things that are dangerous or detrimental. Your children may not have always chosen to obey, and when they didn't, there were consequences. In the same way, God, our heavenly Father, gives us rules to guide us. And there are consequences when we don't follow them.

To keep yourself on the right road, keep your mind set on what the Spirit desires.

Beloved Father, give me the courage to side with the angels, to keep my mind on what Your Spirit desires.

MERCY ME

*Then, at the evening sacrifice, I rose from my self-abasement, with
my tunic and cloak torn, and fell on my knees with my hands
spread out to the LORD my God and prayed:"I am too ashamed and
disgraced, my God, to lift up my face to you, because our sins are
higher than our heads and our guilt has reached to the heavens."*

EZRA 9:5–6 NIV

. . . .

Ezra was a man with many responsibilities. A Jewish scribe, he led a
group of exiles from Judea to Jerusalem, and tried hard to guide them
to follow the teachings of God. Upon arriving in Jerusalem, however, he
found that many had broken the laws set forth in the Torah, and were
otherwise living sinful lives.

Ezra took these things to heart. He seemed at his wit's end. Finally,
he fell to his knees, splayed out before God, and prayed, not only for
himself, but also for the people of Jerusalem. Before all, his voice alone
resonated to God.

Ezra knew that God is merciful, and His mercy endures forever.
You too can rest assured that no matter what your circumstances, God
is listening and He is merciful. You just need to raise your prayers to
Him, and He will listen.

*Dear God, sometimes it is hard to know where to turn.
Sometimes I feel alone and scared. Please remind me to turn
my eyes to heaven and raise my voice to You in prayer.*

WHAT'S IT WORTH?

Do good to your servant according to your word, LORD.
Teach me knowledge and good judgment, for I trust your
commands. . . . You are good, and what you do is good;
teach me your decrees. . . . The law from your mouth is more
precious to me than thousands of pieces of silver and gold.
PSALM 119:65–66, 68, 72 NIV

• •

What's your most valuable possession? A piece of jewelry? A car? Your house? These are all wonderful things, to be sure. But nothing can compare to God's Word, the book given by the Lord of Creation to guide your life.

This most valuable gift is free of charge and is most likely in your possession already. It's the true Word of God, available to you in the Holy Bible.

Yet to have this valuable resource in your possession doesn't benefit you until you read its words and adopt its teachings. Though it may cost you nothing, the wisdom and the peace you receive from its words are a true gift. Proverbs 4:7-9 (NIV) says, "Get wisdom. Though it cost all you have, get understanding. Cherish her, and she will exalt you; embrace her, and she will honor you. She will give you a garland to grace your head and present you with a glorious crown." Make an effort to do so today and every day, and you will find good from the God of good.

Dear God, thank You for Your Word, the guide for
my life. Teach me what You'd have me know.

WONDERFULLY MADE

But who are you, a human being, to talk back to God? "Shall what is formed say to the one who formed it, 'Why did you make me like this?'" Does not the potter have the right to make out of the same lump of clay some pottery for special purposes and some for common use?

ROMANS 9:20–21 NIV

. . . .

If a sculpture could talk, would it have the right to question its creator on why he made her a certain way? If so, surely a sculpture by Picasso, having seen a Michelangelo sculpture, would ask its creator, "Why me?" As amusing as that whimsical example might be, truth be told, the created has no right to question its creator. The sculptor simply took a lump of clay and gave it character and shape based on his desires and specifications, his vision for his creation.

Though some days it is difficult to accept certain things in your life, and you feel justified in questioning why God would do this or that, remember He is in control. He created every inch of you. He is perfect and you are one of His masterpieces (Ephesians 2:10), beautifully and wonderfully made (Psalm 139:14). He sculpted you just as you are, for His own reasons. And He will always have you in His hands, just as He did while He created you.

Dear God, thank You for creating me just as I am,
Your perfect masterpiece, wonderfully made.

CALL ON HIM

*For there is no difference between Jew and Gentile—the same
Lord is Lord of all and richly blesses all who call on Him, for,
"Everyone who calls on the name of the Lord will be saved."*

ROMANS 10:12–13 NIV

. . . .

What a beautiful sentiment! We are all equal in the eyes of God. It doesn't matter who you are or from where you came. Age, gender, ethnicity, education—it just doesn't matter. God is the God of all. And all are His children.

The apostle Paul says that anyone who calls on the name of the Lord will be saved through her faith. Remember, it is not through anything that a person does to earn eternal salvation, but rather God's gift to any and all who believe and call on Him to be saved. It can't get any easier than that!

Today, call on God's name. Answer His invitation, accept His promise to bless you richly. Remember that you are a daughter of God, and He loves you, just as you are.

*Dear God, thank You for reminding me that we—all of us—are equal in
Your eyes, regardless of age, gender, race, education, etc. That all who
call on Your name will be richly blessed and saved. Help me see myself,
and everyone around me, through Your eyes of light and love. Amen.*

GENERATIONS OF FAITHFULNESS

Your faithfulness continues through all generations;
you established the earth, and it endures.

PSALM 119:90 NIV

. . . .

It's reassuring to know that God's faithfulness and righteousness continue for each generation that passes. He was here for all your ancestors, He is here for you now, and He will be here for all generations to come. What a wonderful promise!

God created this earth and it will endure forever. The sun, the "greater light" (Genesis 1:16 NIV), rises and sets each day, the seas ebb and flow, the seasons change according to location, plants bloom, and all in accordance with His enduring laws. Sit under the stars one night and take in God's "lesser light" (Genesis 1:16 NIV). Revel in the fact that God's beautiful creation is here now for you to enjoy and will be here for generations to come.

With every step you take on the solid ground beneath your feet, remember that it's through God's grace and His creation that you can walk securely. Psalm 136:1 (NIV) says, "Give thanks to the LORD, for he is good. His love endures forever." Forever. How wonderful to know you are loved and cared for, forever. And not only you, but all your generations to come.

Dear God, what a wonderful world You've created. I'm grateful
for the promise that Your faithfulness will continue to endure
not only for me, but for my family, for generations to come.

WE CAN SEW!

We have different gifts, according to the grace given to each of us. If your gift is prophesying, then prophesy in accordance with your faith; if it is serving, then serve; if it is teaching, then teach; if it is to encourage, then give encouragement; if it is giving, then give generously; if it is to lead, do it diligently; if it is to show mercy, do it cheerfully.

ROMANS 12:6–8 NIV

. . . .

In the comedy *Three Amigos*, a poor town in Mexico is threatened by banditos planning to overtake their village. The protagonists try to save them by using the strengths of the town. They ask the villagers, "What is it this town is really good at?" Silence. Then comes the response "We can sew!" As unlikely as it seems, that's what saved them in the end.

As the apostle Paul writes, everyone has different gifts. It doesn't matter what they are. What matters is that each person share his or her talent with others.

You have great value as an individual. Consider your talents, your strengths. What God-given abilities can you employ to make this world a better place? What can you share with others to not just gain a sense of your own worth but become the silver lining in someone else's day?

Dear God, thank You for my gifts! Help me share them with others.

WE WILL OVERCOME!

Do not be overcome by evil, but overcome evil with good.
ROMANS 12:21 NIV

. . . .

What a powerful message in one short sentence!

Romans 12:21 reminds us that evil does indeed exist. Every day, we'll likely hear a news report about some kind of evil being perpetrated or perhaps we'll have a personal encounter with evil in our own lives. What we need to remember is that God would have us overcome that evil with good.

You do not have to look far to see people who've done just that. The person who set up a youth sports program in his violence-ridden neighborhood so that the at-risk kids have a positive place to go; kids who raised money for a fellow student battling cancer; communities who joined in a clean-up effort at a location riddled with hate-filled graffiti. For every heartbreaking story of hatred, there are several stories of people who came to the rescue to help out. *That* is the message. *That* is the key.

Fred Rogers, a champion of children everywhere, once said, "When I was a boy and I would see scary things in the news, my mother would say to me, 'Look for the helpers. You will always find people who are helping.'" This is the message Paul is relaying in today's verse. In bad situations, be a helper by overcoming evil with good.

Dear God, inspire me to not fear evil, but to help overcome it with good.

JUDGE-FREE ZONE

You, then, why do you judge your brother or sister? Or why do you treat them with contempt? For we will all stand before God's judgment seat.
ROMANS 14:10 NIV

. . . .

Have you ever been called to jury duty? The responsibility of holding the fate of a fellow human being in your hands can be daunting. You have to weigh all the evidence carefully, and be careful not to judge based on the appearance of the accused alone or on your initial first impression. Whether a person is heavily tattooed or looks like the kid next door, you are called to judge fairly and in accordance with the laws of a particular state or country.

Outside of a jury or courtroom, it's not your responsibility to judge anyone else, to treat them with disdain, to mock them, or assume a position of superiority over them. God alone knows what experiences others have had, their circumstances, their history. He alone can judge.

In Matthew 7:1 (NIV), Jesus says, "Do not judge, or you too will be judged." So unless you received a summons for jury duty, it's best to leave the judging to the One who is qualified, the One true God, the One who sees all, and knows all.

Dear God, it is difficult to not judge others. Please help us to live in harmony with others and leave the judging to You.

FILL 'ER UP

May the God of hope fill you with all joy and peace as you trust in him,
so that you may overflow with hope by the power of the Holy Spirit.
ROMANS 15:13 NIV

. . . .

Have you ever looked down at your gas gauge while driving and realized your tank was dangerously low? You have two choices in this scenario: you can either fill your tank with gas or keep driving, which means you'll eventually run out of gas completely. Certainly, the former is the best choice.

A similar scenario can occur in your walk of faith. Sometimes your spiritual tank may seem near-overflowing. But then something may drastically drain you—maybe some unexpected bad news or a daunting task. Suddenly the low energy indicator light is flashing in your mind and you find you've nothing left to give.

Take heart! The apostle Paul has already put a prayer out there to cover you, asking that God would *fill* you with joy and peace by trusting in God so that your spiritual tank will be *overflowing* by the power of the Holy Spirit.

God is there for you with a spiritual fill-up anytime you need it. To access His supply, simply close your eyes and pray for His Spirit to fill you up—and hope, joy, and peace *will* be restored in you.

Dear God, please keep my tank of hope, joy, and
peace filled to overflowing as I trust in You.

TRUE INNER PEACE

Great peace have those who love your law,
and nothing can make them stumble.
PSALM 119:165 NIV

. . . .

There certainly are a lot of resources for self-help in the world today. At the bookstore, the self-help section is brimming with topics from Acrophobia to Zoophobia and everything in between. There are self-diagnosing websites and toll-free numbers you can call. There are television shows and podcasts on virtually every self-help topic, which seemingly provide a myriad of solutions to eradicate every possible stumbling block. But, according to today's verses, the road to true inner peace is loving God's Word.

The word used in today's scripture for "peace" is the Hebrew *shalom*, which translates to wholeness, tranquility, prosperity, and safety. The psalmist is telling you that you will not stumble once you realize loving God's law is the key to opening the door of inner peace.

If you feel locked out or isolated from the calm and cool God promises, turn to His Word. Love His instructions. Walk as He would have you walk. And you'll not only find yourself sure-footed but possessing great peace.

Dear God, I long for shalom, for the peace only You can
provide, the true peace that comes from loving Your
laws and from believing in You with all my heart.

AMAZING GRACE

I have strayed like a lost sheep. Seek your servant,
for I have not forgotten your commands.
PSALM 119:176 NIV

. . . .

You have probably sung the classic hymn "Amazing Grace" many times. Its lyrics echo the sentiment of today's verse: "I once was lost but now am found." These words are a comfort because they give hope. The author, like the strayed sheep, was lost. But, through prayer and God's "amazing grace," no one remains alone. His lost and humble servants become found through faith.

If you stray from the right path, you may find yourself confused, disoriented. It is easy lose your sense of direction in this troubled world. Many is the time you may feel separated from the flock and struggling to find your way back. You may for some time continue to wander further and further away, unaware of how to return.

Little lamb, know this: God will always look for you. Just do what you can to keep the faith, follow the commands God has laid down in His Word. No matter how alone you may feel, know God is watching for you. Keep His teachings in your heart. And pray. He will hear. He will seek you out.

Dear God, rescue me, when I stray from Your path.
Seek me out. Show me the way to return home to You.

HUMBLE HEROES

Esther again pleaded with the king, falling at his feet and weeping.
She begged him to put an end to the evil plan of Haman the Agagite,
which he had devised against the Jews. . . . Mordecai the Jew was
second in rank to King Xerxes, preeminent among the Jews, and
held in high esteem by his many fellow Jews, because he worked for
the good of his people and spoke up for the welfare of all the Jews.
ESTHER 8:3; 10:3 NIV

. . . .

Mordecai was a regular guy, a good man, an exiled Jew living in Susa, the capital of Persia. He was guardian to his orphaned cousin Esther. With God working behind the scenes, the young, brave, and beautiful Esther became the wife of King Xerxes of Persia.

The humble and God-fearing Mordecai himself earned a place of honor in the kingdom by uncovering an assassination plot against Xerxes. At the same time, he urged Queen Esther to risk her own life to save God's people from being exterminated by the evil Haman.

By doing the right things in difficult situations and believing God could bring good out of the worst situations, both Esther and Mordecai ended up saving the lives of many people. Take a page from their book. Do the right thing, knowing God is with you.

God, help me to be brave like Mordecai and Esther, knowing You
walk with me and will bring the best out of the worst situations.

SMARTER AND STRONGER

For the foolishness of God is wiser than human wisdom,
and the weakness of God is stronger than human strength.
1 CORINTHIANS 1:25 NIV

. . . .

Think of the smartest and strongest person you know. There certainly have been many brilliant minds in the fields of science and medicine. There have been many strong men throughout history, who could lift hundreds of pounds or even pull trucks! But the smartest person you know pales in comparison to the knowledge of God and the strongest person is nowhere near as strong as God the Father, the Creator and Sustainer of the universe and beyond.

The apostle Paul had written this letter to the Corinthians to rebut the idea that God was foolish and weak, having given His only Son to be crucified like a common criminal. Some said a smarter, stronger God could have saved Him! Those who truly believe in God and His message understand God's plan to save the world was the ultimate in wisdom. Christ's immense strength was demonstrated by His remaining on the cross, sacrificing His life so that humankind would have eternal life.

No matter what you may be going through or struggling with, know that God has the wisdom and strength to save, sustain, provide, and prosper you.

Dear God, there is no one wiser or stronger than You. Help me
live my faith with that truth firmly set in my mind and heart.

THE SPIRIT'S POWER

I came to you in weakness with great fear and trembling. My message and my preaching were not with wise and persuasive words, but with a demonstration of the Spirit's power, so that your faith might not rest on human wisdom, but on God's power.

1 CORINTHIANS 2:3–5 NIV

• •

Have you ever had to stand up to speak to a group of people and felt your knees knocking together? Perhaps a bead of sweat started rolling down your back as well. Maybe your hands got cold and clammy. Yet still, something urged you on. Something gave you the power to open your mouth and speak. That was a demonstration of the Spirit's power. And because of that power, your faith rests in God, not in you and your human wisdom.

Psalm 125:1 (NIV) says, "Those who trust in the LORD are like Mount Zion, which cannot be shaken but endures forever." When the going gets tough, when your knees start wobbling, remember God is in control. Let your faith in God render you unshakable, and be at peace knowing He is at the helm, steering you to calmer shores.

Dear God, be my eyes, ears, and mind. Through You, I trust that my path is as it should be. Guide me safely through each day.

THE BEST COUNSELOR

*"Surely God does not reject one who is blameless or
strengthen the hands of evildoers. He will yet fill your
mouth with laughter and your lips with shouts of joy."*

JOB 8:20–21 NIV

. . . .

Job had lost *everything*—his sons and daughters, livelihood, even his
health. He'd reached a point of desperation. Thinking he was offering
sound advice, Bildad told his friend Job that he must have sinned or
otherwise offended God. He insisted Job go to God and make things
right so that laughter and joy can be restored.

There's a flaw in Bildad's logic! Psalm 103:8–10 says, "The LORD is
compassionate and gracious, slow to anger, abounding in love. He will
not always accuse, nor will he harbor his anger forever; he does not treat
us as our sins deserve or repay us according to our iniquities" (NIV). God
doesn't punish you for your deeds. He doesn't hold grudges.

What's more, deep in Job's heart, his faith remained. Though it was
tested, he never renounced his beliefs nor blamed God.

Sometimes the advice of well-meaning friends can lead you in
the wrong direction. When you need wise counsel, you would do better
to follow your heart and keep your faith. God and His Word are the
best advisors.

---

*Dear God, it's so easy to get confused by the advice and
ideas of others. Continually remind me that You are the
best counselor, the only source of truth and light.*

IT'S A WONDERFUL LIFE

*"Why then did you bring me out of the womb? I wish I had
died before any eye saw me. If only I had never come into being,
or had been carried straight from the womb to the grave!"*
JOB 10:18–19 NIV

One of the greatest classic Christmas movies is *It's a Wonderful Life*.
Part of the script could have been taken directly from today's scripture.
So despondent over his dire situation, the lead character George Bailey,
wished he'd never been born. Through the work of an angel, George got
his wish, and saw exactly what the lives of others would have been like
without him. In the end, he realized that no matter what, his life was not
only precious but of value, and his faith was restored.

Job had to have been just as despondent as George Bailey to utter
the words found in today's verses. Have you ever felt that lost? Although
Job suffered greatly, he was never abandoned by God, even though he
must have felt that way. In the end, he was blessed with abundance—great
wealth, more sons and daughters, and a long life.

When you find yourself struggling, take heart! God is with you,
giving you the strength you need in the present, knowing blessings will
be awaiting you when you come out on the other side.

*Dear God, in good times and bad, help keep my faith strong,
knowing that in Your time, not mine, things will be better.*

COUNTING ON THE LORD

*I am counting on the L*ORD*; yes, I am counting on him. I have put my hope in his word. I long for the Lord more than sentries long for the dawn, yes, more than sentries long for the dawn. O Israel, hope in the L*ORD*; for with the L*ORD *there is unfailing love.*

PSALM 130:5–7 NLT

. . . .

When you find yourself in the depts of despair, do as this psalmist did. Call upon God for help.

Step 1: Ask Him to hear your cry, to pay attention to your prayer.

Step 2: Remind yourself that your God is a loving and forgiving God. That He is the One you can count on. He is the One in whose Word you can hope.

Step 3: Hope. And do so with a sense of expectation. Make it a firm fact in your mind that God *will* do something. He *will* forgive and help you. He *will* enfold you within His everlasting arms. He *will* provide what you lack. He *will* see you through this—no matter what "this" may be.

Step 4: Wait. Look for Him around every corner, behind every word in His Book. Know that He holds for you the love that never fails, the mercy that lasts forever.

And lastly, Step 5: Believe.

Lord of my life, thank You for hearing my prayer. For loving me, forgiving me. You are my hope, my love, my light. For You alone I wait and live, knowing You will see me through.

PERSISTENT IN FAITH

"I know that my redeemer lives, and that in the end
he will stand on the earth. And after my skin has
been destroyed, yet in my flesh I will see God."
JOB 19:25–26 NIV

. . . .

Have you ever been so sure of something that you could speak about it with absolute certainty, even when faced with the worst of adversity? That's the situation in which Job found himself. His friends had spent hours talking over Job's dire situation. But none spoke the truth as Job knew it to be. In what was surely the lowest period in his life, Job speaks these words of faith. He *knew* with a certainty that his Redeemer lived, that he would come face-to-face with God someday, that God would keep His promises.

No one, least of all Job, knew why he was suffering so, or what brought about the horrific chain of events that would leave him so despondent. But even in the midst of his trials and tribulations, Job made the decision to *trust* in God, to worship and glorify Him. Though life crumbled all around him, Job had no doubt he would see his Redeemer in the end.

When the going gets tough, the tough remember Job's faith and God's promises. With God in your life, with Him by your side, with your mustard seed of faith, you can and will get through anything.

Dear God, help me to be as persistent in faith as Your servant Job.

PLAN B

"I will allow no sleep to my eyes or slumber to my eyelids, till I find
a place for the LORD, a dwelling for the Mighty One of Jacob."
PSALM 132:4–5 NIV

. . . .

David promised the Lord he would not rest until he found a worthy place for the ark of God. David felt that the ark, the symbol for God's presence on earth, deserved a special place. Being a man of his word and full of holy fervor, David was dedicated to this idea of building a suitable temple worthy of God. But God had other ideas.

God told David that it would be Solomon, David's son, who would build the temple. Yet the Lord was so pleased with David, that He promised David one of his "sons will sit on your throne for ever and ever" (Psalm 132:12 NIV). In the meantime, David remained dedicated to God, even helping collect materials for the new temple.

David's dedication is admirable. While his original goal to build a temple was denied, he continued to remain faithful to God. Though sometimes things don't work out as you hoped or planned, take a page from David's book and never lose your zeal.

Dear God, sometimes what I ask for is denied for reasons
only You know. Help me to trust that You always know best,
and help me to keep my passion in service to You.

NIGHTTIME PRAISE

*Now praise the LORD, all you servants of the LORD who
stand in the LORD's house at night! Lift up your hands
in the holy place and praise the LORD! May the LORD,
Maker of heaven and earth, bless you from Zion.*

PSALM 134:1–3 HCSB

. . . .

When you need a faith-lift, when you need to raise your spirit, free your
soul, and get closer to God, praise Him. At night. In the wee hours. When
it's just you and the Lord.

Lift up your hands where you stand.

You don't have to be in a church. Wherever you meet God, wherever
you feel the Spirit's presence, wherever you sense the breath of Jesus, you
are in a holy place. There in that moment, praise Him. Tell the One who
has formed you, the One who walks beside you, the One who protects,
provides, blesses, and calms, how much you love Him, need Him, and
are in awe of Him. Perhaps better yet, say nothing at all. Just sense the
joy of lingering in His presence, in His light and love. Commune with
Him. Hope in Him. Merge with Him. Lose yourself in Him.

Then, when your body urges you to find a place of rest and you head
to bed, close your eyes, knowing that the Lord, the Maker of heaven and
heart, earth and expectations, has blessed you.

*Lord, Maker of my heart, soul, spirit,
and mind, to You I lift my hands in praise!*

A CHOSEN TREASURE

Praise the LORD, for the LORD is good; sing praise to his name, for that is pleasant. For the LORD has chosen Jacob to be his own, Israel to be his treasured possession. I know that the LORD is great, that our Lord is greater than all gods.

PSALM 135:3–5 NIV

. . . .

Imagine that. God has chosen you to be His own. He sees you as His "treasured possession."

This Lord, the One who does what He pleases, who makes the mist rise, lightning flash, thunder blast, winds blow. . .this sacred being who is a God of so many signs and wonders, the Lord who defeated kings, gave His people a promised land, sacrificed His own Son so that you could freely and boldly come to Him in praise and prayer, is concerned about, cares about you.

You are the supernatural powerhouse's treasure.

You He has chosen to work, move, and love through.

Today, praise that Lord of lords. Thank Him for His attention, time, blessings, strength, provision, and patience. Then pray. . .

Dear God, use me as You please. For I am Your humble, loving servant and daughter. Because You, Abba, are my very own treasure.

GIVE THANKS

*Give thanks to the LORD, for he is good! His faithful
love endures forever. Give thanks to the God of gods.
His faithful love endures forever. Give thanks to the
Lord of lords. His faithful love endures forever.*

PSALM 136:1–3 NLT

. . . .

The psalmist acknowledged that God alone was the One who did mighty
miracles. God was the One worthy of praise, admiration, and thanksgiving. It was God's faithful love that endured forever and ever.

Job and the apostle Paul, they too attested to these truths that God
was good, faithful, and worthy of all praise. For God had brought Job
and Paul—and many people like them—through much hardship. He
had also strengthened them and blessed their lives and their ministries.

So, when your thoughts, heart, and actions seem inconsistent with
what God would have you think, feel, and do, change your perspective
by today's Bible reading in Job 31–33 and 1 Corinthians 9:1–18. Doing
so will remind you that you're not alone. That other children of God also
struggled with their thoughts and actions. But as they sought after God,
He gave them wisdom, bestowed guidance, and performed miracles on
their behalf. And He'll do the same for all who seek Him and rely on
His Word. Your job? To praise, proclaim, and thank Him.

Lord, thank You for being so good to me, for loving me—forever!

ETERNAL GOLD

You've all been to the stadium and seen the athletes race. Everyone runs; one wins. Run to win. All good athletes train hard. They do it for a gold medal that tarnishes and fades. You're after one that's gold eternally.

1 CORINTHIANS 9:24–25 MSG

• •

The apostle Paul was all in for Jesus, his faith clearly the most important thing in his life. Paul compared a walk of faith to running a race. He encouraged his readers to be like an athlete who ran to win, who trained vigorously to be the best version of themselves in and out of the stadium.

Therefore, keep running your race of faith, remembering that at the end of the day, you're not living out your faith for a reward to hang around your neck, or on your wall. You're doing it for that medal "that's gold eternally," the one that never rusts nor fades.

Today, run hard for the finish line, giving your walk of faith all you've got.

Jesus, I want to be all in for You! May the words of the apostle Paul, and Job, inspire me to keep going, keep loving, and keep serving for You. In Jesus' name I pray, amen.

THE POWER OF GOD

"God's voice thunders in marvelous ways; he does great things beyond our understanding. He says to the snow, 'Fall on the earth,' and to the rain shower, 'Be a mighty downpour.'"

JOB 37:5–6 NIV

. . . .

The book of Job recounted the suffering that a man of God endured, the wrestling to comprehend what had happened and the reason, as well as witnessing of God's abundant restoration. An insightful friend of Job's, Elihu, reminded him of God's awesome power, that God was in control of all things, a being that was great and to be feared.

At the end of the book that bears his name, Job got real with God. His thoughts, heart, and actions became authentic. Job talked to God. God listened. And God dialogued with Job. Through it all, Job realized what David and Paul later acknowledged, "'The earth is the Lord's, and everything in it'" (Psalm 24:1; 1 Corinthians 10:26 NIV).

No matter what you're going through, God wants to hear from you. If your thoughts are straying from God's truths, talk it out with Him or seek council. If your heart is heavy, cry out to Him in prayer, alone or with someone you trust. Then, witness the transforming power of God work and move in and through you.

Lord, I want to commit my thoughts, heart, and actions to You. By Your power, change me.

REVIVED BY LOVE

*I will worship toward Your holy temple and praise Your name
for Your loving-kindness and for Your truth and faithfulness;
for You have exalted above all else Your name and Your word
and You have magnified Your word above all Your name!*

PSALM 138:2 AMPC

. . . .

The psalmist knew what it was like to endure times of trouble and sorrow, but to be confident to know that God would revive him (Psalm 138:7). He, like many that have come before and after him, may have wrestled with the challenges of life, endured great suffering, and sought solace.

The Word continually tells us that God saw the struggles of His people and spoke to them directly, through prophets, or through His Word. Sometimes He even transformed everyday challenges into extraordinary miracles.

You too may find there are seasons of life that are more laborious and taxing than others. Such times will stretch and refine your faith. While you're walking in them, remember that God loves you. Then turn your thoughts and heart toward the psalmist's words: "In the day when I called, You answered me; and You strengthened me with strength (might and inflexibility to temptation) in my inner self" (Psalm 138:3 AMPC).

---

*Lord, "though I walk in the midst of trouble, You will revive me;
You will stretch forth Your hand against the wrath of my enemies,
and Your right hand will save me" (Psalm 138:7 AMPC).*

SEASONS

For everything there is a season, and a time for every matter under heaven: a time to be born, and a time to die; a time to plant, and a time to pluck up what is planted; a time to kill, and a time to heal; a time to break down, and a time to build up; a time to weep, and a time to laugh; a time to mourn, and a time to dance.

ECCLESIASTES 3:1–4 ESV

. . . .

The writer of Ecclesiastes, who is identified as "the Teacher" (Ecclesiastes 1:1 NLT), acknowledged that life had many ups and downs, twists and turns, blessings and challenges. That our time is fleeting; that all streams flow into the sea; that history continually repeats itself; that there is really nothing new under the sun (Ecclesiastes 1:4, 7, 9–10).

Amazingly enough, the Teacher was right! Here we are, thousands of years later, and today's verses, as well as many other parts of Ecclesiastes, continue to hold true. And so does the fact that God continues to be faithful to His children.

In all seasons, may your thoughts focus on God's goodness. May your heart jump for joy knowing that God sees you and loves you passionately! And may you celebrate the blessings of God, all the gifts He has given you.

Lord, in all seasons of life I'm committed to You and You alone. May my thoughts, words, actions, and deeds honor You.

WRITTEN DOWN

For it was You who created my inward parts; You knit me
together in my mother's womb. I will praise You because
I have been remarkably and wonderfully made. Your
works are wonderful, and I know this very well.

PSALM 139:13–14 HCSB

. . . .

God has created everything, including you. When you were being formed in your mother's womb, He had a plan and a purpose for your life! All your days were written down.

Thus, God knows everything about you, including when you sit and when you rise, what you think and what you say—even before you've formed any words in your mouth!

Today, praise God for making you in a way that you can't even explain; for His ways are too awesome to fathom. Remember that God has made you with a special gift, one that will enable, strengthen, and edify the church (1 Corinthians 12:27–31).

You, woman of the Way, are special, significant, and a blessing to all those around you! May this truth uplift and encourage your thoughts, heart, and actions toward the One who gave you life. Praise God for what He has done and has yet to do in and through you.

Heavenly Father, I'm so grateful for this life that You have given
me. I'm in awe of all that You have done. May my life glorify You!

WISE LIVING

Search me, God, and know my heart; test me and know
my anxious thoughts. See if there is any offensive way
in me, and lead me in the way everlasting.
PSALM 139:23–24 NIV

. . . .

The psalmist, David, admitted in the beginning of his song that God had already thoroughly searched him (Psalm 139:1). And now here, in his last lines, David invites God to search him again. To examine his heart and test his anxious thoughts. These words portray a humble mind, a vulnerable heart, and an amazing, faith-driven willingness to let God be God in and over every detail of his life—within and without. David's plea, his prayer, reveals his desire to have and live in accordance with God's superior wisdom.

Today's Old Testament reading also acknowledges the importance of wise living: "Wisdom is a shelter as money is a shelter, but the advantage of knowledge is this: Wisdom preserves those who have it" (Ecclesiastes 7:12 NIV).

God makes it clear in His words and songs that living wisely and humbly before God, asking Him in to your innermost being, and being willing to take and obey His instruction is an essential part of being transformed into the likeness of Jesus. For God honors the prayers of His daughters who pray for wisdom.

God, I need Your wisdom! Please give me the guidance to transform
my thoughts, hearts, and actions to be more in line with Yours.

STAND FIRM

*Let me now remind you, dear brothers and sisters, of the Good
News I preached to you before. You welcomed it then, and you
still stand firm in it. It is this Good News that saves you if you
continue to believe the message I told you—unless, of course, you
believed something that was never true in the first place.*

1 CORINTHIANS 15:1–2 NLT

. . . .

The apostle Paul wrote directly to the believers in Corinth about the
importance of standing firm in what they believed in, which was the
resurrection of Christ. For it was the Good News message he preached
that would save them, not some other false doctrine or theology.

These same principles hold true today. There are so many other
religious and spiritual practices out there that look good, feel good, and
sound good. It might seem nice to pick and choose a little from here, a
little from there, and almost make your own good news message. But the
apostle Paul, and the rest of the Bible, is clear: There is only one truth
you need to welcome, only one truth you need to continue to stand firm
in and receive. It's the saving grace message of Jesus.

*Lord, help me stand firm in You. For I want my thoughts,
heart, and actions to completely line up with what Your
Word has to say. And if I drift, I pray Your Holy Spirit
would graciously and gently nudge me back to You.*

THINK STRAIGHT

*Think straight. Awaken to the holiness of life. No more playing
fast and loose with resurrection facts. Ignorance of God is a
luxury you can't afford in times like these. Aren't you embarrassed
that you've let this kind of thing go on as long as you have?*
1 CORINTHIANS 15:34 MSG

. . . .

The resurrection of the dead was a topic worth writing about, because for Paul, it was clear that if there was no resurrection of the dead, then not even Jesus could have been raised. He went on to say that if Jesus wasn't raised from the dead, then the whole Good News message of faith was useless. On a final note, Paul urged those in Corinth to be good witnesses and to not be misled; to think straight when it came to the resurrection.

Why was it that Paul addressed this topic with such great passion and fervor? Probably because a lot of people doubted Jesus really died and rose from the dead. Furthermore, some people probably didn't even believe a resurrection from the dead was possible.

How about you, dear daughter in Christ? Where is your faith? What are you thinking and how is that impacting your heart and actions? Carefully consider today's words from Paul. Pray they may keep you focused and on the straight and narrow path of life in Jesus.

*God, when the world comes at me with its own religious
and spiritual beliefs, may I stay firmly rooted in You.*

LABOR IN THE LORD

*Be strong and immovable. Always work enthusiastically for the
Lord, for you know that nothing you do for the Lord is ever useless..*
1 CORINTHIANS 15:58 NLT

. . . .

When a person died, having faith that their body would one day be
resurrected was not foolish. The apostle Paul wrote:

*Our earthly bodies are planted in the ground when we die, but they
will be raised to live forever. Our bodies are buried in brokenness,
but they will be raised in glory. They are buried in weakness,
but they will be raised in strength. They are buried as natural
human bodies, but they will be raised as spiritual bodies. For just
as there are natural bodies, there are also spiritual bodies.*
1 CORINTHIANS 15:42–44 NLT

With Paul's understanding came a charge to believers that death in
this life wasn't the end, rather it was the route to eternal life with God.
Therefore, in this life it was important to devote oneself fully to God. It
was important to stand firm in the faith because the Lord would give
great victory over sin and death.

As a daughter in Christ, you too are called to stand firm in your
thoughts. You are called to give your heart fully to God. And you're called
to work enthusiastically for the Lord.

*Lord, help me to embrace my faith and share in
the victory that comes from eternal life in You.*

REMAIN OBEDIENT

Hear, O heavens, and give ear, O earth! For the Lord has spoken:
I have nourished and brought up sons and have made them
great and exalted, but they have rebelled against Me and broken
away from Me. The ox [instinctively] knows his owner, and the
donkey his master's crib, but Israel does not know or recognize
Me [as Lord], My people do not consider or understand.
ISAIAH 1:2–3 AMPC

. . . .

The prophet Isaiah prophesied to God's people in Judah about the coming Messiah. He spoke to those who were believing one thing and following another. For example, some people believed in God but took more seriously their earthly kings and idols. Some were offering worthless sacrifices and completely turned against God. Isaiah wanted God's people to turn back to Him.

Perhaps what was going on in Isaiah's day wasn't too far off what our current culture and society is experiencing. Some people believe in many different things. Some people have their hearts turned away from God. Others act out in a way that doesn't please the Lord.

For you, hear Isaiah's message. Hold on to it. Remain obedient to a God who loves you. Think about Him day and night. Call on Him in prayer. Keep your heart soft to His grace and mercy. And act in a way that is a witness for all to see.

Holy Spirit, fill me with Your divine presence.
Enable me to remain obedient to You!

THE GOD OF COMFORT

Blessed be the God and Father of our Lord Jesus Christ, the Father of mercies and God of all comfort, who comforts us in all our affliction, so that we may be able to comfort those who are in any affliction, with the comfort with which we ourselves are comforted by God.

2 CORINTHIANS 1:3–4 ESV

. . . .

The apostle Paul knew what it was like to be the recipient of God's supernatural comfort. He and his companions suffered many things to bring to others the good news of a God who loved him—and them— unconditionally. Paul endured a weakness that he pleaded to God to take away, only to find out that God could still use it. At another time, he tells his readers, he and his companions "were completely overwhelmed— beyond our strength—so that we even despaired of life. Indeed, we personally had a death sentence within ourselves, so that we would not trust in ourselves but in God who raises the dead" (2 Corinthians 1:8–10 HCSB). How amazing that even when imprisoned, Paul's thoughts, heart, and actions continually testified of God's goodness.

When you're going through a hard time, remember that you belong to a Lord who also suffered. That the God who delivered you once will do so again. That He will comfort you as no one else can, and you can hope in Him.

Abba Father, I need Your comfort right now.
Speak to me. Hold me close. May I feel Your presence.

GRACIOUS SPIRIT

Answer me quickly, LORD; my spirit fails. Don't hide Your face from me, or I will be like those going down to the Pit. Let me experience Your faithful love in the morning, for I trust in You. Reveal to me the way I should go because I long for You. Rescue me from my enemies, LORD; I come to You for protection. Teach me to do Your will, for You are my God. May Your gracious Spirit lead me on level ground.
PSALM 143:7–10 HCSB

. . . .

David prayed to God for answers. He prayed for God's loving presence, help, protection, wisdom, and knowledge. He prayed for the grace of the Spirit to lead and guide him.

David's humble pleas revealed just how much he wanted his thoughts, heart, and actions to line up with God's and His call on His life.

Perhaps David's words resonate with you. Perhaps today you are looking to God for an answer, for more of His presence and wisdom, for the power of the Holy Spirit to move in your life and the lives of others, for the Lord's grace to abound, to lead you to level ground?

In this moment, take some time to quiet your mind, heart, and body through prayer. Let God's gracious Spirit touch you in a way that shows you just how precious you—a dearly loved daughter of the King—are.

Gracious God, I come to You now. I need Your wisdom and presence.

NO END

*For unto us a child is born, unto us a son is given: and the government
shall be upon his shoulder: and his name shall be called Wonderful,
Counsellor, The mighty God, The everlasting Father, The Prince of
Peace. Of the increase of his government and peace there shall be no
end, upon the throne of David, and upon his kingdom, to order it,
and to establish it with judgment and with justice from henceforth
even for ever. The zeal of the LORD of hosts will perform this.*

ISAIAH 9:6–7 KJV

· ·

Years before Jesus came down from heaven, Isaiah prophesied to God's
people—those who were not yet wholeheartedly committed to God—
about the coming Prince of Peace.

Isaiah's prophecy summed up what Jesus would be for all humankind.
It acknowledged that Jesus would reign supreme over all governing
authorities. And it provided the assurance of knowing that He would
be the way to eternal life.

May today's verses infuse you with joy. May they remind you of
the blessings to be found in the One who saved humankind. May they
remind you of the unconditional and eternal love that is to be found in
Jesus. May they prompt you to share His love with others.

*Jesus, thank You for coming down from heaven, for demonstrating
how I am to think, love, and act. Thank You for dying on the cross
for the forgiveness of sins so that I will be with You forever!*

GLORIOUS GLORY

*If the old way, which brings condemnation, was glorious,
how much more glorious is the new way, which makes us
right with God! In fact, that first glory was not glorious at all
compared with the overwhelming glory of the new way. So
if the old way, which has been replaced, was glorious, how
much more glorious is the new, which remains forever!*

2 CORINTHIANS 3:9–11 NLT

. . . .

The apostle Paul wrote to those in Corinth about the glory that abounded
from the New Covenant. He was comparing the New Covenant with the
old one. Even though the old one was glorious, the new one was even
better because it replaced the former with a fresher way of living that
would remain forever.

To Paul this was exciting news to share not just among those in
Corinth but to all people. It motivated him to be bold and brave about
his faith in Jesus. Why? Because the same Messiah that Isaiah prophesied
about years ago, and the same God that David exalted in today's psalm,
was the same God from whom Paul received freedom and the forgiveness
of sins.

As a daughter in Christ, may the words written about Jesus long
before His birth give your thoughts comfort. May the praises of David
uplift your heart. And may the actions by Paul to preach the Good News
motivate you to spread the Word wherever you can.

Lord, in all that I think, say, and do, may I give You glory.

ERRAND RUNNERS

*Remember, our Message is not about ourselves; we're proclaiming
Jesus Christ, the Master. All we are is messengers, errand
runners from Jesus for you. It started when God said, "Light up
the darkness!" and our lives filled up with light as we saw and
understood God in the face of Christ, all bright and beautiful.*
2 Corinthians 4:5–6 msg

. . . .

Paul had a very clear vision and understanding of his purpose in Jesus
Christ. He knew what it meant to live for God. Sometimes there would be
suffering and sacrifice. Other times, there would be great joy knowing that
God was on the move and using him for great good and glory in Christ.

It seemed most appropriate for Paul to consider himself, as The
Message translation puts it, an errand runner, or as the Amplified Bible,
Classic Edition says, a servant or a slave. Paul was very accepting of these
terms for he knew that his life was much better with Christ in it.

As you reflect on today's words, think back on some of the things
you've gone through. Perhaps you felt called or compelled to do something
because the prompting of the Holy Spirit assured you to do so. Praise
God for the ability to step out in faith! Think about, and pray in your
heart, what He might want you to do next for Him. And then act in faith.

*Jesus, by Your grace, please help me to
be Your errand runner for Your glory.*

AN AMBASSADOR

This means that anyone who belongs to Christ has become a new person. The old life is gone; a new life has begun! And all of this is a gift from God, who brought us back to himself through Christ. And God has given us this task of reconciling people to him. For God was in Christ, reconciling the world to himself, no longer counting people's sins against them. And he gave us this wonderful message of reconciliation. So we are Christ's ambassadors; God is making his appeal through us.

2 CORINTHIANS 5:17–20 NLT

• •

Paul wrote to the Corinthians, telling them that anyone in Christ was a new person. Their old life was gone and a new one had begun. All because God sent Jesus into the world to reconcile people to Him, no longer counting their sins against them.

You, woman of the Way, are a new creation. You are a new person with a new mind and heart. And God has now tasked you with carrying this message to others around you. You are now an ambassador for Christ.

All of this means that you get to think, love, and act in the way that God compels you to. In doing so, people will want what you have. And in those times when you're tempted to remember past sins and failures—stop and remember, you're a new creation in Christ!

Lord, help me to continually be reconciled to You,
and to be Your mouthpiece to the nations!

PRAISE THE LORD!

*Great is our Lord and of great power; His understanding
is inexhaustible and boundless. The Lord lifts up the
humble and downtrodden; He casts the wicked down
to the ground. Sing to the Lord with thanksgiving;
sing praises with the harp or the lyre to our God!*
PSALM 147:5–7 AMPC

. . . .

God heals those whose hearts are broken, those wounded by pain or sorrow. When you're looking for understanding, He's the Guy to go to. When you're humbled and downtrodden, He's the One who will lift you up.

Yet that's not all. God calls out the stars, each of which He has named. He controls the weather, feeds the animals and birds. And He takes great pleasure in those who worship Him, hope in His mercy and loving-kindness.

Yes, God has indeed done wonderful things and is worthy of praise.

Of course, we, like the apostle Paul, may endure many hardships. Yet if we have faith in our God, we, like Paul, will be willing to go to great lengths to do what He calls us to do.

No matter what challenges, or blessings, you have in your life right now, take a minute to praise the Lord aloud or in writing. Call a friend to pray with. He is your God and wants to hear from you.

*Lord, I take this time to shift my thoughts toward Your goodness.
Whether my heart is happy or down, I choose to praise You.*

KEEP THE PEACE

*You will guard him and keep him in perfect and constant peace
whose mind [both its inclination and its character] is stayed
on You, because he commits himself to You, leans on You, and
hopes confidently in You. So trust in the Lord (commit yourself
to Him, lean on Him, hope confidently in Him) forever; for
the Lord God is an everlasting Rock [the Rock of Ages].*
ISAIAH 26:3–4 AMPC

. . . .

When your peace of mind and heart has flown out the window, Isaiah gives
you some steps to get it back. First, remember that God is the guardian
of your peace. Second, remember that your calm can be recaptured if you
fix your thoughts on the Lord. Third, remember that He is the only one
worthy of your trust.

Then you, like Paul, will find that even if you have "conflicts on the
outside, fears inside" (2 Corinthians 7:5 HCSB), you will find the calm
you crave from "God, who comforts the humble" (2 Corinthians 7:6
HCSB). Then, with the peace and calm from God, you will find yourself,
a person "close to his heart" (Psalm 148:14 NIV), praising "the name of
the LORD, for his name alone is exalted; his majesty is above earth and
heaven" (Psalm 148:13 ESV).

*Heavenly Father, thanks for being the guardian of my
heart and the calmer of my mind. In this moment,
I fix my thoughts on You, the Lord I trust and lean on!*

A NEW SONG

Hallelujah! Sing to the LORD a new song, His praise in the assembly of the godly. Let Israel celebrate its Maker; let the children of Zion rejoice in their King. Let them praise His name with dancing and make music to Him with tambourine and lyre.

PSALM 149:1–3 HCSB

. . . .

According to the psalmist, there was much to rejoice about. Although God's people had endured much, they were committed to singing a new song to the Lord. They focused their thoughts, heart, and actions toward their Creator. They danced and made music! Their praises flowed from inside of them, outwardly toward God.

God-followers like Job, Abraham, Sarah, Elijah, Ruth, Naomi, Hannah, Esther, the disciples, Mary Magdalene and the apostle Paul endured so much for their Creator. Yet they still knew how to shift their mind, heart, and actions toward praising and thanking God.

You too have a new song that you can sing to the Lord. Look back over your life and recount the times God pulled through for you. Consider your present circumstances. Is there anything worth praising God for? Of course, there is! So, sing, dance, make music to the Lord. Then, watch how it changes your perspective from the inside out.

Abba Father, help me to choose to focus on the joy and peace that only comes from You! Today, I lift my voice in a new song of praise to You!

A LIFE WELL LIVED

The fear of the LORD is the beginning of knowledge: but fools despise wisdom and instruction. My son, hear the instruction of thy father, and forsake not the law of thy mother: for they shall be an ornament of grace unto thy head, and chains about thy neck.

PROVERBS 1:7–9 KJV

. . . .

Solomon, who succeeded his father King David to the throne, was just a boy—not in age but in knowledge and understanding—when he became king. One night when God asked what he wanted more than anything, Solomon didn't request fame or success. Rather, he asked God for wisdom. Because of his humble answer, God not only gave Solomon the gift of wisdom but chose to bless him with much success.

Solomon understood what it meant to fear—have reverence or a deep respect for—the Lord. Out of this fear flowed from his heart the words of wisdom that would be penned by him and read by many for thousands of years. These proverbs weren't promises but provided helpful tips and insight into how to live a godly life.

Your heavenly Father wants you to have a life that is well lived in Him. Whether you're reading the book of Proverbs, or any another part of the Bible, read it daily so that it will become a part of you—and you'll experience God's grace and blessings in unimaginable ways!

Lord, reveal Yourself to me in Your Word.

BOAST IN THE LORD

As the Scriptures say, "If you want to boast, boast only about the Lord." When people commend themselves, it doesn't count for much. The important thing is for the Lord to commend them.
2 Corinthians 10:17–18 nlt

. . . .

The apostle Paul had much to boast about the Lord. As Saul, Paul had been going down the wrong path, living a life completely against God's love and goodness. Then, Saul accepted the new way of life in Jesus and was completely changed. He got a new name (Paul) and a brand-new purpose for life. He loved the Lord so much that he committed to the ministry of sharing the Good News to the nations.

Not only did Paul preach the Good News, but he knew his Old Testament scripture. It was Jeremiah, an Old Testament prophet through whom God spoke, who first coined the concept that if there was anything worth boasting about in this life, it was to boast in the Lord (9:24).

What do you tend to boast about? When you do well at something, do you take the credit or give it to God? Hopefully, you acknowledge His work in your life because then you'll be acting as a witness to others.

Heavenly Father, may I boast only in You.
When I do well, may it be for Your glory, not mine.

ON DISPLAY

Wilderness and desert will sing joyously, the badlands will celebrate and flower—like the crocus in spring, bursting into blossom, a symphony of song and color. Mountain glories of Lebanon—a gift. Awesome Carmel, stunning Sharon—gifts. GOD's resplendent glory, fully on display. GOD awesome, GOD majestic.

ISAIAH 35:1–2 MSG

• •

In today's reading, the prophet Isaiah wrote about God's future judgment as well as His great mercy and the restoration of His people. One season would seem dark, gloomy, even scary. Then, another season would give way to abundance, joy, and splendor. Before anything can blossom there must be a time of laying down, letting go, and even letting die. This makes room for new things to grow, for blessings and a harvest.

In autumn, the leaves turn beautiful colors. But these leaves also fall to the ground, making a cover for the earth in preparation for winter, when all will become cold and bare. Then, there is spring, which gives way to new life and beauty. This cycle continues year after year. In life, there are seasons as well. One season can be challenging and another filled with blessings. However, there's goodness in all of it. For the goodness of God created it all.

Lord, from the warm summer sun to the cool autumn breeze, may I be able to see You on display in all seasons of life.

DELIGHT IN WEAKNESS

Three times I pleaded with the Lord to take it away from me. But he said to me, "My grace is sufficient for you, for my power is made perfect in weakness." Therefore I will boast all the more gladly about my weaknesses, so that Christ's power may rest on me. That is why, for Christ's sake, I delight in weaknesses, in insults, in hardships, in persecutions, in difficulties. For when I am weak, then I am strong.
2 CORINTHIANS 12:8–10 NIV

Paul knew what it was like to feel weak. He understood what it meant to pray, even plead, to God to take away a weakness that at times caused him to feel inconvenienced, vulnerable, and frustrated. However, by God's grace, Paul came to accept that his weakness—which God didn't take away—was perhaps a good thing because it kept Paul humble and completely dependent on God. It seemed as though Paul learned to not be a victim of his weakness but to truly delight in it and find strength in it.

Perhaps you yourself have a special weakness or point of vulnerability. Maybe you, like Paul, have pleaded with God to take it away. In the end, remember that God's grace is so big and wonderful that He can take anything that looks and feels messy in your life, and turn it around for great good.

God, please take my weakness and use it for Your divine glory. Help me to delight in my difficulties.

SEEK WISDOM

*If you will receive my words and treasure up my commandments
within you, making your ear attentive to skillful and godly
Wisdom and inclining and directing your heart and mind
to understanding [applying all your powers to the quest for
it]; yes, if you cry out for insight and raise your voice for
understanding, if you seek [Wisdom] as for silver and search
for skillful and godly Wisdom as for hidden treasures, then
you will understand the reverent and worshipful fear of the
Lord and find the knowledge of [our omniscient] God.*

PROVERBS 2:1–5 AMPC

. . . .

Solomon spoke favorably of gaining wisdom, insight, and knowledge
from God. He compared wisdom to treasures. He advocated for a right
way of living and believed it was found in wisdom itself.

Make seeking wisdom your quest. Whatever decision you're trying
to make, whatever words you're trying to say, whatever action you're
taking to serve others in love, look to God for wisdom. Then watch what
God will do.

In the same way that God honored Solomon when he asked for
wisdom, God will honor you. He will bless you in ways beyond what
you can fathom. Keep turning your thoughts, heart, and actions toward
the God of wisdom.

*Lord, when I don't know what to say or do, please give
me Your wisdom in how to act. May my thoughts, heart,
and actions be in tune with You and Your Word.*

CATALYST FOR CHANGE

But you, Israel, my servant, Jacob, whom I have chosen, the offspring of Abraham, my friend; you whom I took from the ends of the earth, and called from its farthest corners, saying to you, "You are my servant, I have chosen you and not cast you off"; fear not, for I am with you; be not dismayed, for I am your God; I will strengthen you, I will help you, I will uphold you with my righteous right hand.

ISAIAH 41:8–10 ESV

. . . .

God was for His people and that was why He used prophets like Isaiah to speak truth into their lives. God loved His children so much that He didn't want them to wander aimlessly wondering where He was, what was He up to, and if He really cared about them. So God used Isaiah to lead the catalytic charge toward righteous living.

In a similar way, God wants to use *you* to be a catalyst for good, for change, for love and good works. Just as God used Deborah, Ruth, Naomi, Hannah, Elizabeth, and Mary, He wants to use you—your thoughts, your heart, and your actions—to make an impact in this world for the better. So, when you feel afraid, remember the same God of the Old and New Testaments is the same God today. The One who tells you not to fear. Trust in Him and He will guide you.

Lord, use me to be Your catalyst for change.

LIVE FOR GOD

For through the law I have died to the law, so that I might live for God. I have been crucified with Christ and I no longer live, but Christ lives in me. The life I now live in the body, I live by faith in the Son of God, who loved me and gave Himself for me.

GALATIANS 2:19–20 HCSB

· ·

The apostle Paul spoke about freedom from the religious law. The law he referred to was the Mosaic law, the Old Testament way of living. Christ freed people from their sins. By accepting the power of the resurrection of the cross at Calvary, people could receive God's forgiveness, have Christ live *within* them, and live *with* Him for eternity.

This crucified life wasn't an easy one. Paul learned what it meant to depend on God and live by faith. He also learned to accept and value God's grace. As a daughter in Christ, you too are called to live for God by faith. This calling means that you thoughtfully accept His free gift of grace and eternal life. It means that you turn your heart toward the things of God and act in a way that allows Christ to have full rein within you. The more you do so, the more your heart, mind, and actions will reflect the love and light of Christ.

Jesus, thank You for dying on the cross for the forgiveness of my sins. Help me to love and live by Your grace.

PRECIOUS TO GOD

*She is more precious than rubies: and all the things thou canst desire
are not to be compared unto her. Length of days is in her right
hand; and in her left hand riches and honour. Her ways are ways of
pleasantness, and all her paths are peace. She is a tree of life to them
that lay hold upon her: and happy is every one that retaineth her.*

PROVERBS 3:15–18 KJV

. . . .

Solomon described what life would be like for those who sought Wisdom.
She would lead the way to honor and a fruitful life. When trouble came,
they wouldn't stumble or fall.

You are a precious child of God. You are His daughter. He loves you
and sent His Son to die for you. He wants you to live a full and abundant
life filled with blessings and goodness. And all through that life, amid
good times and bad, God wants you to seek Him for wisdom.

Precious daughter of God, take some time to let that sink in. No
matter who you are, what you've suffered or endured, rich or poor, plain
or fancy, God adores you! And when you seek after Him and *His* wisdom,
He won't fail you!

*Lord, thank You for loving me unconditionally, for always
looking out for me, for answering my call, for being such
a wonderful Father and guide. Linger with me here as I let
that sink in. Then fill me with Your love and wisdom.*

CHILDREN OF GOD

For you are all children of God through faith in Christ Jesus. And all who have been united with Christ in baptism have put on Christ, like putting on new clothes. There is no longer Jew or Gentile, slave or free, male and female. For you are all one in Christ Jesus. And now that you belong to Christ, you are the true children of Abraham. You are his heirs, and God's promise to Abraham belongs to you.

GALATIANS 3:26–29 NLT

• •

The apostle Paul wrote to the churches in Galatia about being God's children through faith.

Before Jesus Christ died to save us, God's people lived under the religiosity of the old law. But the way of faith in Jesus brought new life and hope into their lives. This was awesome news back in Paul's day, and it's still wonderful news today! To be a child of God with no strings attached and no requirements as far as race, sex, or nationality is an amazing free gift! You don't have to live by rules and rituals to be forgiven and made right with God. You get to do that by simply accepting that Jesus died for you and your sins, confess your sins to God, and ask Him for forgiveness. Then receive His grace and mercy. It's that simple!

Lord, I'm so grateful to be a child of God, to be an heir of Abraham, and to inherit all the promises! All praise and glory to You!

HOLD ON

*"Listen now, you who know right from wrong, you who hold
my teaching inside you: Pay no attention to insults, and when
mocked don't let it get you down. Those insults and mockeries are
moth-eaten, from brains that are termite-ridden, but my setting-
things-right lasts, my salvation goes on and on and on."*

ISAIAH 51:7–8 MSG

. . . .

Isaiah provided words of comfort to God's people that they would be
taken care of. His encouragement was to hold on to the teachings of
God. To focus on God and to not pay attention to the challenging things
going on around them. God was their source of peace and comfort, even
in the most tumultuous of times.

These same words spoken thousands of years ago can be ones that
you hold on to today. When you feel uptight, when everything looks
and feels like a mess, remember that God is holding on to you. Because
you have been reading God's Word, you know right from wrong, you
know His truths. So hold them inside you, allowing them to guide your
thoughts and heart. Let your outward actions demonstrate that you're
secure in Jesus Christ, forever!

*Lord, help me to hold on to You and Your Word. I want my
life be an example of what it means to be passionate about
reading the Bible and taking the words written seriously.*

FINDING OUR FOCUS

My son, pay attention to what I say; turn your ear to my words. Do not let them out of your sight, keep them within your heart; for they are life to those who find them and health to one's whole body. Above all else, guard your heart, for everything you do flows from it. . . . Let your eyes look straight ahead; fix your gaze directly before you.

PROVERBS 4:20–23, 25 NIV

· ·

The long-ago author of the book of Proverbs has good advice for us still today. Like modern-day psychologists, the author understood the connection between our inner and outer lives. The things we focus on in our thoughts and emotions will naturally shape the way we act. If we allow our minds to be filled with negative thoughts, they will influence both our emotions and our behaviors.

Researchers have found that negativity can make us more prone to physical illnesses. Unfortunately, our world bombards us with negative messages, a constant stream of bad news about ourselves and the world in which we live, and it's nearly impossible to shut our ears. We have to make a daily, active effort to listen to God's voice instead, focusing our inner eyes on His message of love.

Lord of Life, teach me to guard my heart and mind. Remind me to occupy my thoughts with Your Word. Be the focus that leads me forward.

GOOD NEWS

*How beautiful on the mountains are the feet of the messenger
bringing good news, breaking the news that all's well,
proclaiming good times, announcing salvation.*
Isaiah 52:7–8 msg

. . . .

In yesterday's Bible reading, we were reminded to guard our hearts and minds against the world's negativity and brokenness (Proverbs 4:20–23, 25). In today's reading, the prophet Isaiah suggests we're called to be carriers of God's good news, replacing the world's constant stream of pain and frustration with the message that God is longing to bless and heal. As we make God and His affection for us the focus of our hearts and minds, His love will spill out into our words and actions, helping others to also guard their hearts and minds against the world's lies. The good news of God's love and salvation has a ripple effect. The message may start small, but only God knows how far it will travel.

How will you use your beautiful feet today to spread the news in your world that all is well in God? What will you do to break that good news?

*Fill my heart with Your Spirit, Lord, so that I can
carry Your good news to everyone I meet today.*

STOP COMPETING!

Each one should test their own actions. Then they can take pride in themselves alone, without comparing themselves to someone else.
GALATIANS 6:4 NIV

. . . .

Our society focuses on competition. It constantly asks us to compare ourselves to our friends, our family, our neighbors, our colleagues. It tells us the lie that we're not good enough if we don't measure up in some way. Maybe we're heavier than our sister. . .or our house isn't as tidy as our neighbor's. . .or we're not quite as good at our jobs as some of our colleagues. We can even feel competitive at church, worrying that we're not as "spiritual" as some of the other church members.

The reverse can be true as well: we can find ourselves taking pride in our own accomplishments, feeling as though we've managed to prove our worth, when our abilities, appearance and wardrobe, or possessions exceed those of the people around us. This habitual pattern of thought is contrary to God's good news, though, and it can throw us off course, emotionally, spiritually, and behaviorally.

The thing is, God doesn't care how we compare to others; He only cares how we measure up to His individual call on each of our lives.

Thank You, God, that You love me as I am. If You never compare me to anyone else, why should I? Remind me that in Your eyes, I'm valuable in my own unique way.

EVERLASTING LIGHT

The LORD rises upon you and his glory appears over you. . . . The sun will no more be your light by day, nor will the brightness of the moon shine on you, for the LORD will be your everlasting light and your God will be your glory. Your sun will never set again, and your moon will wane no more; the LORD will be your everlasting light.

ISAIAH 60:2, 19–20 NIV

. . . .

These verses are often interpreted as referring to our life in eternity—but we can also apply them to our lives today, in the here and now. As human beings, we all tend to depend on unreliable sources of "light." At some point, our physical and mental strength reach their limits; our careers, our roles in life, and even our closest relationships do not endure forever in this world.

Just as the sun and moon rise and set, so do this world's "lights" have their rhythms of ebb and flow. If we depend on them for our sense of security and direction, allowing all our emotions and thoughts to focus on them, then sooner or later, we will find ourselves walking in darkness.

But God's light is always there. It never sets, it never wanes. When we use it to guide our thoughts, emotions, and actions, we live our lives in God's steady illumination.

*Guide my steps, Lord; shape my thoughts,
and inspire my emotions. Be my everlasting Light.*

YOU'RE IRREPLACEABLE!

He creates each of us by Christ Jesus to join him in the work
he does, the good work he has gotten ready for us to do.
EPHESIANS 2:10 MSG

. . . .

As we get older, sometimes we realize that all our big ambitions probably aren't going to materialize. We look at our achievements and our various life roles, and our lives may seem smaller than we dreamed they would be when we were younger.

We judge our outer lives by the world's standards, and then we allow that judgment to tinge our inner lives with discouragement and self-condemnation. But that's not the way God sees our lives. He has a purpose for each of us; we each have our own unique share in the work God is doing in our world.

We may never know until eternity all the ways God uses us to share His love—but God knows. We are each irreplaceable in the Kingdom of Heaven.

Jesus, teach me to find my value in doing the work of love to
which You have called me. May I find my joy in serving You.

FLOODED WITH GOD

*May He grant you out of the rich treasury of His glory to be
strengthened and reinforced with mighty power in the inner man
by the [Holy] Spirit [Himself indwelling your innermost being and
personality]. May Christ through your faith [actually] dwell (settle
down, abide, make His permanent home) in your hearts! May you
be rooted deep in love and founded securely on love, that you may
have the power and be strong to apprehend and grasp with all the
saints [God's devoted people, the experience of that love] what is
the breadth and length and height and depth [of it]; [that you may
really come] to know [practically, through experience for yourselves]
the love of Christ, which far surpasses mere knowledge [without
experience]; that you may be filled [through all your being] unto all the
fullness of God [may have the richest measure of the divine Presence,
and become a body wholly filled and flooded with God Himself]!*

EPHESIANS 3:16–19 AMPC

. . . .

Whenever you feel discouraged, read these verses. This is the life God
is calling you to—a life of strength, energy, and spiritual wealth that
takes root in your inner self, filling your thoughts with the infinite love
of God, allowing you to actively experience God's presence in your life,
inside and out.

Dwell in me, Christ. I want to be completely filled and flooded with You.

IDENTITY

"I knew you before I formed you in your mother's womb. Before you were born I set you apart and appointed you as my prophet to the nations."
JEREMIAH 1:5 NLT

. . . .

Our roles in life go through many changes. We start out as children, dependent on adults' caregiving; we move on to adolescence, struggling now for independence from those same caregivers; and then we journey into adulthood, where we assume a host of new responsibilities: wifehood, homeowning, employment, motherhood, to name just a few. And then, as the years go by, we may find ourselves without a spouse, retired, our children grown. With so many changes, it's hard sometimes to hold on to our sense of identity. Who are we if we no longer bear the name Mommy? Who are we if we aren't a wife anymore? Who are we if we no longer hold a job or its title?

These disturbing thoughts and emotions can throw us into confusion, uncertain how to proceed with our lives. But in this scripture verse, God assures us that *He* knows who we are. He holds our deepest, truest identities safe in His hands. No matter what external roles may come or go, we have a role that will never end—to be a carrier of God's love and truth.

Help me, Lord, to keep my sense of identity rooted in You. Remind me I don't need to depend on my outer roles to define me. May my outer character and actions always flow out from the sure inner knowledge that I am Yours.

A CYCLE OF GRACE

Watch what God does, and then you do it, like children who learn proper behavior from their parents. Mostly what God does is love you. Keep company with him and learn a life of love. Observe how Christ loved us. His love was not cautious but extravagant. He didn't love in order to get something from us but to give everything of himself to us. Love like that.

EPHESIANS 5:1–2 MSG

. . . .

When Paul wrote these directions to the people at Ephesus, he was giving them very practical advice, advice that still applies to our lives today. We can learn to live the way God wants us to live by getting to know Him better. Reading the Gospels and seeing how Jesus acted give us a role model to follow. It teaches us how we too should behave as we interact with others and go about our lives.

Allowing Jesus to have a place in our hearts, we learn from Him how to act—and by acting out of the selfless love He demonstrated, our hearts open to receive an ever-greater awareness of His presence. Our inner experience of God's love produces love in action in our outer lives, and love in action leads to more love in our inner lives. It's the opposite of a vicious cycle; the reciprocal action between our inner and outer lives forms a cycle of grace.

Fill my heart, Jesus, with Your extravagant love, so that I can spread Your selfless, unconditional love out into the world.

PROTECTED

*Be strong in the Lord [be empowered through your union with Him];
draw your strength from Him [that strength which His boundless
might provides]. Put on God's whole armor [the armor of a heavy-
armed soldier which God supplies], that you may be able successfully
to stand up against [all] the strategies and the deceits of the devil.*

Ephesians 6:10–11 AMPC

. . . .

God doesn't call very many of us to be hermits who serve Him in constant solitude. Instead, He asks most of us to serve Him in the midst of busy lives, lives filled up with relationships and work.

When the apostle Paul wrote his letter to the Ephesians, he understood that for most of us, our relationship with God will be expressed actively, in our marriages and homes, as well as out in the world. But Paul also knew we can't live in alignment with God's Spirit if we head out each day unprotected, our hearts and minds vulnerable to the onslaught of voices that tear down our courage and make us weak. That's why Paul tells us in these verses that we must put on God's "armor."

When our inner lives are deeply rooted in God's love, then we will have the strength to live our lives according to His plan. Our relationship with God will protect our thoughts and emotions. He will give us the power and courage we need each morning to face even the most demanding days.

*Remind me each morning, Lord, to put on Your
armor. Surround me with Your shield of love.*

RELATIONSHIPS

*Every time you cross my mind, I break out in exclamations
of thanks to God. Each exclamation is a trigger to prayer.
I find myself praying for you with a glad heart.*
PHILIPPIANS 1:3 MSG

. . . .

Often, sadness, fear, and other difficult emotions are the triggers that
send us to God in prayer. God is always ready to meet us amid life's
challenges, but He also longs for us to come to Him with our joys as well.
Some relationships, for example, are sources of great happiness. Whether
it's a close friend or our spouse, children, or another family member,
just thinking about certain people in our lives can bring smiles to our
faces. God wants to share our pleasure in these relationships—and one
way to make Him a part of them is to use thoughts of our loved ones as
reminders to turn to God.

Each time we find ourselves smiling about something our husband
said, remembering a friend's kindness, or delighting in the memory of
a child's imagination, we can, first, thank God for this person's presence
in our lives, and, second, ask God to bless them.

*God of Love, thank You for the wonderful people You have
brought into my life. I am so grateful for the way You bless me
through them, and I pray You will use me to bless them as well.
May each of these relationships draw me closer to You.*

SEEKING GOD

Those who seek me early and diligently shall find me.
PROVERBS 8:17 AMPC

. . . .

It's not always easy to sense God's presence in our lives. Often our own emotions may get in our way, clouding our spiritual vision. Other times, it may be intrusive and worrisome thoughts that distract us from the knowledge that God is always with us. Or it could be the constant rush of our busy lives that seems to hide God.

In reality, of course, God is *always* with us—and He promises us that when we make the effort to seek Him consciously and diligently each day (even if that means getting up early in the morning in order to have alone time with Him), sooner or later we *will* find Him. Our awareness of His presence will be restored.

Thank You, Lord, that You never abandon me. When I complain that I don't feel You with me, remind me I need to find time to be alone in prayer. Open my eyes so that I may see You more clearly, hear Your voice, and sense Your loving presence.

THE SOURCE OF LIFE

For whoever finds me finds life. . . .
But those who miss me injure themselves.
PROVERBS 8:35, 36 NLT

. . . .

Our society often gives us the unspoken message that a life of following God is a life of restriction, a life of saying no to pleasures other people get to enjoy. That attitude is found nowhere in the Bible, though. Instead, the fullness of life is constantly equated with living in the presence of God.

When we turn away from God's presence, we don't find more to enjoy in life but less. We end up hurting ourselves, emotionally, spiritually, and even physically. God knows what is best for us—and He wants to give it to us, if we will only let Him.

Life-Giver, may I never forget You are the source of all life—
all joy, all wholeness, all well-being. Keep me spiritually close
to You, so that my thoughts, emotions, and actions will all
fall in line with Your constant love. Remind me that You alone
know what is best for me. And that You alone will give me
the best, if only I open myself to You and Your presence.

FREED FROM THE PAST

I don't mean to say that I have already achieved these things or that I have already reached perfection. But I press on to possess that perfection for which Christ Jesus first possessed me. No, dear brothers and sisters, I have not achieved it, but I focus on this one thing: Forgetting the past and looking forward to what lies ahead, I press on to reach the end of the race and receive the heavenly prize for which God, through Christ Jesus, is calling us.

PHILIPPIANS 3:12–14 NLT

• •

The apostle Paul was not always the great Christian teacher we remember him as today. Before meeting Christ, he was a judgmental, angry man unable to accept that God was speaking in a new way through Christ and His followers. Paul (then known as Saul) had dedicated his life to tracking down and punishing Christians, sometimes even putting them to death. After his conversion, he could have let his guilt over his past weigh him down; it might have convinced him he wasn't equipped to be a leader in the new church.

Yet Paul didn't let those old memories get in the way of his present-day actions. He released his thoughts of the past so that he was free to follow Jesus in the present.

When thoughts about my past threaten to interfere with my life today, Jesus, dragging me down emotionally, holding me back from acting on Your behalf, remind me to follow Paul's example. I give yesterday to You.

SECURITY FROM NEGATIVE THOUGHTS

They will fight against you like an attacking army, but I will make you as secure as a fortified wall of bronze. They will not conquer you, for I am with you to protect and rescue you. I, the LORD, have spoken!

JEREMIAH 15:20 NLT

. . . .

We may think that our spiritual enemies attack us from the outside—but sometimes, our own thoughts can be like a destructive army, pulling us down spiritually. When anxiety and fear beset us, when our thoughts are crowded with frustration or resentment, or when guilt and self-doubt make us question ourselves, our thoughts and emotions can rob us of the strength we need to live with love and courage. But God understands— after all, He created our human nature—and He promises to help us. His Spirit can act as a "wall" between our thoughts and our true and deepest identities. With God on our side, we don't have to be defeated by our own thoughts.

Protect me from my obsessive thoughts, Lord.
Rescue me from my overwhelming emotions.
May Your presence surround my heart and mind.

JOYFUL ANTICIPATION

The lines of purpose in your lives never grow slack, tightly tied
as they are to your future in heaven, kept taut by hope.
COLOSSIANS 1:5 MSG

. . . .

Hope isn't just a warm fuzzy feeling that makes us feel good about life. When the Bible speaks of hope, it's not referring to an emotion. Instead, the Greek word our English Bibles translate as *hope* meant, literally, "confident expectation" or "joyful anticipation." It's similar to the way we might feel as we wait for a beloved friend to arrive at our house, confident she will not disappoint us. Or we could compare the biblical meaning of *hope* to the way a child feels before Christmas: no matter how dismal life may be at this moment, Christmas always comes!

In today's verse, the apostle Paul tells us that as we live our lives with our minds filled with the joyful anticipation of eternity, that awareness will shape our actions today. It will give us a greater sense of perspective, allowing us to rise above the negative emotions that so often overcome us. No matter what happens today, we can be confident that something wonderful lies ahead.

Thank You, Beloved Lord, that You have tied my life to heaven. May I
live each day in joyful anticipation of all You will do, in me and around
me. Remind me to always look at life through the eyes of eternity.

JESUS IS THE ROAD MAP

*Everything of God gets expressed in [Jesus],
so you can see and hear him clearly.*
COLOSSIANS 2:9 MSG

. . . .

It's not always easy to know how God wants us to live our lives. When faced with a decision, we may wish God would write a message in giant letters across the sky. Other times, we might find ourselves caught up in arguments with other Christians, disagreeing about how God wants us to act. Scripture can be interpreted in various ways; how can we be sure which interpretation is correct when sometimes they differ so much?

Fortunately, we don't have to let confusion cloud our minds or throw us off God's path. Instead, the Bible tells us to focus on Jesus. Study the way He lived His life. Use Him as an example of how to think, feel, and act.

Read and reread Jesus' words in the Gospel. Remember: His life is the road map God wants us to follow.

Thank You, Father God, for sending us Jesus so we could see and hear You more clearly. Prompt me to read about Your Son, to take in the words He spoke, to live my life using Him as my road map.

NOURISHING CONVERSATIONS

The lips of the righteous nourish many.
PROVERBS 10:21 NIV

. . . .

Many of us spend most of our waking hours talking. We may be communicating with someone directly at work or home, or we might be texting, emailing, or commenting on social media, but it all counts as talking. Words pour out of us in a continuous stream, and we often give them very little thought. Again and again, though, the Bible tells us that our words matter.

The things we say have the power to do great harm—or great good. Our words can tear down others, spread gossip, or extend arguments. They can cause hurt feelings and anger, opening up chasms of division between people. But God would have us use our words to build bridges of understanding, to connect our hearts with others. He would have us speak words that build others up, come from a place of truth, and encourage peace. The great advantage there is that, when we are careful to speak only words that nourish others, our own hearts and souls are enriched as well.

Today, Lord, may I be on the watch for any negative or hurtful words that might fall from my lips. Please use my conversations, both in person and remotely, to bless others, to bless me, and most of all, to bless You.

GREED

Don't be greedy, for a greedy person is an
idolater, worshiping the things of this world.
Colossians 3:5 nlt

. . . .

The first of the Ten Commandments given to Moses in the Old Testament tells us we are to have no other gods before God—and now, in the New Testament, we see that money and possessions can become the "gods" we worship instead of the Lord of Life. It's not easy, though, to resist the pull of money and the things it buys.

Our society insists we need *more* of everything: if we have a house, we need a bigger house; if we drive a car, we need a newer, more expensive car; if we have a good job, we need a more important job that pays more money. This wanting *more* is endless, because businesses make money by convincing us there's always something bigger and better than the thing we already have. Without us realizing, this attitude can end up shaping the way we live our lives.

It takes conscious effort to disengage our hearts and minds from what society tells us. When we do, though, we realize only God can truly satisfy the desires of our hearts.

Lord, draw my attention to all the ways greed drives
my heart, mind, and actions. Show me how to step
away and instead, be driven only by Your love.

PLANTED

My eyes will watch over them for their good. . . . I will build them up and not tear them down; I will plant them and not uproot them. I will give them a heart to know me, that I am the LORD.

JEREMIAH 24:6–7 NIV

. . . .

Some of us grew up with the idea that God was out to get us. We imagined He was just waiting for us to trip up, so He could punish us for our sins. That concept of God is a false one.

God wants only to build us up and make us stronger and more whole. He wants our inner and outer lives to be healthy and joyful. And He knows that the best—in fact, the only—way that happens is when we come to know Him. As we allow Him to live within our hearts and minds, our entire lives will flourish and grow. Our thoughts, our emotions, and our behaviors will all be shaped by the Spirit of Love living within us.

Thank You, God, that You are keeping an eye on me, looking out for my good. I'm glad, Lord, that I have a God-shaped hole inside me. Please fill it with Your love.

GOSSIP

*Whoever derides their neighbor has no sense, but the one
who has understanding holds their tongue. A gossip betrays
a confidence, but a trustworthy person keeps a secret.*

PROVERBS 11:12–13 NIV

. . . .

Yet again the Bible reminds us that it's not enough to be "spiritual" on the inside, if our words and actions are not in line with God's love. A little bit of gossip with a friend may seem so harmless, but scripture makes clear how destructive it can be. In fact, the Bible contains more than 130 verses speaking against gossip, while it has only 60-some about murder!

Gossip is deadly. It can destroy friendships and hurt others' self-concepts. It overshadows the selfless love God calls us to have for our neighbors, and it can weaken our own relationship with God. As followers of Christ, we need to be careful that our words reflect His love.

*Christ, the next time my friends and I start to gossip, remind
me to hold my tongue or to just walk away. May I be worthy
in my thoughts, words, and deeds to bear Your name.*

GOD'S ECONOMY

A generous person will prosper; whoever
refreshes others will be refreshed.
PROVERBS 11:25 NIV

. . . .

The wisdom we find in the book of Proverbs often runs contrary to the "common-sense" attitudes of our society. Our culture says we need to take care of ourselves first. It assumes that the way to get ahead is by carefully guarding our resources. But divine wisdom points us in a different direction. Instead of working from the world's assumption that there's not enough to go around for everyone, God's economy is built on the infinite bounty of His love. The more we give away our resources (whether they be time, energy, talents, possessions, or money), the more space we have in our hearts and lives for all that God is longing to give us.

God wants us to reflect the same generosity He has shown to us. How might you find a way to do that today?

Strengthen my trust in Your love, Lord, as You also
heighten my love for others. May I give to others as
unselfishly as You have given Yourself to me.

THE REAL GOD

God has not appointed us to [incur His] wrath [He did not select us to condemn us], but [that we might] obtain [His] salvation through our Lord Jesus Christ (the Messiah).
1 Thessalonians 5:9 AMPC

. . . .

Sometimes the "God" who lives in our heads is quite different from the God the Bible describes. Some of the primary shapers of our individual ideas about God are our parents. Those of us who are fortunate to have loving parents who affirmed us and delighted in our growth are more likely to accept that God loves us unconditionally—while those of us who grew up with critical, distant, neglectful, or abusive parents, may unconsciously expect God to be the same.

Our image of God will shape how we feel about ourselves, and it will also influence how we interact with others. That's why it's important we spend time with scripture, letting God's true nature soak into our hearts and minds, replacing any false images that may be lurking there.

God does not condemn or withhold His love. His only goal is to make us whole.

I'm so glad, Jesus, that You came to earth to show us a God of love. I ask that You heal any wounds I carry in my heart, so that I can get to know the real You.

ALWAYS!

Always be joyful. Never stop praying. Be thankful in all circumstances,
for this is God's will for you who belong to Christ Jesus.
1 THESSALONIANS 5:16–18 NLT

. . . .

Verses like these tell us God cares about our inner experience. He wants our hearts and minds to be filled with joy, prayer, and gratitude. Obviously, though, we can't manufacture a constantly happy mood, nor does God consider our more negative emotions (such as anger, fear, sorrow) to be sins. So what did the apostle Paul mean when he wrote these words?

In the original Greek language, the word translated as "joyful" in today's verses has some extra layers of meaning. According to *The Discovery Bible*, the word implies "a leaning toward God's grace; a conscious and experiential awareness of that grace." This awareness can exist side-by-side with sorrow and frustration and even anger.

In a similar way, although we can't always be on our knees in prayer, we can keep the lines of communication always open between our hearts and God's.

And finally, though we can be thankful *for* all circumstances, we can choose to continue in gratitude for God's grace *in* all circumstances.

Remind me, Lord, not to skip over verses like this that seem impossible to experience in real life. Instead, teach me to meditate on them, unpacking their meaning in my life little by little, until I truly understand what it means to be always joyful, always prayerful, always grateful.

THE POWER OF THOUGHTS

Evil scheming distorts the schemer;
peace-planning brings joy to the planner.
PROVERBS 12:20 MSG

. . . .

We often feel we have very little control over our thoughts. They're like a constant river flowing through our minds, while we passively stand by, letting both pure and polluted water rush through us. Psychologists, however, tell us we *can* learn to control our thoughts, replacing negative, self-defeating "self-talk" with positive and creative affirmations.

The wisdom of Proverbs reinforces this modern idea, reminding us that when we allow ourselves to nurture fantasies of revenge or hatred, those thoughts have an effect: they warp our hearts, restrict our spiritual vision, and shape our behaviors. Dwelling on plans for building peace in the world, however, even in small ways, expands our hearts, widens our spiritual perspectives, and helps us perceive new opportunities for action.

Lord of Wisdom, I ask for Your help today as I seek to choose the thoughts that linger in my mind. Remind me that my inner thoughts have power to shape the outer world. And show me how to transform my negative thoughts into positive ones, thoughts that will widen my perspective and help me see new avenues of opportunity.

PATIENT ENDURANCE

May the Lord lead your hearts into a full understanding and expression of the love of God and the patient endurance that comes from Christ.

2 THESSALONIANS 3:5 NLT

. . . .

Notice that this verse speaks of hearts, understanding, and expression, linking our emotions, our mind, and our actions into one unified spiritual journey whose destination is the love of God. Paul, who wrote this letter to the church at Thessaloniki, knew from personal experience that the spiritual pathway is filled with both joy and challenges.

We live in a culture that values speed and looks for instant gratification, but when Paul spoke of "patient endurance," he was talking about a willingness to wait, a commitment to keep going even when our progress is so slow it hardly seems we're going anywhere at all. This is a perspective that measures success not by showy achievements but rather by a quiet determination that's rooted deeply in our relationship with Christ.

Jesus, teach me Your patience, Your willingness to endure pain and loneliness and misunderstanding. May I come to understand Your love more and more—and may my life express Your love to everyone I encounter.

CAREFUL WORDS

*The good acquire a taste for helpful conversation; bullies
push and shove their way through life. Careful words make
for a careful life; careless talk may ruin everything.*
PROVERBS 13:2–3 MSG

. . . .

The Bible tells us over and over that our words matter. They have power.

When we think before we speak, choosing words that affirm and
give life, those words shape not only others' lives but our own hearts and
lives as well. They help us carve out careful and care-giving habits in our
thoughts and actions. On the other hand, when we speak carelessly, letting
words spill out of us without regard to their effects, we can damage both
the lives of others and ourselves.

We're not only to look before we leap but to think before we speak.

---

*Teach me to be careful with my words, Lord. May I make
a habit of thinking before I speak—and may my words
always express Your love, kindness, and care.*

EVERYONE'S INCLUDED!

I urge you, first of all, to pray for all people. Ask God to help them; intercede on their behalf, and give thanks for them. Pray this way for kings and all who are in authority so that we can live peaceful and quiet lives marked by godliness and dignity. This is good and pleases God our Savior, who wants everyone to be saved and to understand the truth.

1 TIMOTHY 2:1–4 NLT

. . . .

God's love leaves out no one. He loves each of us unconditionally, regardless of our politics or skin color, religious beliefs or social media comments. His heart is open to us all, and He extends His hand to each of us, welcoming us into His presence.

God wants us to have the same attitude. As human beings, that's not always easy—but the apostle Paul tells his friend Timothy that the first step is prayer. The more we pray for *all* people, the more we will be able to feel concern for them in our hearts.

When our prayers shape our thoughts, allowing us to look past our differences, our thoughts will shape our behaviors, empowering us to reach out to everyone with God's love.

God, remind me daily to pray for all people—the ones I like and don't like, the ones who share my beliefs and the ones who don't, the ones I understand and those I don't. May my prayers open my heart wider to receive and give Your love.

THE GOODNESS OF THE CREATED WORLD

Everything God has created is good, and nothing is to be thrown away or refused if it is received with thanksgiving.
1 TIMOTHY 4:4 AMPC

. . . .

When God created the physical world, He affirmed that it was all good (Genesis 1).

There is nothing in physical reality that is innately sinful, and nothing that has the power in and of itself to separate us from God. The trouble we encounter with material objects comes instead from within our own hearts. If we allow *things* to become more important to us than God, accumulating them and hoarding them, then we have turned them into idols, false gods that take God's place in our hearts and lives.

The apostle Paul knew the secret for avoiding this pitfall: gratitude. When we look at everything in the physical world—our homes, our possessions, the world of nature, everything and everyone—and thank God for it all, we acknowledge that we did nothing to deserve the physical blessings we've received.

Gratitude sees God's love everywhere we turn. It connects our hearts and lives to the One who loves us.

I thank You, Lord, for all You have given me. May I receive each aspect of my physical life as an expression of Your love.

DOWN THROUGH THE GENERATIONS

A good life gets passed on to the grandchildren.
PROVERBS 13:22 MSG

. . . .

The way we think and feel shapes our actions—and then our lives touch everyone with whom we come in contact. This is the amazing power of God's love. But this power isn't limited to the people we encounter physically; it spreads out in ripples from us to people we don't even know. It even travels forward to people we may never meet, especially our descendants: our grandchildren, our great-grandchildren, our great-great-grandchildren. . .and on through the generations.

How we choose to think and speak and act today will affect the lives of those who come after us. It is the legacy we leave behind.

How will you choose to think and speak and act today?

Father God, I pray for the generations that will come after me, people I may never meet. May I build a strong foundation of love for them to grow from.

TRUE WEALTH

As for the rich in this world, charge them not to be proud and
arrogant and contemptuous of others, nor to set their hopes
on uncertain riches, but on God, Who richly and ceaselessly
provides us with everything for [our] enjoyment.

1 TIMOTHY 6:17 AMPC

. . . .

Here again, Paul affirms the goodness of physical reality, as he did in an earlier passage, one we read a couple of days ago. At the same time, he reminds us that taking pride in our possessions—as though they somehow prove we are better, more important people—is a false perspective.

Physical reality is rich with God's blessing, and He wants us to enjoy the world He created—but that world can never give us real security and fulfillment. Only God's love can do that.

Teach me to enjoy all You have given me, God, while at the same
time I recognize I can take no credit for any of it; it is all a gift from
You. I choose to set my heart and mind on spiritual riches rather
than this world's empty so-called wealth. I choose to set my hope on
You, for You alone provide me with all I need—and so much more!

THE STRENGTH TO GOD'S LOVE

For God did not give us a spirit of timidity (of cowardice, of craven and cringing and fawning fear), but [He has given us a spirit] of power and of love and of calm and well-balanced mind and discipline and self-control.

2 Timothy 1:7 ampc

. . . .

Our emotions come and go—but they do not always tell the truth about spiritual reality.

All of us experience feelings of depression and fear sometimes, but we need to remember that those emotions are not messages from God. Those feelings try to tell us we're not good enough, not strong enough, not smart enough; they say that the world is a frightening and hopeless place.

We can be gentle with those feelings, loving our own selves with God's unconditional love, but we need to remember that they are only feelings, not reality. And as we draw closer to God, He will replace those feelings with His Spirit of power, love, and wisdom. These are the qualities that give us the strength to choose the way we speak and act. And then, as our words and actions line up with God's love, we will find that our minds are calmer. Heart, mind, and action support one another in God's service.

I don't want my anxieties to rule my life anymore, God. Fill me instead with Your Spirit. I know Your love is stronger than all my fears.

KEEP IN MIND

*Think over these things I am saying [understand them
and grasp their application], for the Lord will grant
you full insight and understanding in everything.
Constantly keep in mind Jesus Christ (the Messiah).*
2 TIMOTHY 2:7–8 AMPC

. . . .

What's mostly filling your mind these days? Is it concerns about work
or school? The husband and kids? Friends or finances? Politics or health
care? Diet or aging?

If you've got a lot of worldly questions, thoughts, ideas, fears, longings,
doubts, and suspicions rolling around in your head, chances are you're
seeing the world through the limited perspective of humankind. For a
change of mind and focus, you need to dig into God's Word. And not
just today. But every day.

No need to take giant mouthfuls of the Gospel. Just enough in the
morning to give you something to mull over for the rest of the day and
pray about that night. Perhaps start at Matthew 1:1 or Genesis 1:1 or
Psalms 1:1. Keep reading until you find a morsel that gives you a taste
of Jesus, the Lord of love and light.

Just something to keep in mind.

*Here I am, Lord, sitting before You. Show me what good words
You would have me see, read, consider. Open my mind and
heart, helping me to grasp their implication and application.
Help me keep my focus, Lord, on You and Your Word.*

LIFE AND HEALTH

*He who is slow to anger has great understanding, but he
who is hasty of spirit exposes and exalts his folly. A calm and
undisturbed mind and heart are the life and health of the body,
but envy, jealousy, and wrath are like rottenness of the bones.*

PROVERBS 14:29–30 AMPC

• •

How often has your temper gotten the best of you? How many times have
you wanted to take back the words you've said—even while they were
still tumbling out of your mouth? On what occasions has your health—
mentally, physically, emotionally, and spiritually—suffered because you
couldn't keep your cool within or without?

Proverbs reminds us that instead of responding with rapid rage, we
should pause and try to understand people and situations. That we are to
think before we speak. That we are to not to compare ourselves and our
lives to those of others but to enjoy where we are so that our mind and
heart will be calm, lacking in envy and anger, and our body will be healthy!

How do we get there from here? We continue in what we've learned,
what we truly and strongly believe. We keep our heads and hearts buried
in God's Word.

Let's begin today!

*Lord, help me to keep my entire being ensconced in Your truths,
precepts, love, and light. For when I am in You, I know I will find the
life and health, the peace and strength, the calm and cool I long for.*

STAND BY

At my first defense no one came to stand by me, but all deserted
me. May it not be charged against them! But the Lord stood by
me and strengthened me, so that through me the message might
be fully proclaimed and all the Gentiles might hear it. So I was
rescued from the lion's mouth. The Lord will rescue me from every
evil deed and bring me safely into his heavenly kingdom.
2 TIMOTHY 4:16–18 ESV

. . . .

Sometimes, when we're in the thick of it and have to face an uncomfortable
situation, we may look around and realize we're standing all alone. Those
who promised to always be by our side through thick and thin are nowhere
to be found. At that point our knees may begin to buckle, our voice to
tremble, and our head to spin.

That's when we must remember we need never stand alone. Even
though our fellow humans may desert us, we can always count on the
Lord to stand by us. Why? Because "He [God] Himself has said, I will
not in any way fail you *nor* give you up *nor* leave you without support.
[I will] not, [I will] not, [I will] not in any degree leave you helpless nor
forsake *nor* let [you] down (relax My hold on you)! [Assuredly not!]"
(Hebrews 13:5 AMPC).

Let those emphatic truths from God's Word ring in your heart,
mind, spirit, and soul.

With You standing by me, Lord, I can endure anything!

A GLAD HEART

A glad heart makes a happy face; a broken heart crushes the spirit. A wise person is hungry for knowledge, while the fool feeds on trash. For the despondent, every day brings trouble; for the happy heart, life is a continual feast.

PROVERBS 15:13–15 NLT

. . . .

It's clear from today's verses that God wants us to have a glad heart. Yet how many times have you turned to someone in church and seen that person's habitual frown? You turn away from him, wondering why he's such a sourpuss when there are so many blessings to be gleaned from God's hand.

In that same moment, assess your own self. Before you run to judge the sourpuss next to you, consider your own face. Is your brow furrowed? A frown fixed below your nose? Chances are, it might slip through everyone once in a while.

So what's a woman to do? Simple. Put a smile on your face. How? By digging into all the blessings God has waiting for you in His Word. By feeding yourself on His promises, His goodness, His insatiable love for you. The more you do, the happier your heart, face, God, and perhaps your fellow pew-sitter will be! (Smiling is contagious, you know!)

Lord, as I open up Your Word today, lead me to Your good news. Point me toward Your abundant blessings. Nourish me with Your promises. Give me a glad heart!

GOOD DEEDS

Look forward with hope to that wonderful day when the glory of our great God and Savior, Jesus Christ, will be revealed. He gave his life to free us from every kind of sin, to cleanse us, and to make us his very own people, totally committed to doing good deeds.

TITUS 2:13–14 NLT

• •

So many people are looking for meaning to their lives, to understanding their purpose in this world. How wonderful that you, a daughter of God and sister of Christ, already know your purpose: to be right with God, free to access His presence, call upon His help, walk His way, and do good deeds. That's how you can find hope and meaning in this world, by changing it—as well as yourself and those whose lives you touch—for the better.

Yet the blessings don't stop there. For by looking forward with hope, living in freedom, and doing good deeds, not only will you find yourself growing closer and closer to God but His ears will be open to your prayers (Proverbs 15:29). For the more you walk as He would have you walk, the more your prayers will be aligned with His will. And the more your prayers are aligned with His will, the more His answer and vision will fit yours.

Thank You, Lord, for giving up Your life for me. Now, show me what good I can do in Your name today!

HIS SWEET MERCY

We ourselves were once foolish, disobedient, led astray, slaves to various passions and pleasures, passing our days in malice and envy, hated by others and hating one another. But when the goodness and loving kindness of God our Savior appeared, he saved us, not because of works done by us in righteousness, but according to his own mercy, by the washing of regeneration and renewal of the Holy Spirit, whom he poured out on us richly through Jesus Christ our Savior.

TITUS 3:3–6 ESV

Mercy. What a beautiful word—it makes the whole of our being relax and smile. Since we are to think on good and lovely things in this life, then the concept of mercy should be one of those "things." How many times have people shown us grace? How many times have we extended compassion to others? Of course, the ultimate mercy is what God did for humankind through Jesus Christ.

Yes, God's sweet mercy came down from heaven and nothing in the world will ever, ever be the same again.

Dear God, I thank You for sending Your Son to die for me, to save me from my sins, to give me eternal life. I can never repay You for such a sacrifice, but I intend to serve You and love You for all time. Amen.

AN IMPOSSIBLE DREAM MADE POSSIBLE

A man's mind plans his way, but the Lord
directs his steps and makes them sure.
PROVERBS 16:9 AMPC

. . . .

Even when we are very young, we start the dreaming process. You know, all the many things we want to accomplish—all the way from constructing a tiny house made with colorful plastic blocks on the floor to designing a building complex in downtown USA.

Somewhere in this unfolding journey, hopefully we will recognize and thank God for the many gifts and talents He offers us to fulfill our purpose. We should, of course, add in faith, prayer, training, and perseverance. And then along with His perfect will and timing, the Lord promises to direct our steps and turn that dream—of being all that God created us to be—into a reality.

Oh, to delight daily with the Lord in our purposed-filled work—well, can you think of a better or more positive way to live this life?

Almighty God, I thank You for giving me purpose and the talents and abilities to fulfill Your will for my life. Please guide me in all that I do and direct my every step. May my life's work bring You delight and glorify Your name for You alone are worthy of my worship. In Jesus' holy name I pray. Amen.

SEARCHING FOR THE GOOD

He who deals wisely and heeds [God's] word and counsel shall find good, and whoever leans on, trusts in, and is confident in the Lord—happy, blessed, and fortunate is he.
PROVERBS 16:20 AMPC

· ·

As Christians, each morning (hopefully) we are on the hunt for what is good. We like good things to eat for breakfast. We like to hear words that are lovely rather than words full of anger. We like a hug before we head out for the day. We like to plan for hopeful and excellent things that will happen at the office or home or wherever we will be. If there are major problems, we spend time trying to transform them into what is true and helpful. In other words, as Christ-followers, our souls long for what is good.

If we find ourselves turning away from that godly ideal, it could be that we have fallen into some kind of snare. But with the help of the Holy Spirit, we can be freed of the unhealthy patterns and negative traps we may find ourselves in. We can learn to live the words of today's verse, and we can discover how to be free and happy in the Lord!

Lord, Your holy Word is a wonderful guidebook for living a healthy and satisfying and hope-filled life in You. Thank You for that—and so much more besides! Amen.

SWEETNESS TO THE SOUL

Gracious words are like a honeycomb,
sweetness to the soul and health to the body.
PROVERBS 16:24 ESV

· ·

Our modern-day society is in great need of gracious words, not only in the context of the words we speak to each other as individuals but on social media and the news. How wonderful it would be to make it a point each day to ask the Lord to help us speak words of healing to all, in that way demonstrating to the world what gracious words sound like and how they feel to the soul.

Let us change this very day and may our new watchword be "gracious." May that new way of life not only change our own soul but all those souls who cross our paths. May the ripple effects be powerful and transforming. May those sweeter-than-honeycomb words reflect back to the One who love us and cares for us and knows us by name—Jesus Christ.

Dear Lord, thank You for being so gracious to me. I in turn want to be gracious to others. Show me how to do that. Grant me Your supernatural aid to combat the negative and the hurtful words in this world. Help me to be a voice of love and compassion and healing. May my words be like honeycomb, and may they point to You and Your glory. Amen.

SOFTENED HEARTS

We have become fellows with Christ (the Messiah) and share in all He has for us, if only we hold our first newborn confidence and original assured expectation [in virtue of which we are believers] firm and unshaken to the end. Then while it is [still] called Today, if you would hear His voice and when you hear it, do not harden your hearts.

HEBREWS 3:14–15 AMPC

. . . .

It's easy to wander away from the Shepherd, to lose our way after our initial finding of Him. But that's when we begin to get into trouble and become weak in our faith, open to fears and doubts. Thus, we are encouraged to hold on to that firm faith that we started out with. As we do so, we will remain unshaken in our heart, body, mind, spirit, and soul. Then our ears will be more open to His voice, His movement, His light, and His Spirit. Then when we hear His call, His message, our hearts will be soft, willing to obey, open to His direction.

Today think back to when you first believed. Remember the confidence you had in Christ. Then seek His presence. Listen to all He has to say. Do what He would have you do. Trust Him, knowing His way is *the* way.

Christ, speak to me, Spirit to spirit. My ears are open to Your voice, my soul to Your way, my mind to Your wisdom. Whisper to my softened heart. I will listen and believe.

LIVING UNFETTERED

Love prospers when a fault is forgiven,
but dwelling on it separates close friends.
PROVERBS 17:9 NLT

. . . .

Have you ever had a friend—or been a friend—who could not let go of a past offense? Just. Couldn't. Let. It. Go. It leaves you with such a residue in your spirit, you may eventually find yourself walking away from the friendship.

Fortunately, the Bible has lots of tips on living, and Proverbs reminds us that a friendship will wilt if you keep dwelling on how your friend has wronged you. But love will bloom and flourish if you let the offense go and let God deal with it.

The Love Chapter also says it well: "Love is patient and kind. Love is not jealous or boastful or proud or rude. It does not demand its own way. It is not irritable, and it keeps no record of being wronged" (1 Corinthians 13:4–5 NLT).

May we become so busy with creating and laughing and loving and eating and praying and singing and working that we totally forget to keep a record of wrongs. May we toss those old lists away and start living anew—unfettered and free!

Lord, help me not dwell on the wrongs committed against me
or occurring around me. Help me to think good thoughts, to
focus on the good things happening. Show me how to live an
unfettered life, one in which I am free to love more! Amen.

GREAT CONFIDENT AND HOPE

God also bound himself with an oath, so that those who received the promise could be perfectly sure that he would never change his mind. So God has given both his promise and his oath. These two things are unchangeable because it is impossible for God to lie. Therefore, we who have fled to him for refuge can have great confidence as we hold to the hope that lies before us.

HEBREWS 6:17–18 NLT

. . . .

Ever get discouraged, wondering if God is going to make good on all the promises He has made to His children? Consider Abraham. He had to wait twenty-five years for the promises of a son to become a reality!

So, woman of the Way, hang on! God will come through. He will not change His mind. He cannot, does not lie. Those promises God made all those thousands of years ago, will be fulfilled, some in your own lifetime. Because God said, "I am the LORD! If I say it, it will happen" (Ezekiel 12:25 NLT).

If there's any person you can take at His word, who's honest as the day is long and a tried-and-true keeper of promises, it's the Lord of the universe, your Creator and Sustainer. Yahweh. So hang on to that great confidence and hope you have in Him.

Thank You, Lord, for being so true to Your Word and promises. Because You do what You say, I have confidence and hope!

AN ACT OF KINDNESS

For it was indeed fitting that we should have such a high priest,
holy, innocent, unstained, separated from sinners, and exalted
above the heavens. He has no need, like those high priests, to offer
sacrifices daily, first for his own sins and then for those of the
people, since he did this once for all when he offered up himself.

HEBREWS 7:26–27 ESV

. . . .

Has anyone ever offered you an act of kindness that was so guileless and so loving and so unconditionally generous that it made you weep? When that happens, we may never forget it, because it is so wonderful and memorable.

Then here comes Jesus, innocent and holy in the midst of our brokenness, missteps, and problems. Jesus offers us not only love but everything in heaven and on earth. Even His life. Even though we deserved none of it.

How can we thank this Jesus for this wonderous gift? How can we ever? By loving as He loved, giving as He gave, speaking as He spoke, thinking as He thought, doing as He did.

Doing someone a kindness today is the perfect place to start.

Almighty God, thank You for sending Your Son to offer Himself
as a perfect sacrifice once for all, all before You knew me.
Thank You so much for Your grace-filled gift! Now, Lord,
show me today, who needs a little kindness? Amen.

INNERMOST MIND AND HEART

This is the covenant that I will make with the house of Israel after those days, says the Lord: I will imprint My laws upon their minds, even upon their innermost thoughts and understanding, and engrave them upon their hearts; and I will be their God, and they shall be My people.

HEBREWS 8:10 AMPC

. . . .

Under the old covenant God had made with humankind, He wrote His laws to His people upon tablets of stone. But now, under this new covenant of grace, of which Jesus is mediator, God imprints His laws on His peoples' minds. He writes them directly upon their hearts.

Under this new covenant, God promises to help you to understand, to know, to believe His laws of love. He promises to give you a heart to love those laws, the power to put them into action, the courage to live your life in accordance with them, and the memory to retain them.

Never feel you are going through this life ill-prepared or unguided. For God has equipped your innermost heart and mind to lean, learn, love, and live His way.

Thank You, Lord, for imprinting Your laws of love and life upon my mind, for engraving them upon my heart. With Your handwritten message deep within me, I know I will neither lose my way nor Your love.

A STRONG TOWER

The name of the Lord is a strong tower; the [consistently]
righteous man [upright and in right standing with God]
runs into it and is safe, high [above evil] and strong.

PROVERBS 18:10 AMPC

. . . .

The "name of the Lord" is the expression for the entire character of God, the person He has revealed Himself to be. That's why His name is a strong tower, a place of safety, high above this world of humankind.

When you're afraid, you can run to the Lord, your Rock of Refuge. When you're in want, run to the Lord Will Provide. When you're broken, run to the Lord That Heals. When you need guidance and protection, run to the Lord My Shepherd. When you're anxious, run to the Lord Is Peace. When you feel ignored or invisible, run to the Lord Who Sees or Watches Over Me. When you need wisdom and calm, go to the Wonderful Counselor and Prince of Peace. When you need a path to understanding, head to the Teacher.

When you have a particular need, run to and pray in the name of that aspect of God you require. You will find all you need in the name of the Lord.

Strong Tower, it is to You I run when I am troubled in mind,
hurting in heart, out of sync in spirit. Reveal Yourself to
me in all Your many aspects. You are all I need.

GODLY CONNECTIONS

Let us think of ways to motivate one another to acts of
love and good works. And let us not neglect our meeting
together, as some people do, but encourage one another.
Hebrews 10:24–25 nlt

· ·

Not only are we to think of good and worthy things in our own minds and hearts. We're reminded to think of ways to spur one another to actions of love and good works. To encourage each other.

Today, find a way to connect to a fellow churchgoer. To encourage or to inspire him or her to act in love or do a good work. Even if you cannot find a way to meet one another in person due to conflicting schedules, pandemics, or other obstacles, you can still connect with someone online, over the phone, or while participating in activities other than those at church. You can write letters and send cards, perhaps text or email. The main point here is not to just connect to another spirit, but to connect with a common purpose in the presence of an uncommon God. To encourage, motivate, and inspire one another.

The more you step out and build up another person as you walk upon this earth, the better, the richer, the more godly your world will be—within and out.

Tell me, Lord, who You would have me connect with
today. Tell me who You would have me motivate, inspire,
and encourage to do good, to love in Your name!

FINDING GOOD

*He who gains Wisdom loves his own life; he who
keeps understanding shall prosper and find good.*
PROVERBS 19:8 AMPC

• •

There's a lot of good stuff packed into this one sentence, this one verse from Proverbs. It contains echoes of scriptures such as Proverbs 4:5, which tells us to "Get skillful and godly Wisdom, get understanding" (AMPC). Proverbs 16:20 says, "He who deals wisely and heeds [God's] word and counsel shall find good, and whoever leans on, trusts in, and is confident in the Lord—happy, blessed, and fortunate is he" (AMPC).

How wonderful this advice is! How great that God is telling us to do what we are endeavoring to do within these pages! We're putting ourselves out there to find the wisdom in the Word, knowledge that will help us to keep our eyes, heart, mind, and feet on the good path God has set before us. A path upon which we are to love God with all we are and others as ourselves. It is this seeking after God and His goodness that will help us to prosper in this world and the one beyond.

Begin today. Seek out wisdom in God's Word. Ask Him to help you understand what you're reading. Then make an effort to keep that wisdom in the forefront of your mind. In so doing, you cannot help but find good!

*Lord of love and light, help me gain wisdom within
Your Word. May it then work in my heart and mind.*

A POWERHOUSE OF FAITH

*Now faith is the assurance (the confirmation, the title deed)
of the things [we] hope for, being the proof of things [we] do
not see and the conviction of their reality [faith perceiving as
real fact what is not revealed to the senses]. For by [faith—
trust and holy fervor born of faith] the men of old had divine
testimony borne to them and obtained a good report.*

HEBREWS 11:1–2 AMPC

. . . .

This passage on faith is reassuring in this ever-changing and challenging world. And as you read all of Hebrews 11 you will see a spectacular overview of faith throughout the ages. The biblical heroes that are depicted in this chapter did not always prove themselves to be perfect specimens of humanity, but they did prove themselves to have great faith in God.

God counts faith as righteousness, and when we look at James 5:16, we find even more comfort: "The earnest (heartfelt, continued) prayer of a righteous man makes tremendous power available [dynamic in its working]" (AMPC).

So, not only is a life of faith in God the most beautiful way to live; it's also the way for our prayers to have great power. So, may we walk by faith, may we grow daily as we trust in Christ, and may our prayers be effective for His glorious kingdom!

*Dear God, I want to be a powerhouse of faith.
Show me the way. In Jesus' name I pray. Amen.*

A HEART HUG—AND MORE!

*If you help the poor, you are lending to
the LORD—and he will repay you!*
PROVERBS 19:17 NLT

. . . .

Have you ever helped someone who was needy? Perhaps you worked in a soup kitchen, handing out meals to the hungry. Maybe you spearheaded a clothing and blanket–drive for people who suffered through a hurricane. Or perhaps you financially supported an organization that ministers to the homeless. This glorious feeling of giving is like none other. It's like a warm embrace for the soul. Makes you want to do it again and again.

Doing for or giving to others is not only a heart hug for you but a way of life that pleases the Lord. And amazingly enough, God will repay you for lending to the poor, if not in this life, you will be blessed in the life to come. For God's Word is sure and His promises endure forever. Amen!

Lord, sometimes I get so deeply involved in my own life and all my own daily problems that I forget to notice the needs of others. Help me to have a sensitivity when it comes to the poor and the needy. May I always have compassion and kindness and generosity for I know this attitude pleases You. And I know when I offer these acts of kindness, in a way, I am doing these deeds for You too. Amen.

BORN TO RUN

*Let us strip off every weight that slows us down, especially the
sin that so easily trips us up. And let us run with endurance
the race God has set before us. We do this by keeping our eyes on
Jesus, the champion who initiates and perfects our faith.*

HEBREWS 12:1–2 NLT

. . . .

What is it in your life that is weighing you down? Perhaps something
from your past keeps tripping you up. Maybe a memory that just won't
die. Or perhaps there's a touch of unforgiveness, one that impedes the
work the Holy Spirit is attempting to perform in and through you. Maybe
there are worries of the future that are fogging your vision of who God
wants you to be, what He wants you do to.

No matter what is slowing you down, the message is clear: Strip
it off. Then run the race God has set before you, keeping your focus on
Jesus, the living Word, as you do so.

Today, spend some time in prayer before God. Ask Him what might
be hindering your progress in your spiritual life, what might be obscuring
your vision of who God sees when He looks at the true you. Then run
the race you were born to run.

*I pray, Lord, that You would reveal what might be hindering me
from running the race You have put before me. Then help me
rid myself of that encumbrance as I fix my eyes on Jesus.*

OH, THOSE WEEDS

Make sure no one gets left out of God's generosity. Keep
a sharp eye out for weeds of bitter discontent. A thistle or
two gone to seed can ruin a whole garden in no time.
HEBREWS 12:15 MSG

. . . .

Are you a Naomi or a Ruth?

Because of a drought, Naomi and her family had fled Bethlehem. Relocated to the hostile territory of Moab, Naomi's two sons grew up and married two Moabite women. Then tragedy strikes again: Naomi's husband and sons die. Now homeless, widowed, and childless, Naomi decides to walk back to Bethlehem.

At first her widowed daughters-in-law follow her. Naomi is able to convince Orpah to go back to her family. But Ruth sticks with Naomi, refusing to part with her. Together they arrive in Bethlehem where Naomi tells the local women, "Don't call me Naomi; call me Bitter. The Strong One has dealt me a bitter blow. I left here full of life, and GOD has brought me back with nothing but the clothes on my back. Why would you call me Naomi? God certainly doesn't. The Strong One ruined me" (Ruth 1:20–21 MSG). In the end, Ruth's continued love of, respect for, and kindness to Naomi saved both herself and her mother-in-law from the bane of bitterness.

Are you a Ruth or a Naomi?

Lord, show me where I may need to do some
weeding in my life—within and without.

THE GIFT OF HOSPITALITY

Let love for your fellow believers continue and be a fixed practice with you [never let it fail]. Do not forget or neglect or refuse to extend hospitality to strangers [in the brotherhood— being friendly, cordial, and gracious, sharing the comforts of your home and doing your part generously], for through it some have entertained angels without knowing it.

HEBREWS 13:1–2 AMPC

. . . .

Hebrews 13 reminds us that there is an unseen world out there. And that sometimes that other realm opens up to us—whether God lifts the veil and allows us a glimpse of what is happening in the supernatural world or God allows that world to connect with ours. Sounds kind of far out there. Almost too hard to believe, right? But if we take out all of the supernatural elements of the Bible, we take God, His ways, and His plan out of our story.

So, when God talks about being hospitable, and in doing so we may have entertained angels, He means it! It is a mind-blowing thought. What would we say if somehow we encountered someone who was indeed an angel? What would the angel wear or eat or say? A thousand questions come to mind. But whether we entertain an angel or not in our lifetime, either way, we as Christians, are to be kind and generous to all folks.

And a welcome mat might be nice too.

Dear Lord, please show me how to offer hospitality. Amen.

OUR TRUE COLORS

Consider it a sheer gift, friends, when tests and challenges come at you from all sides. You know that under pressure, your faith-life is forced into the open and shows its true colors. So don't try to get out of anything prematurely. Let it do its work so you become mature and well-developed, not deficient in any way.

JAMES 1:2–4 MSG

. . . .

No one likes to be uncomfortable. Or to be tweaked or tested in their faith. We'd rather have an easy life with comfortable overstuffed furniture and a full pantry with lovely things to eat. And friends and family and coworkers with whom we get along fabulously. Or—well, you get the picture.

Yet sometimes life isn't all that comfortable. Sometimes it's messy. And when we are tested in this life, our true colors do show. And sometimes those colors are a dull, lifeless cloudlike gray, not the way they were meant to be, such as the bright, brilliant, swirling colors of, say, a van Gogh painting!

When we are challenged and cornered by life, what colors do we show? Hopefully we will see our trials as a positive, as a gift to make us grow and bloom with new life.

Oh, Lord, please give me courage. Help me be grateful for the blessings as well as the challenges that come my way, seeing the latter as a sort of gift that will grow me into a mature and well-developed woman of faith! Amen.

NO PARTIALITY

Show no partiality as you hold the faith in our Lord Jesus
Christy. . . . For if a man wearing a gold ring and fine clothing
comes into your assembly, and a poor man in shabby clothing
also comes in, and if you pay attention to the one who wears
the fine clothing and say, "You sit here in a good place,"
while you say to the poor man, "You stand over there," or,
"Sit down at my feet," have you not then made distinctions
among yourselves and become judges with evil thoughts?

JAMES 2:1–4 ESV

. . . .

We've all done it. You see someone at a party and automatically judge her. *She's well dressed and must have important friends. I should meet her.* Or, say, someone strolls in who looks a little rough around the edges. *Hmm. Not sure she's worth my time.*

Since childhood we learn from the world how to judge people. Yet the worst in appearance might have a beautiful heart and the spirit of a saint. And by a quick judgment, we may miss a glorious chance to gain the friend of a lifetime.

When we encounter others, let's strive to see the best in each—no matter what they look like on the outside.

Lord, remind me to treat all people the
same for I know that pleases You. Amen.

TENDER TRANSPLANTS

And I will give you a new heart, and I will put a new spirit in you. I will take out your stony, stubborn heart and give you a tender, responsive heart. And I will put my Spirit in you so that you will follow my decrees and be careful to obey my regulations.

Ezekiel 36:26–27 nlt

. . . .

Some people are embarrassed about having a tender heart. They feel (or perhaps have been told) that in this world they need to be tougher. That they cannot be led by compassion. That they must be realists, have a stiff upper lip. That's the only way they'll get through life.

Yet a tender heart is exactly what God is looking for. What the world may see as a defect, He considers an asset. For it is only that tender heart that will seek Him, listen to what He has to say, and then actually do what He has told them to do.

When you came to Jesus, you received a new heart and a new spirit. And those transplants are what's going to make you a mighty woman for God. A courageous yet kindhearted female who when God says, "Who will go for me?" will respond obediently with a warm, "Send me, Lord. Send me."

Thank You, Lord, for making me a courageous yet kindhearted female who will willingly serve You. In Jesus' name. Amen.

CLOSE TO YOU

Draw near to God, and He will draw near to you.
JAMES 4:8 HCSB

. . . .

God longs to be so gracious to us (Isaiah 30:18). Like the prodigal son's father, He stands waiting at the gate, constantly looking down that road, hoping that we will soon be coming around the corner. Then He suddenly sees us drawing closer and closer. But He cannot help Himself. He breaks into a run and encloses us in His everlasting arms of love. Before we can even get an explanation out of our mouths, before we can explain why we ran off as we did and how terribly things turned out, He begins preparing a celebration in honor of our homecoming.

Once again in His presence, our worries ease, our negative thoughts evaporate, our doubts disappear. His grace, mercy, love, and forgiveness showered upon us make us humble and ever so glad to have come home.

If you've drifted off, away from the power, light, and love you need to grow into the woman of God you were created to be, run back home. Throw yourself into God's welcoming arms. Draw near to Him, and He will be ever closer to you.

---

*Lord, I want to come close, to be held in Your welcoming
arms, to lay my head upon Your shoulders, to feel
Your breath upon my cheek. Hold me, Lord.*

UNDEFEATABLE GOD

*Nothing clever, nothing conceived, nothing contrived,
can get the better of GOD. Do your best, prepare for
the worst—then trust GOD to bring victory.*
PROVERBS 21:30–31 MSG

. . . .

When it feels as if there's no way you can win the battle against negative thoughts, when it seems there's no way out of the predicament you're in, when you begin to believe that the bad guys are truly going to win the day, remember: nothing and no one, no plan or plot, no power or foe can win against God.

How do we know this? God has proven it over and over again. He did so when He drowned Pharoah and his chariots in the Red Sea and brought His own people safely through that same sea and onto dry land (Exodus 14). The Lord stilled the sun and moon for Joshua, bringing His victory to Joshua over the Amorites (Joshua 10). He brought victory to Deborah and Barak, defeating Sisera and his 900 iron chariots (Judges 4). He made it possible for a shepherd boy to kill a giant (1 Samuel 17).

So no need to ever worry about anything, child of God. You're Dad? He's so got this.

Continually remind me, Lord, that as long as I dwell in Your secret place, I'll be fine because You are the "Almighty [Whose power no foe can withstand]" (Psalm 91:1 AMPC).

A WOMAN OF INTEGRITY

A sterling reputation is better than striking it rich;
a gracious spirit is better than money in the bank.
PROVERBS 22:1 MSG

. . . .

Most people will admit that they love to be held in high esteem. Who wouldn't? It means people think highly of you because you are trustworthy and diligent, courageous, and full of compassion. Friends and family members or coworkers may call you up for advice or help or prayer or comfort. You may even have a place of honor when attending parties and gatherings, all because your reputation is stellar and people admire you for all your wise words and generous deeds, they trust that you will do as you say and that all you say and do is good.

If you're not yet where you'd like to be, no worries. Just focus on walking the walk with God humbly by your side, not just talking the talk—as the old saying goes. Live your lives so that Christ is not merely that "someone special" for Sundays, but the One who's front and center in your life. Always.

Dear God, help me become a glowing woman of integrity, to please You in all things. Grow me up into a woman who has a gracious spirit and who follows You always and loves You above all others. In Jesus' powerful and holy name, I pray. Amen.

READ, HEED, AND LEAD

Listen to the words of the wise; apply your heart to
my instruction. For it is good to keep these sayings
in your heart and always ready on your lips.
PROVERBS 22:17–18 NLT

. . . .

One very good way to keep your mind focused on the positive, your heart tender, and your actions good is to "listen to the words of the wise." And where will you find such words? In the Bible, the bestselling book of all time as of 1995, according to *Guinness World Records*.

Read, then heed the words of God. Allow them to guide you through life. Spend time memorizing what you read, especially the verses that truly move you. Storing such words up in your heart during times of contentment will serve to keep you calm during times of chaos. When the stinging words of others or your own discouraging thoughts threaten your peace of mind, being able to recite God's words aloud will be a balm to not just your spirit and soul but to others who hear God's spoken wisdom.

So remember to read God's Word, heed His wisdom, and allow both to lead your heart and mind to a better place.

Bring to my attention, Lord, those words of wisdom
You'd like me to store in my heart. Then show me ways in
which I can incorporate those words into my life, to Your
glory and my peace. In Jesus' name I pray, amen.

CHOSEN

You are the ones chosen by God, chosen for the high calling of priestly work, chosen to be a holy people, God's instruments to do his work and speak out for him, to tell others of the night-and-day difference he made for you—from nothing to something, from rejected to accepted.

1 PETER 2:9–10 MSG

. . . .

When the comments of others or perhaps even the thoughts generated by your own mind, lead you to think you are nothing, remember who you are in Christ.

You are a confident woman of the Way who has been chosen by God for a holy task, for a purpose. You are here for God to work through you in whatever color, shape, or form He desires. You are a woman who has been saved and accepted by Christ for a purpose, so that you can tell others of the wonders He works in your life.

The knowledge that you are special or something of value in God's eyes means that you are not nothing but something; you are not rejected but have been accepted. Allow this knowledge to lead you to a higher spiritual plane, a place where you will find the confidence and courage to allow God to mold you into a woman who is firm in her faith and strong in the Word, ready to bow to her Master and do what He's called her to do.

Thank You, Lord, for choosing me to be an instrument for You. Let's begin. Amen.

PRIORITIES

*Cast but a glance at riches, and they are gone, for they will
surely sprout wings and fly off to the sky like an eagle.*
PROVERBS 23:5 NIV

. . . .

Sometimes even though we know in our minds we should fix our eyes on Jesus, it is easy to fall into the trap of looking to our left and right instead of straight ahead to our Savior. We see others around us building the bigger house, driving the newer car, and wearing the latest fashions. We give in to the temptation to desire those things above our walk with the Lord. In the end, though, worldly things will never satisfy.

When you feel jealousy creeping in, remember this. Riches are fleeting. They are gone as quickly as they come. The greatest blessings in this life do not have a price tag. They are worth immeasurably more than mere dollars and coins.

Lean into the Lord and recall the words of the old hymn by Helen H. Lemmel that says: "Turn your eyes upon Jesus. Look full in His wonderful face. And the things of earth will grow strangely dim in the light of His glory and grace."

Lord, fill my life with true riches such as faith, family, and friends, I pray.

REPAY EVIL WITH BLESSING

Finally, all of you, be like-minded, be sympathetic, love one another, be compassionate and humble. Do not repay evil with evil or insult with insult. On the contrary, repay evil with blessing, because to this you were called so that you may inherit a blessing.

1 Peter 3:8–9 NIV

. . . .

It's so much easier to retaliate. After all, it's human nature to rise up in anger and lash out. And often it's our tongues that get us into more trouble than our fists! Words fly out quickly and can bring about great destruction. When someone hurts us, it does not take any self-control to jump into the ring and fight back—physically or verbally.

It takes more than *self*-control to act in love when we are hurt. It takes *God* control. That's right. We have to rely on a strength beyond what is humanly possible, a strength that God gives us when we seek Him.

The next time you are wronged (and it could be today!), rather than repaying evil for evil...stop and pray. In that very moment before you speak a word or take any action, turn everything you are thinking and feeling over to God. He'll empower you to remain silent or to speak a word that restores peace in the situation.

Father in Heaven, may I show kindness when I am wronged.

EVEN IF HE DOESN'T

If we are thrown into the blazing furnace, the God we serve is able to deliver us from it, and he will deliver us from Your Majesty's hand. But even if he does not, we want you to know, Your Majesty, that we will not serve your gods or worship the image of gold you have set up."

Daniel 3:17–18 niv

. . . .

It's one thing to declare that your God is able. It's another to stand firm in your faith when He might not do what you're hoping He does.

Shadrach, Meshach, and Abednego knew that God was able to save them, but what they did not know is if He would. They walked out of a fiery furnace alive because the Lord chose to spare them that day. That might not have been the case.

We cannot always understand the ways of God, but as believers, we can trust Him. Proverbs 3:5–6 (niv) says: "Trust in the Lord with all your heart and lean not on your own understanding; in all your ways submit to him, and he will make your paths straight."

That's what these three young men did in the face of death. They leaned into God rather than relying on their own understanding. Our heavenly Father may not always act in the way we hope, but He will always come through for us. He is faithful.

Help me to trust in Your will for my life, Lord, no matter what.

TRAITS TO DEVELOP

*If you possess these qualities in increasing measure, they will keep you
from being ineffective and unproductive in your knowledge of our
Lord Jesus Christ. But whoever does not have them is nearsighted and
blind, forgetting that they have been cleansed from their past sins.*

2 Peter 1:8–9 niv

. . . .

In school, children learn cause and effect. The teacher gives if-then statements to explain the concept. "*If* you are late to school, *then* you will receive a tardy slip. *If* the three bears return home, *then* Goldilocks will be frightened away." It's a simple concept to learn, but it's not always as easy to apply to the spiritual life.

Take note of the cause-and-effect relationship Peter lays out for us in 2 Peter 1:8–9. *If* certain traits increase in our lives, *then* we'll be effective and productive in our knowledge of the Savior. *If* not, *then* we won't. Wow!

The qualities referred to here are found in 2 Peter 1:5–7 (niv): "Make every effort to add to your faith goodness; and to goodness, knowledge; and to knowledge, self-control; and to self-control, perseverance; and to perseverance, godliness; and to godliness, mutual affection; and to mutual affection, love."

Pay attention to these characteristics. Write them down. Pray for them to be true of you. Seek out scripture to guide you in developing them in your life. The payoff is great.

*Grow these important traits in me, Lord,
so that I might know more of Jesus daily. Amen.*

BUILDING YOUR HOUSE

*By wisdom a house is built, and through understanding
it is established; through knowledge its rooms are
filled with rare and beautiful treasures.*

PROVERBS 24:3–4 NIV

. . . .

As a woman, you play an important role in the lives of those closest to you. You represent the Lord and serve as a role model to those around you. You are an example every single day. You build a reputation over time, and your family and friends learn what matters most to you through your reactions to life's circumstances, both the blessings and the trials.

When a house is built, it must stand on a firm foundation. If your life is built upon the foundation of faith, it will shine before others and provide strength for them as well.

Resist the urge to focus on the outward and be content with less than those around you materially. True treasures are not found through online shopping but by tapping into the power source of your Lord and Savior.

Seek the wisdom of the Father through His holy Word and through prayer. Associate with other believers in the Christian community. Find time to rest and set yourself apart from the busy, busy, busy of this world. These things will help you to establish a house built with wisdom as its basis.

Lord, may I build my life upon a foundation of faith in You.

AN HONEST ANSWER

An honest answer is like a kiss on the lips.
PROVERBS 24:26 NIV

. . . .

Many of us have heard it said that honesty is the best policy. The Bible goes a little bit further with today's pearl of wisdom, telling us "an honest answer is like a kiss on the lips."

Honesty can be tricky, though, in actual practice. Have you ever found it hard to tell someone the truth? We all struggle with this now and again. For there are times when it's just easier to avoid being honest.

Instead of flattering a friend by agreeing with everything she says, you may want to try listening more than you speak. Then, if and when advice is asked of you, take the opportunity to speak into another's life seriously. Give wise counsel rather than just going along with what you know the other person wants to hear. This can be a tall order! No one wants to rub a friend or relative the wrong way. Yet it is our responsibility as believers to be honest and to point others down the right path, the one that will ultimately lead them to Jesus.

As you invest in a daily quiet time with the Lord, He will grow your faith and wisdom. You can then use that wisdom to pour into the lives of those who seek your honest answers.

Lord, may I be honest with my family and friends—and You—always.

THE ETERNAL

The world and its desires pass away,
but whoever does the will of God lives forever.
1 JOHN 2:17 NIV

• •

Today find hope in the eternal. Although this world is fleeting, God is forever—the same yesterday, today, and tomorrow. You, believer, are saved and you stand solid and strong upon a foundation of faith in an eternal God who loves you with an everlasting love. Seek His will and carry it out day by day, moment by moment, until He calls you home to Himself.

Certainly you are in the world, but you are not of the world, nor do you belong to the world (John 17:14–16; 15:19). You are a citizen of heaven and you are a child of the Creator. One day you will be with Him in glory. For now, He has purposes for you on this earth.

As you move through your day, focus on the eternal that is before you. People. Relationships. The Bible. Your walk with Jesus. Pour yourself into that which is lasting. Don't let that which fades hinder you, because time is too precious. This world will not last. The things that people chase such as fame and fortune will all fade one day. They will be no more. Like wood, hay, and stubble, they will quickly burn away. But the one who does the Father's will lives forever.

Father, fix my focus on the eternal, I ask. Amen.

CONFIDENT AND UNASHAMED

And now, dear children, continue in him, so that when he appears
we may be confident and unashamed before him at his coming.

1 JOHN 2:28 NIV

• •

Confident and unashamed. That is how the believer can appear before the Lord when He returns. When Jesus comes again, we want to be found doing His will.

There will be many who will be surprised at His coming. Those who have rejected Christ all their lives will go to their knees for, as the Bible tells us, every knee shall bow (Isaiah 45:23; Romans 14:11; Philippians 2:10–11). How glorious for you because you are already choosing to bow before Jesus!

As you live your day-to-day life, look to Jesus to strengthen you. "Continue in him"—keep on keeping on, believer! Stand strong on the promises given to you in scripture. The temptation to sin is sometimes overwhelming, but the Holy Spirit is alive and well in those who have accepted Christ as Savior. You have what it takes to say no to sin.

When Jesus returns, may you be found saying yes to the things of the Lord and no to sin. May you be ready so that you might stand before your Lord confident and unashamed.

Lord, may I resist sin and stand firm in my faith until You return. Amen.

YOU BELONG TO GOD

*See what great love the Father has lavished on us, that we should
be called children of God! And that is what we are! The reason
the world does not know us is that it did not know him.*

1 JOHN 3:1 NIV

. . . .

If you're a parent, you know that there is no love greater than the love of a parent for a child. And yet in the frailty of our human condition, even we cannot love perfectly. But God, who is sovereign over all of creation, calls us His children. He loves us with a perfect, unconditional love. He knows us and He loves us still, enough to sacrifice His beloved Son on a cross that we might have life.

Our heavenly Father calls us sons and daughters. He calls us His own. We need not search for our identity in career or social status. Whether we are beautiful according to this world's standards or not makes no difference to our God. If others do not value you, that is because they do not value the almighty God.

Rest assured this day and each day that you live that your Father is watching over you. He knows your comings and your goings. He rejoices with you in victories and He shelters you with His wing when times are hard. He loves you and is a good, good Father.

Lord, remind me of my great worth because I belong to You. Amen.

THE IMPORTANCE OF SELF-CONTROL

*Like a city whose walls are broken through
is a person who lacks self-control.*
PROVERBS 25:28 NIV

· ·

There's a children's song whose lyrics include, "Once I had a knot in my shoe, and it would not come loose. I tried and tried and pried and pried, but it would not come loose." The frustrated child then became so angry he kicked a door and stubbed his little toe!

Just like the child in this song, we may all get frustrated at times. This life definitely has its challenges, both great and small, which seem to present themselves all too often.

Self-control is like the secret weapon of a superhero. If we possess it, we can pull it out when it is necessary to use. The Bible says a person without self-control is like a city whose walls are broken through. Those who do not have self-control leave a path of destruction in their wake. Relationships can be destroyed through words and actions not under the control of the Holy Spirit.

Even if a lack of self-control is a major weakness in your life, God can change that through His Holy Spirit. Ask Him to set a guard over your tongue and to help you find ways to think before you act in those times when you feel angry.

Lord, help me demonstrate self-control today. Amen.

LEARN FROM YOUR MISTAKES

As a dog returns to its vomit, so fools repeat their folly.
PROVERBS 26:11 NIV

. . . .

When we make a mistake, it feels good to be told, "That's okay. Everyone makes mistakes. After all, you're only human," which is certainly true. Yet at other times we may be told, "Don't make the same mistake twice." For the second time one makes a mistake, it's no longer a mistake but a choice.

Proverbs warns us against repeating our folly. *Folly* is defined as a "lack of good sense; foolishness." Can you look back over the years and remember a time you made a foolish choice or mistake? We all can! Perhaps we've hurt someone deeply or broken a promise. Maybe we got caught up in temptation and found ourselves living outside of God's will for our life. Perhaps our lack of good sense caused us—and maybe others—to suffer dire consequences.

The Lord wants us to learn from our mistakes and to draw near to Him. We can learn to walk closer with God by remembering our errors and asking Him to guide us in His ways.

Making a mistake is one thing. Returning to it and repeating the same mistake over and over is another. Take this opportunity to learn and grow, lean into the Lord, seek His wisdom on the matter, and move forward on a better path.

God, help me to learn from rather than repeat my mistakes. Amen.

LOVE ONE ANOTHER

*And now I ask you, dear lady—not as though I were
writing you a new commandment, but the one we have
had from the beginning—that we love one another.*

2 JOHN 5 ESV

. . . .

This verse reminds us to love other people. Doing so may sound simple but be hard to live out on a daily basis. Love is so much more than just a word. Love acts. It sacrifices. It sees the best, gives the benefit of the doubt, empathizes, and truly cares.

Have you snapped at your spouse or child recently and later realized that your irritation was unwarranted? Have you lost your cool with a fast-food drive-through worker who messed up your order? Have you looked to your own interests over those of others? Have you failed at loving well?

Do not fret. We all have. We are human and we live in a fallen world.

However, the world will sometimes tell you that it's okay to hurt someone else. It will pat you on the back, suggest pills or therapy, remind you that you did not mean to do it, and send you on your way. The Lord's advice, though, remains tried-and-true the same through the ages. He tells us to keep on loving.

Father, help me to love those around me well. Amen.

IMITATORS OF GOOD

Beloved, do not imitate evil but imitate good. Whoever does good is from God; whoever does evil has not seen God.

3 JOHN 11 ESV

. . . .

Parrots are interesting creatures. They can be taught to say, "Polly want a cracker." For when parrots hear something, they will often repeat it. They are imitators of humans.

Yet aren't we all copycats? Consider that young children imitate not only what we adults say but also what we do. When the driver ahead of you doesn't immediately move when the traffic light turns green and your child yells out, "C'mon. Go already, lady!" from the backseat, you may shudder in the realization that he or she is copying you!

God's Word warns us against imitating evil. Instead, He would have us imitate what's good. How do we do this? Immersing ourselves in God's Word is one way. Choosing our models—live and prerecorded—wisely is another. For what goes in has a tendency to be what comes out. Thus, it would benefit us to avoid TV shows and movies with foul language, and to choose friends who are a positive Christian influence on us.

How will you imitate what is good? How will you avoid letting evil seep into your lifestyle and language?

Lord, help me to stay connected to You through reading Your Word daily. I pray You would guide me as I choose positive influences. Amen.

IRON SHARPENS IRON

Iron sharpens iron, and one man sharpens another.
PROVERBS 27:17 ESV

. . . .

In Old Testament days, one would use one iron blade to sharpen another until both were sharper tools. The improvement could not take place with just one blade. It required two.

In the same way as "iron sharpens iron," we are to sharpen one another as believers in Christ. We can do that by being connected in a Christian community where we need never walk alone. By spending time with like-minded, godly individuals, we will find the support and accountability we need to grow in God.

We become more effective witnesses for Christ when we allow others to come close to us. It's so easy to just drift into church a few times per year, sit alone at the back, and slip out before the last song has ended. When we take this approach, we miss out on the sharpening of our character that can only happen when we allow other people to know us well. We must also allow people we have grown to trust to speak into our lives.

Who sharpens you in this life?

*Lord, help me to establish and nurture Christian friendships
so that I might have accountability in my life. Amen.*

GOD NEVER CHANGES

*"I am the Alpha and the Omega," says the Lord God, "who
is and who was and who is to come, the Almighty."*
REVELATION 1:8 ESV

. . . .

So many things in life change. We move. Our home changes. We get
married, have a baby, experience divorce, lose a parent, or bury a child.
Our family changes. We grow older with each passing year. We are not
able to be as active or stay up as late as we once did. We drift apart from
friends. We grow closer to others. Our friendships change.

Life is constantly throwing changes at us left and right. Sometimes
it is hard to keep up!

Yet there is one thing that never changes: the Lord. He is the same
yesterday, today, and tomorrow. He is the Beginning and the End. He is
sovereign. Not only has He always been, but He will always be. He who
calls Himself the Great I Am is what you need in each moment. He is
the Prince of Peace and the King of Glory. He will never ever leave or
forsake you. He will never ever change.

*Lord, You are the Alpha and Omega, the Beginning
and the End. I will put my trust in You alone. Amen.*

INTEGRITY MATTERS

*Better is a poor man who walks in his integrity
than a rich man who is crooked in his ways.*
PROVERBS 28:6 ESV

. . . .

This world would have us believe that material wealth is what matters most. We are constantly bombarded with advertisements for the latest cars, cell phones, robot vacuum cleaners, and other gadgets. Social media feeds that highlight our friends' trips to exotic places cause us to long for expensive travels as well. But money and the things it can buy do not begin to stack up against a good name.

It's clear in Proverbs 28:6 that integrity matters. What you do when no one is looking makes a difference. Your reputation is worth more than riches.

Work toward a life that is marked by integrity. Do this by avoiding even little white lies. Be honest. Live humbly. Resist the urge to make much of yourself, even if you accomplish great things. Make much of Jesus by focusing on those around you and their needs. Live for the Lord. Others will take notice. And in the end, the things that money can buy are nothing but wood, hay, and stubble.

Walk in a way that pleases the Lord. Walk with integrity.

*Father, strengthen my character, I pray. I want to be known as
one whose word means something and whose reputation is solid
in Your eyes. Remind me each day that integrity matters. Amen.*

JESUS IS A GENTLEMAN

*Here I am! I stand at the door and knock. If anyone
hears my voice and opens the door, I will come in
and eat with that person, and they with me.*

REVELATION 3:20 NIV

· ·

Today's verse speaks of Jesus standing at the door of your heart and knocking. He does not and will not barge into your life and make Himself Lord over you—even though He could. Instead, Jesus chooses to be a gentleman. He waits. He longs for you to hear His call upon your life and open the door, but He will not push His way in. He wants you to open the door of your heart.

Maybe you have been a Christian for many years. You heard the call of the Lord and opened your heart to Him once upon a time. But since that time, you have forgotten about His presence in your life. You have become caught up in the world. Your career, family, and hobbies have overshadowed that true salvation experience. Take heart! It's never too late to return to the table with Jesus.

Just like a parent who is always glad to see his son at the door, coming home to share a meal, Jesus is always ready to reunite with you. Make your relationship with Christ a priority. Start today!

*Jesus, I have missed our close fellowship. Join me at the
table again. I long to walk closely with You again. Amen.*

HARD WORK PAYS OFF

Whoever works his land will have plenty of bread, but he who follows worthless pursuits will have plenty of poverty.

PROVERBS 28:19 ESV

. . . .

Have you ever considered everything you do is for the Lord? The endless loads of laundry, errands, household chores. . . All those hours you put in at the job or your home office. . . Then there's the kids, doctor's appointments, car rides, meal planning. . . It's all for the Lord.

In Proverbs we're reminded hard work is blessed by God. And we're warned against following "worthless pursuits." Have you ever had that person who constantly has a "get rich quick" scheme she wants to tell you about? She'd love to drag you into her plans with her, wouldn't she? But you resist, sticking to your current course, even accepting that, to a degree, there may be some monotony in the everyday, knowing you have responsibilities and that most of those schemes are too good to be true. That's wisdom.

Pursue that which you know God has given you to do. Whether it's raising children, working in a business setting, serving as a church leader, or something unique to your circumstances. Don't look to the left or right. Just keep your eyes on Jesus. He'll provide for your needs, and your perseverance won't go unnoticed by your Savior.

Jesus, help me to be wise in my decisions so my family will be blessed with what we need day by day. Amen.

TRUST IN THE LORD

Those who trust in themselves are fools,
but those who walk in wisdom are kept safe.
PROVERBS 28:26 NIV

. . . .

Repeatedly in scripture, we find admonitions to trust in God. And today's scripture makes it clear only a fool trusts in herself.

An earlier verse in Proverbs states: "In their hearts humans plan their course, but the LORD establishes their steps" (16:9 NIV). This tells us that it's good to plan for the future. Certainly, we're not meant to just stagger into each day haphazardly. But God clearly reminds His children that ultimately, we must pray for His will. He knows what's best.

When your plans regarding work or relationships seem to fall apart, resist the urge to panic. Trust not in those plans you had carefully laid for yourself. Trust in God. Later on, even if it's years down the road, when you look back, you'll see that what seemed to be a disaster at the time was, in fact, a blessing. God makes no mistakes!

The Lord assures us that when we seek wisdom, we'll find it (James 1:5). So seek God's will for your life, make plans, and then consistently lay those plans at the feet of the Almighty. Ask Him to open and close doors in your life as He sees fit. You'll be amazed at the peace that follows.

Sovereign God, please help me to walk in wisdom
according to Your will all the days of my life. Amen.

CALMING THE STORM

Mockers can get a whole town agitated, but the wise will calm anger.
PROVERBS 29:8 NLT

. . . .

It takes a wise person to bring calm to a situation rather than escalating it.

Consider some situations in which you have the choice to remain calm when others are upset. It may be at home. When your spouse, children, or other relatives are upset, how do you handle it? Do you join in and add to the drama, or does your presence introduce peace to the situation? Some people just have a way of remaining calm in stressful moments. Think of such a person. What is it that he or she does when things go haywire in order to bring balance back into play?

It may be at your workplace where you need to calm anger. Perhaps you work with or for someone who is rather hotheaded. You feel as if you're walking on eggshells all the time, fearing an explosion of that person's emotions may interrupt your day at any point. By refusing to get involved and even sometimes simply remaining silent, you can calm anger. No one can fault you for silence!

It may be that the anger you sometimes face comes from within. In that case, pray especially for God to step in and bring the calm His presence alone can conjure.

*Lord, help me to be one who brings calm within and without.
I pray in the powerful name of Your Son, Jesus. Amen.*

IS VENTING A GOOD IDEA?

Fools vent their anger, but the wise quietly hold it back.
PROVERBS 29:11 NLT

• •

Proverbs warns us that fools vent their anger. The wise quietly hold their anger back.

Consider the result of each path. If you vent to a friend, what might the effect be? Do you really feel better afterward, or has fuel just been added to the fire? Often we're looking to our audience to agree with us as we rant, to jump on the bandwagon, whatever grievance it is we're expressing. Is venting a godly choice? Is it something necessary for all of us to do from time to time? Or could it be considered sin?

Now think about the alternative, which is quietly holding back anger. In that scenario, no one else becomes involved. We don't risk slandering and gossiping. We don't damage anyone else's reputation. Nor do we show poor character ourselves.

Yet how in the world do you hold back anger? Try praying for the person with whom you are angry. Ask the Lord to help you see things from his or her point of view. It may just bring your frustration level down a notch or two.

God, forgive me for venting too often and stirring others up with my anger. Please help me to gain and sustain a gentle spirit. Help me to show grace and to hold back my anger. Amen.

HUMILITY IS GREATER THAN PRIDE

Pride ends in humiliation, while humility brings honor.
PROVERBS 29:23 NLT

. . . .

Proverbs 16:18 (NIV) cautions, "Pride goes before destruction, a haughty spirit before a fall." Then in Proverbs 29 we read another warning against pride. We're encouraged to lean toward humility rather than pride, for humility is said to bring honor.

Think about some people in the Bible who demonstrated humility—the widow who gave all she had, John the Baptist who said he was not worthy even to untie the sandals of the Messiah, Ruth who served her mother-in-law. Consider the humility within Paul, David, Joseph, Moses. . . . And Jesus Himself who was a servant leader. One who dined with sinners. A Man who was approachable even though He was the Son of the almighty God.

Now consider the people full of pride. Think about the giant Goliath who was felled by a shepherd boy's stone. Even in folktales and cartoons we see the prideful characters fall, don't we? Think of the hare who laughs at the tortoise and yet ends up losing the race! Better yet, consider "The Emperor's New Clothes"!

If pride ends in humiliation and humility brings honor, how do we become humbler? We start by thinking of others. Considering their needs above ours. Also by remembering that every good and perfect gift—including your abilities and intellect—has come to you from God.

Lord, replace pride in my heart with
humility, I pray in Jesus' name. Amen.

GOD IS OUR JUDGE

Many seek an audience with a ruler,
but it is from the LORD that one gets justice.
PROVERBS 29:26 NIV

. . . .

In the end, God alone is our judge. It's His opinion we care about. So don't get caught up in what important people say of you. Instead, focus on serving the Lord and living according to His statutes. If God is pleased with your life, that's ultimately all that matters.

God made you. He has given you abilities and gifts. He places opportunities in your path. He expects you to use those talents and your time and your treasures (financial resources) for His glory. If this is what your life reflects, then you have nothing to fear, even if an earthly leader or ruler disapproves.

Keep on loving God. Keep on serving Him. Spend time in His Word daily. Find a community of Christians that helps you grow. Help your fellow sojourners grow as well. Encourage one another. Study the Bible. Serve in your church—and go beyond its walls. Spread the good news of Jesus wherever you are—work, home, and in your community. Who knows? Perhaps you will be used to take the Gospel to faraway lands.

Remember that God alone is your judge. So put your trust in Him. Seek to please Him. You serve an audience of One.

God, help me remember that You are far more
important than any leader or ruler on this earth. Amen.

GOD IS OUR SHIELD

Every word of God is pure: he is a shield
unto them that put their trust in him.
PROVERBS 30:5 KJV

. . . .

Protection. We all seek it. We build homes with walls of brick and strong rooftops to shelter us. We carry umbrellas, wear coats and gloves, and don masks. We lock our doors and install alarm systems. We secure our children in car seats.

In today's proverb, we read that God's Word is a shield for those who put their trust in Him. Every word of the Lord is pure. It's not diluted or tainted; not half-truth but solid and strong. You can count on it, stand on it. It's a trustworthy foundation; holy, right, steadfast, never-changing.

Take up your shield, Christian. Your protection does not lie in the things of this world. It cannot be purchased or borrowed, bought or bartered for. Your refuge is in the almighty God, the Maker of heaven and earth. You're protected by His wings, held in His arms, shielded from harm. Whatever touches your life must be filtered first through the strong hands of the One who breathed life into you in the first place.

So have no fear. Dwell on the words of Jehovah Jireh, your Protector who provides for you. Eat and drink His holy scriptures. Don't hurry through the meal. Let it digest and nourish you. Trust in the Lord your God. He alone is your shield.

Be my protection, Father. Guide me in Your Word and ways. Amen.

DAILY BREAD

"Two things I ask of you, LORD. . . . Keep falsehood and lies
far from me; give me neither poverty nor riches, but give me
only my daily bread. Otherwise, I may have too much and
disown you and say, 'Who is the LORD?' Or I may become
poor and steal, and so dishonor the name of my God."

PROVERBS 30:7–9 NIV

. . . .

Daily bread. It's that which is enough for today and today alone, without worrying about that which is needed in order to sustain you tomorrow.

Jesus, who was also God, came into this world as an infant, humbly, quietly, unnoticed by most. He'd no bed for a crib, was laid in a feeding trough for animals. He relied upon His heavenly Father to sustain Him.

Daily bread keeps us dependent on our Father. For it's just what we need, nothing less and nothing more. He gives us bread for each day. Were we to hoard away more, we might forget our utter dependence on Him and think that we could rely upon our careful plans and resources, upon ourselves.

God rebuked the Israelites for attempting to save up manna rather than accepting it each new day from His hand. Trust in your Father to nourish you in every way, day by day. Thank Him tonight for your daily bread.

God, thank You for providing for me day by day.
May I learn to trust in You far more than I trust in myself.

TURN FROM SINFUL WAYS

*"Do not be like your ancestors, to whom the earlier prophets
proclaimed: This is what the LORD Almighty says: 'Turn
from your evil ways and your evil practices.' But they would
not listen or pay attention to me, declares the LORD."*

ZECHARIAH 1:4 NIV

. . . .

God offers each individual the free gift of salvation through Christ. He also stands ready to forgive and to guide those who turn from sin. At the same time, He bestows upon us free will. It's up to each individual to accept the free gift of salvation through Christ and to decide whether she will walk in the ways of this world or in the ways of God.

If your parents and their parents before them were believers, then you have a great heritage. If you had great models growing up, you've been blessed. But if you did not, if those who came before you in your family lived according to the flesh and not the spirit, make a commitment today to change that in your own life.

Don't be like those who live according to their own desires, which lead them far from God. Instead choose to serve the Lord. Give Him your life. Read and study His Word. He longs to see you detour off the crooked paths your ancestors followed and start a new life with Him.

*God, keep me walking in Your Way, Lord. Forgive
my sins, and help me always to heed You. Amen.*

LISTEN TO THE LORD

*"They made their hearts as hard as flint and would not listen
to the law or to the words that the LORD Almighty had sent by
his Spirit through the earlier prophets. So the LORD Almighty
was very angry. " 'When I called, they did not listen; so when
they called, I would not listen,' says the LORD Almighty."*

ZECHARIAH 7:12–13 NIV

• •

God was angered by the Israelites of old when they did not listen to Him. We should heed this as a warning ourselves. God does not change. He's the same yesterday, today, and tomorrow. He's still angered today when people turn from Him and ignore His calling.

When your heart is open, it's soft and tender. You are eager to learn and ready to listen. You follow hard after God. But when, like the Israelites, your heart is as hard as stone, it is displeasing to the Lord.

Are you so busy trying to keep up with the Joneses that you are missing God's calling on your life? Does social media distract you from reading the Bible? Be sure that you are not so fixated on climbing the ladder or chasing your dreams that you neglect the purposes God has for you.

*Lord, may I always have a soft heart and listening ears.
May I not only hear Your call but heed it. Amen.*

STIRRING UP ANGER

"For as churning cream produces butter, and as twisting the nose produces blood, so stirring up anger produces strife."
PROVERBS 30:33 NIV

. . . .

Have you ever been guilty of stirring up trouble? We all know deep down when we are doing it, but something in us (called a sin nature) tells us to carry on. It can seem a small offense at the time. After all, what's a little gossip shared in the office? What is the big deal about teasing? Can't your spouse take a joke? And so you were a little tough on the kids…they still don't have the right to lose their cool just because they felt agitated with you. Right? Or…perhaps, if we are honest, we know it is *not so right*….

The Bible warns us about stirring up anger. In Proverbs we read that it creates strife. Do you really want to live with conflict and friction in your relationships? Like many things, this can result in a snowball effect. What starts out as a "joke" or harmless "tidbit of knowledge" can cause a bit of discord, which then may bring about major division.

Take God's Word at face value. Stay far away from things like rumor spreading and sarcasm. Instead, be found as one with a gentle and quiet spirit that's pleasing to the Lord.

Lord, set a guard over my lips. I want to be a peacemaker not a peace breaker.

SPEAK UP

Speak up for those who cannot speak for themselves, for the rights of all who are destitute. Speak up and judge fairly; defend the rights of the poor and needy.
PROVERBS 31:8–9 NIV

. . . .

Sometimes as women we feel hesitant to speak up. Granted, there are times to remain silent. But there are also times when we should stand up for what is right and just. For some cannot defend themselves—the orphan, the widow, the elderly, those with special needs, and more.

You may think so many people are in need of help that there's nothing you can do to make a difference. But that's not true. God clearly calls us to speak for others. And once you get that through your head, your heart and actions will follow.

Speaking up does not have to look like carrying a large sign on a picket line. Far from it! It may mean volunteering at a pregnancy crisis center, opening your home to a foster child, or becoming an advocate for a special needs individual.

Spend some time in prayer about this. Ask God where He wants to use you. Ask Him to remove distractions in your life and provide opportunities for you to serve others and defend the destitute. Then be ready to do so in love.

Lord, help me to see those around me who are not able to speak up for themselves. Show me where You need me, and give me the boldness to say "yes."

WISE WOMAN

She considers a field and buys it;
out of her earnings she plants a vineyard.
PROVERBS 31:16 NIV

. . . .

If you are like most women, you've likely struggled with the concept of the Proverbs 31 woman. You wonder how you could ever be pleasing to God if this list of requirements is what it takes! After all, this woman sounds like Superwoman! How you could ever "do it all"? So you give up, and chalk it up as, without a doubt, unattainable.

But let's take a closer look. Often, we focus on only certain parts of the description given in the final chapter of Proverbs. We remember the part about getting up early and taking care of her family. We see her sewing and food preparation and overlook that she's also savvy in business dealings!

Could it be that the Proverbs 31 woman looks a little more like you than you realize? Some women have a knack for handling the finances in their home. You may not buy a field and plant a vineyard with your earnings. . .but do you clip coupons and shop sales to save money? Have you created a budget that helps your family stay on track monetarily?

Today ask the Lord to help you grow in the areas where He sees the need, but don't sell yourself short too quickly!

Father, help me to be a Proverbs 31 woman in the unique
ways in which You have created me, I pray. Amen.

LOOKING FORWARD TO A NEW YEAR

She is clothed with strength and dignity;
she can laugh at the days to come.
PROVERBS 31:25 NIV

. . . .

As women, we often find ourselves weighed down by concerns regarding our families, careers, friendships, and other aspects of our lives. We worry about illness, whether our kids will have friends in school, and if we should change jobs. We try to make sure we're saving the right amount of money and planning correctly for the future.

There's nothing wrong with planning and preparing. But God would have us clothed with strength and dignity, and able to laugh at the future. If that's the complete opposite of your current existence, it's time to slow down, grab a coffee, and spend more time in the Word of God.

God doesn't want you to live in a constant state of panic about the future. He tells us in Matthew 6:34: "Therefore do not worry about tomorrow, for tomorrow will worry about itself. Each day has enough trouble of its own" (NIV).

So breathe in deep and exhale all those worries away. Clear your head and heart. God's got you! Plan and prepare. But cast your worries on His shoulders. Be so completely confident in Him that you can laugh at the days to come!

Lord, help me to lay my concerns at Your feet. To put all my days in Your hands. I pray You would replace my worry with laughter. Amen.

CONTRIBUTORS

Born in Paraguay, **TERRY ALBURGER** resides in Bucks County, Pennsylvania with her husband and black Lab. She has always had a passion for writing, which has blossomed in her position at Brittany Pointe Estates. Terry enjoys writing and directing their theatrical productions and is also a columnist for local newspapers. She enjoys spending time with her grandchildren. Terry's devotions appear in the month of August.

EMILY BIGGERS is a Tennessee native living in Bedford, Texas. She is mom to Lucy and a teacher facilitator for a local school district. She loves to spend time with family and friends. Emily's devotions appear in the month of December.

ANITA HIGMAN, an award-winning and bestselling author from Texas, has authored or coauthored fifty-plus books, and she has a BA in the combined fields of speech communication, psychology, and art. A few of Anita's favorite things are fairy-tale castles, steampunk clothes, traveling, antiquing, exotic teas, gardening, and laughing with her family and friends! Please drop by Anita's website at anitahigman.com. She would love to hear from you! Anita's devotions appear in the months of May and November.

DONNA K. MALTESE is a freelance writer, editor, and writing coach. Mother of two children, grandmother of one very active grandchild, and caretaker of two rescue animals, she resides in Bucks County, Pennsylvania, with her husband. When not reading or writing, Donna, an avid knitter and crocheter, can be found frequently wrestling yarn from her cat. You can check out her website at donnakmaltese.com. Her devotions appear in the months of January, May, June, and November.

KELLY MCINTOSH is a wife, twin mom, and editor from Ohio. She loves books, the beach, and everything about autumn (but mostly pumpkin spice lattes). Kelly's devotions appear in the month of April.

CAREY SCOTT is an author, speaker, and certified Biblical Life Coach. With authenticity and humor, she challenges women to be real, not perfect, and reminds them to trust God as their Source above all else. Carey is a single mom with two kids in college and lives in Colorado. You can find her at CareyScott.org. Carey's devotions appear in the month of July.

RAE SIMONS has been writing for Barbour Publishing for nearly thirty years. She is the author of many books, including educational books for children and young adults. She and her husband (along with several animals) make their home in upstate New York. Rae's devotions appear in the months of February and October.

Married since 2005, **STACEY THUREEN** is a mom of three young children. She has contributed to, and soloed, book projects published by Barbour Publishing. In addition, Stacey has contributed to Focus on the Family. To find out more about her, and to connect with Stacey, please visit www.staceythureen.com. Stacey's devotions appear in the month of September.

ELLIE ZUMBACH is a freelance writer and actor in northeastern Ohio. She earned a BA in creative writing from Malone University in Canton, Ohio. She has previously published two books with Barbour Publishing: *180 Prayers for a Woman of Confidence* and *God Calls You Strong, Girl*. She has always believed that stories are some of the most important things in the world, and spent her years growing up on a small dairy farm reading as many as she could. Ellie's devotions appear in the month of March.

READ THRU THE BIBLE IN A YEAR PLAN

1-Jan	Gen. 1-2	Matt. 1	Ps. 1
2-Jan	Gen. 3-4	Matt. 2	Ps. 2
3-Jan	Gen. 5-7	Matt. 3	Ps. 3
4-Jan	Gen. 8-10	Matt. 4	Ps. 4
5-Jan	Gen. 11-13	Matt. 5:1-20	Ps. 5
6-Jan	Gen. 14-16	Matt. 5:21-48	Ps. 6
7-Jan	Gen. 17-18	Matt. 6:1-18	Ps. 7
8-Jan	Gen. 19-20	Matt. 6:19-34	Ps. 8
9-Jan	Gen. 21-23	Matt. 7:1-11	Ps. 9:1-8
10-Jan	Gen. 24	Matt. 7:12-29	Ps. 9:9-20
11-Jan	Gen. 25-26	Matt. 8:1-17	Ps. 10:1-11
12-Jan	Gen. 27:1-28:9	Matt. 8:18-34	Ps. 10:12-18
13-Jan	Gen. 28:10-29:35	Matt. 9	Ps. 11
14-Jan	Gen. 30:1-31:21	Matt. 10:1-15	Ps. 12
15-Jan	Gen. 31:22-32:21	Matt. 10:16-36	Ps. 13
16-Jan	Gen. 32:22-34:31	Matt. 10:37-11:6	Ps. 14
17-Jan	Gen. 35-36	Matt. 11:7-24	Ps. 15
18-Jan	Gen. 37-38	Matt. 11:25-30	Ps. 16
19-Jan	Gen. 39-40	Matt. 12:1-29	Ps. 17
20-Jan	Gen. 41	Matt. 12:30-50	Ps. 18:1-15
21-Jan	Gen. 42-43	Matt. 13:1-9	Ps. 18:16-29
22-Jan	Gen. 44-45	Matt. 13:10-23	Ps. 18:30-50
23-Jan	Gen. 46:1-47:26	Matt. 13:24-43	Ps. 19
24-Jan	Gen. 47:27-49:28	Matt. 13:44-58	Ps. 20
25-Jan	Gen. 49:29-Exod. 1:22	Matt. 14	Ps. 21
26-Jan	Exod. 2-3	Matt. 15:1-28	Ps. 22:1-21
27-Jan	Exod. 4:1-5:21	Matt. 15:29-16:12	Ps. 22:22-31
28-Jan	Exod. 5:22-7:24	Matt. 16:13-28	Ps. 23
29-Jan	Exod. 7:25-9:35	Matt. 17:1-9	Ps. 24
30-Jan	Exod. 10-11	Matt. 17:10-27	Ps. 25
31-Jan	Exod. 12	Matt. 18:1-20	Ps. 26
1-Feb	Exod. 13-14	Matt. 18:21-35	Ps. 27
2-Feb	Exod. 15-16	Matt. 19:1-15	Ps. 28
3-Feb	Exod. 17-19	Matt. 19:16-30	Ps. 29
4-Feb	Exod. 20-21	Matt. 20:1-19	Ps. 30
5-Feb	Exod. 22-23	Matt. 20:20-34	Ps. 31:1-8
6-Feb	Exod. 24-25	Matt. 21:1-27	Ps. 31:9-18
7-Feb	Exod 26-27	Matt. 21:28-46	Ps. 31:19-24
8-Feb	Exod. 28	Matt. 22	Ps. 32
9-Feb	Exod. 29	Matt. 23:1-36	Ps. 33:1-12
10-Feb	Exod. 30-31	Matt. 23:37-24:28	Ps. 33:13-22
11-Feb	Exod. 32-33	Matt. 24:29-51	Ps. 34:1-7
12-Feb	Exod. 34:1-35:29	Matt. 25:1-13	Ps. 34:8-22
13-Feb	Exod. 35:30-37:29	Matt. 25:14-30	Ps. 35:1-8
14-Feb	Exod. 38-39	Matt. 25:31-46	Ps. 35:9-17
15-Feb	Exod. 40	Matt. 26:1-35	Ps. 35:18-28
16-Feb	Lev. 1-3	Matt. 26:36-68	Ps. 36:1-6
17-Feb	Lev. 4:1-5:13	Matt. 26:69-27:26	Ps. 36:7-12
18-Feb	Lev. 5:14 -7:21	Matt. 27:27-50	Ps. 37:1-6
19-Feb	Lev. 7:22-8:36	Matt. 27:51-66	Ps. 37:7-26
20-Feb	Lev. 9-10	Matt. 28	Ps. 37:27-40
21-Feb	Lev. 11-12	Mark 1:1-28	Ps. 38
22-Feb	Lev. 13	Mark 1:29-39	Ps. 39
23-Feb	Lev. 14	Mark 1:40-2:12	Ps. 40:1-8
24-Feb	Lev. 15	Mark 2:13-3:35	Ps. 40:9-17
25-Feb	Lev. 16-17	Mark 4:1-20	Ps. 41:1-4
26-Feb	Lev. 18-19	Mark 4:21-41	Ps. 41:5-13
27-Feb	Lev. 20	Mark 5	Ps. 42-43
28-Feb	Lev. 21-22	Mark 6:1-13	Ps. 44
1-Mar	Lev. 23-24	Mark 6:14-29	Ps. 45:1-5
2-Mar	Lev. 25	Mark 6:30-56	Ps. 45:6-12
3-Mar	Lev. 26	Mark 7	Ps. 45:13-17
4-Mar	Lev. 27	Mark 8	Ps. 46
5-Mar	Num. 1-2	Mark 9:1-13	Ps. 47
6-Mar	Num. 3	Mark 9:14-50	Ps. 48:1-8
7-Mar	Num. 4	Mark 10:1-34	Ps. 48:9-14
8-Mar	Num. 5:1-6:21	Mark 10:35-52	Ps. 49:1-9
9-Mar	Num. 6:22-7:47	Mark 11	Ps. 49:10-20
10-Mar	Num. 7:48-8:4	Mark 12:1-27	Ps. 50:1-15
11-Mar	Num. 8:5-9:23	Mark 12:28-44	Ps. 50:16-23

6-Aug	2 Chron. 35:20-36:23	Ps. 118:24-29
7-Aug	Ezra 1-3	Ps. 119:1-8
8-Aug	Ezra 4-5	Ps. 119:9-16
9-Aug	Ezra 6:1-7:26	Ps. 119:17-32
10-Aug	Ezra 7:27-9:4	Ps. 119:33-40
11-Aug	Ezra 9:5-10:44	Ps. 119:41-64
12-Aug	Neh. 1:1-3:16	Ps. 119:65-72
13-Aug	Neh. 3:17-5:13	Ps. 119:73-80
14-Aug	Neh. 5:14-7:73	Ps. 119:81-88
15-Aug	Neh. 8:1-9:5	Ps. 119:89-104
16-Aug	Neh. 9:6-10:27	Ps. 119:105-120
17-Aug	Neh. 10:28-12:26	Ps. 119:121-128
18-Aug	Neh. 12:27-13:31	Ps. 119:129-136
19-Aug	Esther 1:1-2:18	Ps. 119:137-152
20-Aug	Esther 2:19-5:14	Ps. 119:153-168
21-Aug	Esther. 6-8	Ps. 119:169-176
22-Aug	Esther 9-10	Ps. 120-122
23-Aug	Job 1-3	Ps. 123
24-Aug	Job 4-6	Ps. 124-125
25-Aug	Job 7-9	Ps. 126-127
26-Aug	Job 10-13	Ps. 128-129
27-Aug	Job 14-16	Ps. 130
28-Aug	Job 17-20	Ps. 131
29-Aug	Job 21-23	Ps. 132
30-Aug	Job 24-27	Ps. 133-134
31-Aug	Job 28-30	Ps. 135
1-Sep	Job 31-33	Ps. 136:1-9
2-Sep	Job 34-36	Ps. 136:10-26
3-Sep	Job 37-39	Ps. 137
4-Sep	Job 40-42	Ps. 138
5-Sep	Eccles. 1:1-3:15	Ps. 139:1-6
6-Sep	Eccles. 3:16-6:12	Ps. 139:7-18
7-Sep	Eccles. 7:1-9:12	Ps. 139:19-24
8-Sep	Eccles. 9:13-12:14	Ps. 140:1-8
9-Sep	SS 1-4	Ps. 140:9-13
10-Sep	SS 5-8	Ps. 141
11-Sep	Isa. 1-2	Ps. 142
12-Sep	Isa. 3-5	Ps. 143:1-6
13-Sep	Isa. 6-8	Ps. 143:7-12
14-Sep	Isa. 9-10	Ps. 144
15-Sep	Isa. 11-13	Ps. 145
16-Sep	Isa. 14-16	Ps. 146
17-Sep	Isa. 17-19	Ps. 147:1-11
18-Sep	Isa. 20-23	Ps. 147:12-20
19-Sep	Isa. 24:1-26:19	Ps. 148
20-Sep	Isa. 26:20-28:29	Ps. 149-150
21-Sep	Isa. 29-30	Prov. 1:1-9
22-Sep	Isa. 31-33	Prov. 1:10-22
23-Sep	Isa. 34-36	Prov. 1:23-26
24-Sep	Isa. 37-38	Prov. 1:27-33
25-Sep	Isa. 39-40	Prov. 2:1-15
26-Sep	Isa. 41-42	Prov. 2:16-22
27-Sep	Isa. 43:1-44:20	Prov. 3:1-12
28-Sep	Isa. 44:21-46:13	Prov. 3:13-26
29-Sep	Isa. 47:1-49:13	Prov. 3:27-35
30-Sep	Isa. 49:14-51:23	Prov. 4:1-19
1-Oct	Isa. 52-54	Prov. 4:20-27
2-Oct	Isa. 55-57	Prov. 5:1-14
3-Oct	Isa. 58-59	Prov. 5:15-23
4-Oct	Isa. 60-62	Prov. 6:1-5
5-Oct	Isa. 63:1-65:16	Prov. 6:6-19
6-Oct	Isa. 65:17-66:24	Prov. 6:20-26
7-Oct	Jer. 1-2	Prov. 6:27-35
8-Oct	Jer. 3:1-4:22	Prov. 7:1-5
9-Oct	Jer. 4:23-5:31	Prov. 7:6-27
10-Oct	Jer. 6:1-7:26	Prov. 8:1-11
11-Oct	Jer. 7:26-9:16	Prov. 8:12-21
12-Oct	Jer. 9:17-11:17	Prov. 8:22-36
13-Oct	Jer. 11:18-13:27	Prov. 9:1-6
14-Oct	Jer. 14-15	Prov. 9:7-18
15-Oct	Jer. 16-17	Prov. 10:1-5
16-Oct	Jer. 18:1-20:6	Prov. 10:6-14
17-Oct	Jer. 20:7-22:19	Prov. 10:15-26
18-Oct	Jer. 22:20-23:40	Prov. 10:27-32

Rom. 3:27-4:25	
Rom. 5	
Rom. 6:1-7:6	
Rom. 7:7-25	
Rom. 8:1-27	
Rom. 8:28-39	
Rom. 9:1-18	
Rom. 9:19-33	
Rom. 10:1-13	
Rom. 10:14-11:24	
Rom. 11:25-12:8	
Rom. 12:9-13:7	
Rom. 13:8-14:12	
Rom. 14:13-15:13	
Rom. 15:14-21	
Rom. 15:22-33	
Rom. 16	
1 Cor. 1:1-25	
1 Cor. 1:26-2:16	
1 Cor. 3	
1 Cor. 4:1-13	
1 Cor. 4:14-5:13	
1 Cor. 6	
1 Cor. 7:1-16	
1 Cor. 7:17-40	
1 Cor. 8	
1 Cor. 9:1-18	
1 Cor. 9:19-10:13	
1 Cor. 10:14-11:1	
1 Cor. 11:2-34	
1 Cor. 12:1-26	
1 Cor. 12:27-13:13	
1 Cor. 14:1-22	
1 Cor. 14:23-15:11	
1 Cor. 15:12-34	
1 Cor. 15:35-58	
1 Cor. 16	
2 Cor. 1:1-11	
2 Cor. 1:12-2:4	
2 Cor. 2:5-17	
2 Cor. 3	
2 Cor. 4	
2 Cor. 5	
2 Cor. 6	
2 Cor. 7	
2 Cor. 8	
2 Cor. 9	
2 Cor. 10	
2 Cor. 11	
2 Cor. 12:1-10	
2 Cor. 12:11-13:14	
Gal. 1	
Gal. 2	
Gal. 3:1-18	
Gal 3:19-29	
Gal 4:1-11	
Gal. 4:12-31	
Gal. 5	
Gal. 6	
Eph. 1	
Eph. 2	
Eph. 3:1-4:16	
Eph. 4:17-32	
Eph. 5	
Eph. 6	
Phil. 1:1-26	
Phil. 1:27-2:18	
Phil 2:19-30	
Phil. 3	
Phil. 4	
Col. 1:1-23	
Col. 1:24-2:15	
Col. 2:16-3:4	
Col. 3:5-4:1	

SCRIPTURE INDEX

OLD TESTAMENT

NEW TESTAMENT